Is the Rectum a Grave?

and Other Essays

LEO BERSANI

Is the Rectum a Grave?
and Other Essays

THE UNIVERSITY OF CHICAGO PRESS • CHICAGO AND LONDON

LEO BERSANI is professor emeritus of French at the University of California, Berkeley. He is the author of *Homos* and coauthor, with Adam Phillips, of *Intimacies*, the latter also published by the University of Chicago Press.

The University of Chicago Press, Chicago 60637
The University of Chicago Press, Ltd., London
© 2010 by The University of Chicago
All rights reserved. Published 2010
Printed in the United States of America

16 15 14 13 12 11 10   1 2 3 4 5

ISBN-13: 978-0-226-04352-4 (cloth)
ISBN-13: 978-0-226-04354-8 (paper)

ISBN-10: 0-226-04352-5 (cloth)
ISBN-10: 0-226-04354-1 (paper)

Library of Congress Cataloging-in-Publicaion Data

Bersani, Leo.
Is the rectum a grave? : and other essays / Leo Bersani.
p. cm.
Includes index.
ISBN-13: 978-0-226-04352-4 (alk. paper)
ISBN-13: 978-0-226-04354-8 (pbk. : alk. paper)
ISBN-10: 0-226-04352-5 (alk. paper)
ISBN-10: 0-226-04354-1 (pbk. : alk. paper) 1. Sex (Psychology) 2. Psycho-
analysis and art. 3. Gender identity. 4. Queer theory. 5. Cruising (Sexual
behavior) 6. Psychoanalysis. 7. Aesthetics. I. Title.
BF175.5.S48B47 2010
155.3—dc22

2009021307

For Kaja Silverman

Contents

Preface

The thematic coherence of this book lies in the connections I have been try-ing to establish, over the past twenty years or so, among three major topics: sexuality, psychoanalysis, and aesthetics. In part 1, "Is the Rectum a Grave?" and the other essays address issues that have been discussed with consider-able originality (and a sense of urgency) since the advent of the AIDS epi-demic and the birth of queer theory. Chief among these issues are questions concerning gender, identity, and sexuality. Perhaps my principal contribu-tion to these discussions has been my ambivalent response to positions that, in my view, have been too rapidly and uncritically accepted in readings of some brilliant yet also problematic texts of queer theory. In particular, the frequently incisive questioning of dominant assumptions about sexual iden-tity were, especially in the early years of queer theory, accompanied by what seem to me oversimplified (or, as I have called them, pastoral) versions of a nonidentitarian sexuality and subjectivity. "Is the Rectum a Grave?" and, among my books, *Homos* (1995) most specifically embody these responses on my part, although chapters 4 and 5 of part 1 complicate and, I hope, refine my own views.

The refinements and complications were in large part of the result of my conviction that questions regarding subjectivity (and, in particular, sexual identity) could not be adequately discussed without an appeal to psycho-analysis. My treatment of how this might be done is, once again, ambivalent, this time in regard to my commitment to psychoanalysis. Psychoanalysis had been central to my early work, mostly in connection with literary texts (especially in *Baudelaire and Freud* [1977] and *The Freudian Body* [1986]); more recently, it has seemed to me important to address the suspicion, even rejection, of psychoanalytic theory in certain queer and feminist thinkers. Undeniably, psychoanalysis has played a role in the modern project, ana-lyzed by Foucault, of normativizing the human subject. As perhaps the most important modern reflection on subjectivity, psychoanalysis can hardly fail to play a significant role in promoting or obstructing our attempts to re-imagine the subject and to invent what Foucault called "new relational modes." I take

Foucault's summoning us to rethink the relational as a political and moral imperative (a precondition of durable social transformations), and in my writing I have attempted to define how psychoanalytic notions might both invigorate and impede this project. (The mobility of my thought between psychoanalysis and a non- or antipsychoanalytic current best exemplified in Foucault is most succinctly illustrated in chapter 9, "Fr-oucault and the End of Sex.")

Questions of identity are inseparable from questions about how we relate to both the human and the nonhuman world. Subjectivity is inherently relational. What we are is largely a function of how we connect to the world. The tracing of these connections — perceptual, psychic, communal — is inescapably the tracing of formal mobilities, of the "shape" of how we position ourselves both physically and psychically in the world. Art therefore becomes a crucial model or guide (not, however, in a narrowly formalistic sense) in the invention of "new relational modes." My most recent work (especially chapter 10 and the Godard section of chapter 11) are attempts to rethink the aesthetic, not as a category restricted to works more or less officially designated as "works of art," but as enabling and exemplifying the ethical positions and commitments which, it seems to me, this entire collection seeks to articulate.

PART
I
The Sexual Subject

1

Is the Rectum a Grave?

To the memory of Robert Hagopian

These people have sex twenty to thirty times a night. . . . A man
comes along and goes from anus to anus and in a single night will
act as a mosquito transferring infected cells on his penis. When
this is practised for a year, with a man having three thousand
sexual intercourses, one can readily understand this massive
epidemic that is currently upon us.

PROFESSOR OPENDRA NARAYAN, THE JOHNS HOPKINS MEDICAL SCHOOL

I will leave you wondering, with me, why it is that when a
woman spreads her legs for a camera, she is assumed to
be exercising free will.

CATHARINE A. MACKINNON

Le moi est haïssable. . . .

PASCAL

There is a big secret about sex: most people don't like it. I don't have any
statistics to back this up, and I doubt (although since Kinsey there has been
no shortage of polls on sexual behavior) that any poll has ever been taken in
which those polled were simply asked, "Do you like sex?" Nor am I suggesting
the need for any such poll, since people would probably answer the question
as if they were being asked, "Do you often feel the need to have sex?" and one
of my aims will be to suggest why these are two wholly different questions.

Originally published in *October* 43 (Winter 1987): 197–222.

I am, however, interested in my rather irresponsibly announced findings of our nonexistent poll because they strike me as helping to make intelligible a broader spectrum of views about sex and sexuality than perhaps any other single hypothesis. In saying that most people don't like sex, I'm not arguing (nor, obviously, am I denying) that the most rigidly moralistic dicta about sex hide smoldering volcanoes of repressed sexual desire. When you make this argument, you divide people into two camps, and at the same time you let it be known to which camp you belong. There are, you intimate, those who can't face their sexual desires (or, correlatively, the relation between those desires and their views of sex), and those who know that such a relation exists and who are presumably unafraid of their own sexual impulses. Rather, I'm interested in something else, something both camps have in common, which may be a certain *aversion*, an aversion that is not the same thing as a repression and that can coexist quite comfortably with, say, the most enthusiastic endorsement of polysexuality with multiple sex partners.

The aversion I refer to comes in both benign and malignant forms. Malignant aversion has recently had an extraordinary opportunity both to express (and to expose) itself, and, tragically, to demonstrate its power. I'm thinking of course of responses to AIDS — more specifically, of how a public health crisis has been treated like an unprecedented sexual threat. The signs and sense of this extraordinary displacement are the subject of an excellent book just published by Simon Watney, aptly entitled *Policing Desire*.[1] Watney's premise is that "AIDS is not only a medical crisis on an unparalleled scale, it involves a crisis of representation itself, a crisis over the entire framing of knowledge about the human body and its capacities for sexual pleasure" (p. 9). *Policing Desire* is both a casebook of generally appalling examples of this crisis (taken largely from government policy concerning AIDS, as well as from press and television coverage, in England and America) and, most interestingly, an attempt to account for the mechanisms by which a spectacle of suffering and death has unleashed and even appeared to legitimize the impulse to murder.

There is, first of all, the by now familiar, more or less transparent, and ever-increasing evidence of the displacement that Watney studies. At the highest levels of officialdom, there have been the criminal delays in funding research and treatment, the obsession with testing instead of curing, the singularly unqualified members of Reagan's (belatedly constituted) AIDS commission,[2] and the general tendency to think of AIDS as an epidemic of the future rather than a catastrophe of the present. Furthermore, "hospital policies," according to a New York City doctor quoted by Watney, "have more to do with other patients' fears than a concern for the health of AIDS patients" (p. 38). Doctors have refused to operate on people known to be infected with the HIV virus, schools have forbidden children with AIDS to attend classes, and recently citizens of the idyllically named town of Arcadia, Florida, set fire to the house of a family with three hemophiliac children apparently infected with HIV. Television and the press continue to confuse AIDS with the HIV virus, to speak of AIDS as if it were a venereal disease, and consequently to suggest that one catches it by being promiscuous. The effectiveness of the media as an educating force in the fight against AIDS can be measured by the results of a poll cited by Watney in which 56.8 percent of *News of the World* readers came out "in favour of the idea that 'AIDS carriers' should be 'sterilised and given treatment to curb their sexual appetite,' with a mere fifty-one percent in favour of the total recriminalisation of homosexuality" (p. 141). Anecdotally, there is, at a presumably high level of professional expertise, the description of gay male sex—which I quote as an epigraph to this essay—offered to viewers of a BBC *Horizon* program by one Opendra Narayan of the Johns Hopkins Medical School (background in veterinary medicine). A less colorfully expressed but equally lurid account of gay sex was given by Justice Richard Wallach of New York State Supreme Court in Manhattan when, in issuing the temporary restraining order that closed the New St. Marks Baths, he noted: "What a bathhouse like this sets up is the orgiastic behavior of multiple partners, one after the other, where in five minutes you can have five contacts."[3] Finally, the story that gave me the greatest morbid delight appeared in the London *Sun* under the headline "I'd Shoot My Son if He Had AIDS, Says Vicar!" accompanied by a photograph of a man holding a shotgun at a boy at pointblank range. The son, apparently more attuned to his father's penchant for violence than the respectable

2. Comparing the authority and efficiency of Reagan's AIDS commission to the presidential commission on the Space Shuttle accident, Philip M. Boffey wrote: "The staff and resources available to the AIDS commission are far smaller than that provided the Challenger commission. The Challenger panel had a staff of 49, including 15 investigators and several other professionals, operating on a budget of about $3 million, exclusive of staff salaries. Moreover, the Challenger commission could virtually order NASA to perform tests and analyses at its bidding, thus vastly multiplying the resources at its disposal. In contrast, the AIDS commission currently has only six employees, although it may well appoint 10 to 15 in all, according to Dr. Mayberry, the former chairman. Its budget is projected at $950,000, exclusive of staff salaries. Although the AIDS commission has been promised cooperation by all Federal agencies, it is in no position to compel them to do its work" (*New York Times*, October 16, 1987, p. 10).

3. "Court Orders Bath House in Village to Stay Shut," *New York Times*, December 28, 1985, p. 11.

reverend himself, candidly added, "Sometimes I think he would like to shoot me whether I had AIDS or not" (quoted pp. 94–95).

All of this is, as I say, familiar ground, and I mention these few disparate items more or less at random simply as a reminder of where our analytical inquiry starts, *and* to suggest that, given the nature of that starting point, analysis, while necessary, may also be an indefensible luxury. I share Watney's interpretive interests, but it is also important to say that, morally, the only *necessary* response to all of this is rage. "AIDS," Watney writes, "is effectively being used as a pretext throughout the West to 'justify' calls for increasing legislation and regulation of those who are considered to be socially unacceptable" (p. 3). And the unacceptable ones in the AIDS crisis are, of course, male homosexuals and IV drug users (many of the latter, are, as we know, poor blacks and Hispanics). Is it unjust to suggest that *News of the World* readers and the gun-toting British vicar are representative examples of the "general public's" response to AIDS? Are there more decent heterosexuals around, heterosexuals who don't awaken a passionate yearning not to share the same planet with them? Of course there are, but—and this is particularly true of England and the United States—*power* is in the hands of those who give every sign of being able to sympathize more with the murderous "moral" fury of the good vicar than with the agony of a terminal KS patient. It was, after all, the Justice Department of the United States that issued a legal opinion stating that employers could fire employees with AIDS if they had so much as the suspicion that the virus could be spread to other workers, regardless of medical evidence. It was the American Secretary of Health and Human Services who recently urged Congress to defer action on a bill that would ban discrimination against people infected with HIV, and who also argued against the need for a federal law guaranteeing the confidentiality of HIV antibody test results.

To deliver such opinions and arguments is of course not the same thing as pointing a gun at your son's head, but since, as it has often been said, the failure to guarantee confidentiality will discourage people from taking the test and thereby make it more difficult to control the spread of the virus, the only conclusion we can draw is that Secretary Otis R. Bowen finds it more important to have the names of those who test positive than to slow the spread of AIDS into the sacrosanct "general public." To put this schematically: having the information necessary to lock up homosexuals in quarantine camps may be a higher priority in the family-oriented Reagan Administration than saving the heterosexual members of American families from AIDS. Such a priority suggests a far more serious and ambitious passion for violence than what are after all the rather banal, rather normal son-killing impulses of the Reverend Robert Simpson. At the very least, such things as the Justice Department's near recommendation that people with AIDS be thrown out of their jobs suggest that if Edwin Meese would not hold a gun to the head of a man with AIDS, he might not find the murder of a gay man with AIDS (or without AIDS?) intolerable or unbearable. And this is precisely what can be said of millions of fine Germans who never participated in the murder of Jews (and of homosexuals), but who *failed to find the idea of the holocaust unbearable*. That was the more than sufficient measure of their collaboration, the message they sent to their Führer even before the holocaust began but when the *idea* of it was around, was, as it were, being tested for acceptability during the '30s by less violent but nonetheless virulent manifestations of anti-Semitism, just as our leaders, by relegating the protection of people infected with HIV to local authorities, are telling those authorities that anything goes, that the federal government does not find the idea of camps — or perhaps worse — intolerable.

We can of course count on the more liberal press to editorialize against Meese's opinions and Bowen's urgings. We can, however, also count on that same press to give front-page coverage to the story of a presumably straight health worker testing positive for the HIV virus and — at least until recently — almost no coverage at all to complaints about the elephantine pace at which various drugs are being tested and approved for use against the virus. Try keeping up with AIDS research through TV and the press, and you'll remain fairly ignorant. You will, however, learn a great deal from the tube and from your daily newspaper about heterosexual anxieties. Instead of giving us sharp investigative reporting — on, say, 60 *Minutes* — on research inefficiently divided among various uncoordinated and frequently competing private and public centers and agencies, or on the interests of pharmaceutical companies in helping to make available (or helping to keep unavailable) new antiviral treatments and in furthering or delaying the development of a vaccine,[4] TV treats us to nauseating processions of yuppie women announcing

4. On November 15, 1987 — a month after I wrote this — 60 *Minutes* did, in fact, devote a twenty-minute segment to AIDS. The report centered on Randy Shilts's recently published tale of responses and nonresponses — both in the government and in the gay community — to the AIDS crisis (*And the Band Played On*, New York, St. Martin's Press, 1987). The report presented a sympathetic view of Shilts's chronicle of the delayed and half-hearted efforts to deal with the epidemic, and also informed viewers that not a single official of the Reagan Administration would agree — or was authorized — to talk on 60 *Minutes* on the politics of AIDS. However, nearly half of the segment — the first half — was devoted to the murderously naughty sexual habits of Gaetan Dugas, or "Patient Zero," the French-Canadian airline steward who, Shilts claims, was responsible for 40 of the first 200 cases of AIDS reported in the US. Thus the report was sensationalized from the very start with the most

to the world that they will no longer put out for their yuppie boyfriends unless these boyfriends agree to use a condom. Thus hundreds of thousands of gay men and IV drug users, who have reason to think that they may be infected with HIV, or who know that they are (and who therefore live in daily terror that one of the familiar symptoms will show up), or who are already suffering from an AIDS-related illness, or who are dying from one of these illnesses, are asked to sympathize with all those yuppettes agonizing over whether they're going to risk losing a good fuck by taking the "unfeminine" initiative of interrupting the invading male in order to insist that he practice safe sex. In the face of all that, the shrillness of a Larry Kramer can seem like the simplest good sense. The danger of not exaggerating the hostility to homosexuality "legitimized" by AIDS is that, being "sensible," we may soon find ourselves in situations where exaggeration will be difficult, if not impossible. Kramer has recently said that "if AIDS does not spread out widely into the white non-drug-using heterosexual population, as it may or may not do, then the white non-drug-using population is going to hate us even more — for scaring them, for costing them a fucking fortune, for our 'lifestyle,' which they say caused this."[5] What a morbid, even horrendous, yet perhaps sensible suggestion: only when the "general public" is threatened can whatever the opposite of a general public is hope to get adequate attention and treatment.

Almost all the media coverage of AIDS has been aimed at the heterosexual groups now minimally at risk, as if the high-risk groups were not part of the audience. And in a sense, as Watney suggests, they're not. The media targets "an imaginary national family unit which is both white and heterosexual" (p. 43). This doesn't mean that most TV viewers in Europe and America are *not* white and heterosexual and part of a family. It does, however, mean, as Stuart Hall argues, that representation is very different from reflection: "It implies the active work of selecting and presenting, of structuring and shaping: not merely the transmitting of already-existing meaning, but the more active labour of *making things mean*" (quoted p. 124). TV doesn't make the

---

repugnant image of homosexuality imaginable: that of the irresponsible male tart who willfully spread the virus after he was diagnosed and warned of the dangers to others of his promiscuity. I won't go into — as of course 60 *Minutes* (which provides the *best* political reporting on American network television) didn't go into — the phenomenon of Shilts himself as an overnight media star, and the relation between his stardom and his irreproachably respectable image, his longstanding willingness, indeed eagerness, to join the straights in being as venomous toward those at an exceptionally high risk of becoming afflicted with AIDS (gay men) as toward the government officials who seem content to let them die.

    5. Quoted from a speech at a rally in Boston preceding a gay pride celebration; reprinted in, among other publications, the San Francisco lesbian and gay newspaper *Coming Up!*, vol. 8, no. 11 (August 1987), p. 8.

family, but it makes the family *mean* in a certain way. That is, it makes an exceptionally sharp distinction between the family as a biological unit and as a cultural identity, and it does this by teaching us the attributes and attitudes by which people who thought they were already in a family actually only *begin to qualify* as belonging to a family. The great power of the media, and especially of television, is, as Watney writes, "its capacity to manufacture subjectivity itself" (p. 125), and in so doing to dictate the shape of an identity. The "general public" is at once an ideological construct and a moral prescription. Furthermore, the definition of the family *as an identity* is, inherently, an exclusionary process, and the cultural product has no obligation whatsoever to coincide exactly with its natural referent. Thus the family identity produced on American television is much more likely to include your dog than your homosexual brother or sister.

The peculiar exclusion of the principal sufferers in the AIDS crisis from the discourse about it has perhaps been felt most acutely by those gay men who, until recently, were able to feel that they could both be relatively open about their sexuality and still be thought of as belonging to the "general public," to the mainstream of American life. Until the late '60s and '70s, it was of course difficult to manage both these things at the same time. There is, I believe, something salutary in our having to discover the illusory nature of that harmonious adjustment. We now know, or should know, that "gay men," as Watney writes, "are officially regarded, in our entirety, as a disposable constituency" (p. 137). "In our entirety" is crucial. While it would of course be obscene to claim that the comfortable life of a successful gay white businessman or doctor is as oppressed as that of a poverty-stricken black mother in one of our ghettoes, it is also true that the power of blacks *as a group* in the United States is much greater than that of homosexuals. Paradoxically, as we have recently seen in the vote of conservative Democratic senators from the South against the Bork nomination to the Supreme Court, blacks, by their sheer number and their increasing participation in the vote, are no longer a disposable constituency in those very states that have the most illustrious record of racial discrimination. This obviously doesn't mean that blacks have made it in white America. In fact, some political attention to black interests has a certain tactical utility: it softens the blow and obscures the perception of a persistent indifference to the always flourishing economic oppression of blacks. Nowhere is that oppression more visible, less disguised, than in such great American cities as New York, Philadelphia, Boston, and Chicago, although it is typical of the American genius for politically displaced thought that when white liberal New Yorkers (and white liberal columnists such as Anthony Lewis) think of racial oppression, they probably always have images of South Africa in mind.[6] Yet, some blacks are needed in positions of prominence or power, which is not at all true for gay people. Straights can very easily portray gays on TV, while whites generally can't get away with passing for black and are much less effective than blacks as models in TV ads for fast-food chains targeted at the millions of blacks who don't have the money to eat anywhere else. The more greasy the product, the more likely some black models will be allowed to make money promoting it. Also, the country obviously needs a Civil Rights Commission, and it just as obviously has to have blacks on that commission, while there is clearly no immediate prospect for a federal commission to protect and promote gay ways of life. There is no longer a rationale for the oppression of blacks in America, while AIDS has made the oppression of gay men seem like a moral imperative.

In short, a few blacks will always be saved from the appalling fate of most blacks in America, whereas there is no political need to save or protect any homosexuals at all. The country's discovery that Rock Hudson was gay changed nothing: nobody needs actors' votes (or even actors, for that matter) in the same way Southern senators need black votes to stay in power. In those very cities where white gay men could, at least for a few years, think of themselves as decidedly more white than black when it came to the distribution of privileges in America, cities where the increasingly effective ghettoization of blacks progresses unopposed, the gay men who have had as little trouble as their straight counterparts in accepting this demographic and economic segregation must now accept the fact that, unlike the underprivileged blacks all around them whom, like most other whites, they have developed a technique for not seeing, they — the gays — have no claims to power at all. Frequently on the side of power, but powerless; frequently affluent, but politically destitute; frequently articulate, but with *nothing but a moral argument* — not even recognized as a moral argument — to keep themselves in the protected white enclaves and out of the quarantine camps.

On the whole, gay men are no less socially ambitious, and, more often than we like to think, no less reactionary and racist than heterosexuals. To want sex with another man is not exactly a credential for political radicalism — a fact both recognized and denied by the gay liberation movement of the late '60s

6. The black brothers and sisters on behalf of whom Berkeley students demonstrate in Sproul Plaza are always from Johannesburg, never from East Oakland, although signs posted on Oakland telephone poles and walls, which these same students have probably never seen, now announce — dare we have the optimism to say "ominously"? — "Oakland is South Africa."

and early '70s. Recognized to the extent that gay liberation, as Jeffrey Weeks has put it, proposed "a radical separation . . . between homosexuality, which was about sexual preference, and 'gayness,' which was about a subversively political way of life."[7] And denied in that this very separation was proposed by homosexuals, who were thereby at least implicitly arguing for homosexuality itself as a privileged locus or point of departure for a political-sexual identity not "fixed" by, or in some way traceable to, a specific sexual orientation.[8] It is no secret that many homosexuals resisted, or were simply indifferent to, participation in "a subversively political way of life," to being, as it were, de-homosexualized in order to join what Watney describes as "a social identity defined not by notions of sexual 'essence,' but in oppositional relation to the institutions and discourses of medicine, the law, education, housing and welfare policy, and so on" (p. 18). More precisely — and more to the point of an assumption that radical sex means or leads to radical politics — many gay men could, in the late '60s and early '70's, begin to feel comfortable about having "unusual" or radical ideas about what's OK in sex without modifying one bit their proud middle-class consciousness or even their racism. Men whose behavior at night at the San Francisco Cauldron or the New York Mineshaft could win five-star approval from the (mostly straight) theoreticians of polysexuality had no problem being gay slumlords during the day and, in San Francisco for example, evicting from the Western Addition black families unable to pay the rents necessary to gentrify that neighborhood.

I don't mean that they *should* have had a problem about such combinations in their lives (although I obviously don't mean that they should have felt comfortable about being slumlords), but I do mean that there has been a lot of confusion about the real or potential political implications of homosexuality. Gay activists have tended to deduce those implications from the status of homosexuals as an oppressed minority rather than from what I think are (except perhaps in societies more physically repressive than ours has been) the more crucially operative continuities between political sympathies on the one hand and, on the other, fantasies connected with sexual pleasure.

---

7. Jeffrey Weeks, *Sexuality and Its Discontents: Meanings, Myths and Modern Sexualities*, London, Boston, and Henley, Routledge & Kegan Paul, 1985, p. 198.

8. Weeks has a good summary of that "neat ruse of history" by which the "intent of the early gay liberation movement . . . to disrupt fixed expectations that homosexuality was a peculiar condition or minority experience" was transformed, by less radical elements in the movement, into a fight for the legitimate claims of a newly recognized minority, "of what was now an almost 'ethnic' identity." Thus "the breakdown of roles, identities, and fixed expectations" was replaced by "the acceptance of homosexuality as a minority experience," an acceptance that "deliberately emphasizes the ghettoization of homosexual experience and by implication fails to interrogate the inevitability of heterosexuality" (ibid., pp. 198–199).

Thanks to a system of gliding emphases, gay activist rhetoric has even managed at times to suggest that a lust for other men's bodies is a by-product or a decision consequent upon political radicalism rather than a given point of departure for a whole range of political sympathies. While it is indisputably true that sexuality is always being politicized, the ways in which *having sex* politicizes are highly problematical. Right-wing politics can, for example, emerge quite easily from a sentimentalizing of the armed forces or of blue-collar workers, a sentimentalizing which can itself prolong and sublimate a marked sexual preference for sailors and telephone linemen.

In short, to put the matter polemically and even rather brutally, we have been telling a few lies — lies whose strategic value I fully understand, but which the AIDS crisis has rendered obsolescent. I do not, for example, find it helpful to suggest, as Dennis Altman has suggested, that gay baths created "a sort of Whitmanesque democracy, a desire to know and trust other men in a type of brotherhood far removed from the male bondage of rank, hierarchy, and competition that characterise much of the outside world."[9] Anyone who has ever spent one night in a gay bathhouse knows that it is (or was) one of the most ruthlessly ranked, hierarchized, and competitive environments imaginable. Your looks, muscles, hair distribution, size of cock, and shape of ass determined exactly how happy you were going to be during those few hours, and rejection, generally accompanied by two or three words at most, could be swift and brutal, with none of the civilizing hypocrisies with which we get rid of undesirables in the outside world. It has frequently been suggested in recent years that such things as the gay-macho style, the butch-fem lesbian couple, and gay and lesbian sadomasochism, far from expressing unqualified and uncontrollable complicities with a brutal and misogynous ideal of masculinity, or with the heterosexual couple permanently locked into a power structure of male sexual and social mastery over female sexual and social passivity, or, finally, with fascism, are in fact subversive parodies of the very formations and behaviors they appear to ape. Such claims, which have been the subject of lively and often intelligent debate, are, it seems to me, totally aberrant, even though, in terms probably unacceptable to their defenders, they can also — indeed, must also — be supported.

First of all, a distinction has to be made between the possible effects of these styles on the heterosexual world that provides the models on which they are based, and their significance for the lesbians and gay men who perform them. A sloganesque approach won't help us here. Even Weeks, whose

9. Dennis Altman, *The Homosexualization of America, The Americanization of the Homosexual,* New York, St. Martin's Press, 1982, pp. 79–80.

work I admire, speaks of "the rise of the macho-style amongst gay men in the 1970s . . . as another episode in the ongoing 'semiotic guerilla warfare' waged by sexual outsiders against the dominant order," and he approvingly quotes Richard Dyer's suggestion that "by taking the signs of masculinity and eroticizing them in a blatantly homosexual context, much mischief is done to the security with which 'men' are defined in society, and by which their power is secured."[10] These remarks deny what I take to be wholly non-subversive intentions by conflating them with problematically subversive effects. It is difficult to know how "much mischief" can be done by a style that straight men see — if indeed they see it at all — from a car window as they drive down Folsom Street. Their security as males with power may very well not be threatened at all by that scarcely traumatic sight, because nothing forces them to see any relation between the gay-macho style and their image of their own masculinity (indeed, the very exaggerations of that style make such denials seem plausible). It may, however, be true that to the extent that the heterosexual male more or less secretly admires or identifies with motorcycle masculinity, its adoption by faggots creates, as Weeks and Dyer suggest, a painful (if passing) crisis of representation. The gay-macho style simultaneously invents the oxymoronic expression "leather queen" and denies its oxymoronic status; for the macho straight man, leather queen is intelligible, indeed tolerable, only *as* an oxymoron — which is of course to say that it must remain unintelligible. Leather and muscles are defiled by a sexually feminized body, although — and this is where I have trouble with Week's contention that the gay-macho style "gnaws at the roots of a male heterosexual identity"[11] — the macho male's rejection of his representation by the leather queen can also be accompanied by the secret satisfaction of knowing that the leather queen, for all his despicable blasphemy, at least *intends* to pay worshipful tribute to the style and behavior he defiles. The very real potential for subversive confusion in the joining of female sexuality (I'll return to this in a moment) and the signifiers of machismo is dissipated once the heterosexual recognizes in the gay-macho style a *yearning* toward machismo, a yearning that, very conveniently for the heterosexual, makes of the leather queen's forbidding armor and warlike manners a *per*version rather than a *sub*version of real maleness.

Indeed, if we now turn to the significance of the macho-style for gay men, it would, I think, be accurate to say that this style gives rise to two reactions, both of which indicate a profound respect for machismo itself. One is the

10. Weeks, p. 191.
11. Ibid.

classic put-down: the butch number swaggering into a bar in a leather get-up opens his mouth and sounds like a pansy, takes you home, where the first thing you notice is the complete works of Jane Austen, gets you into bed, and — well, you know the rest. In short, the mockery of gay machismo is almost exclusively an internal affair, and it is based on the dark suspicion that you may not be getting the real article. The other reaction is, quite simply, sexual excitement. And this brings us back to the question not of the reflection or expression of politics in sex, but rather of the extremely obscure process by which sexual pleasure *generates* politics.

If licking someone's leather boots turns you (and him) on, neither of you is making a statement subversive of macho masculinity. Parody is an erotic turn-off, and all gay men know this. Much campy talk is parodistic, and while that may be fun at a dinner party, if you're out to make someone you turn off the camp. Male gay camp is, however, largely a parody of women, which, obviously, raises some other questions. The gay male parody of a certain femininity, which, as others have argued, may itself be an elaborate social construct, is both a way of giving vent to the hostility toward women that probably afflicts every male (and which male heterosexuals have of course expressed in infinitely nastier and more effective ways) *and* could also paradoxically be thought of as helping to deconstruct that image for women themselves. A certain type of homosexual camp speaks the truth of that femininity as mindless, asexual, and hysterically bitchy, thereby provoking, it would seem to me, a violently antimimetic reaction in any female spectator. The gay male bitch desublimates and desexualizes a type of femininity glamorized by movie stars, whom he thus lovingly assassinates with his style, even though the campy parodist may himself be quite stimulated by the hateful impulses inevitably included in his performance. The gay-macho style, on the other hand, is intended to excite others sexually, and the only reason that it continues to be adopted is that it frequently succeeds in doing so. (If, especially in its more extreme leather forms, it is so often taken up by older men, it is precisely because they count on it to supplement their diminished sexual appeal.)

The dead seriousness of the gay commitment to machismo (by which I of course don't mean that all gays share, or share unambivalently, this commitment) means that gay men run the risk of idealizing and feeling inferior to certain representations of masculinity on the basis of which they are in fact judged and condemned. The logic of homosexual desire includes the potential for a loving identification with the gay man's enemies. And that is a fantasy-luxury that is at once inevitable and no longer permissible. Inevitable because a sexual desire for men can't be merely a kind of culturally neutral attraction to a Platonic Idea of the male body; the object of that desire necessarily includes a socially determined and socially pervasive definition of what it means to be a man. Arguments for the social construction of gender are by now familiar. But such arguments almost invariably have, for good political reasons, quite a different slant; they are didactically intended as demonstrations that the male and female identities proposed by a patriarchal and sexist culture are not to be taken for what they are proposed to be: ahistorical, essential, biologically determined identities. Without disagreeing with this argument, I want to make a different point, a point understandably less popular with those impatient to be freed of oppressive and degrading self-definitions. What I'm saying is that a gay man doesn't run the risk of loving his oppressor *only* in the ways in which blacks or Jews might more or less secretly collaborate with their oppressors — that is, as a consequence of the oppression, of that subtle corruption by which a slave can come to idolize power, to agree that he should be enslaved because he is enslaved, that he should be denied power because he doesn't have any. But blacks and Jews don't *become* blacks and Jews as a result of that internalization of an oppressive mentality, whereas that internalization is in part constitutive of male homosexual desire, which, like all sexual desire, combines and confuses impulses to appropriate and to identify with the object of desire. An authentic gay male political identity therefore implies a struggle not only against definitions of maleness and of homosexuality as they are reiterated and imposed in a heterosexist social discourse, but also against those very same definitions so seductively and so faithfully reflected by those (in large part culturally invented and elaborated) male bodies that we carry within us as permanently renewable sources of excitement.

There is, however, perhaps a way to explode this ideological body. I want to propose, instead of a denial of what I take to be important (if politically unpleasant) truths about male homosexual desire, an arduous representational discipline. The sexist power that defines maleness in most human cultures can easily survive social revolutions; what it perhaps cannot survive is a certain way of assuming, or taking on, that power. If, as Weeks puts it, gay men "gnaw at the roots of a male heterosexual identity," it is not because of the parodistic distance that they take from that identity, but rather because, from within their nearly mad identification with it, *they never cease to feel the appeal of its being violated.*

To understand this, it is perhaps necessary to accept the pain of embracing, at least provisionally, a homophobic representation of homosexuality.

Let's return for a moment to the disturbed harmonies of Arcadia, Florida, and try to imagine what its citizens — especially those who set fire to the Rays' home — actually saw when they thought about or looked at the Rays' three boys. The persecuting of children or of heterosexuals with AIDS (or who have tested positive for HIV) is particularly striking in view of the popular description of such people as "innocent victims." It is as if gay men's "guilt" were the real agent of infection. And what is it, exactly, that they are guilty of? Everyone agrees that the crime is sexual, and Watney, along with others, defines it as the imagined or real promiscuity for which gay men are so famous. He analyzes a story about AIDS by the science correspondent of the *Observer* in which the "major argument, supported by 'AIDS experts in America,' [is] against 'casual sexual encounters.'" A London doctor does, in the course of the article, urge the use of condoms in such encounters, but "the main problem . . . is evidently 'promiscuity,' with issues about the kinds of sex one has pushed firmly into the background" (p. 35). But the kinds of sex involved, in quite a different sense, may in fact be crucial to the argument. Since the promiscuity here is homosexual promiscuity, we may, I think, legitimately wonder if what is being done is not as important as how many times it is being done. Or, more exactly, the act being represented may itself be associated with insatiable desire, with unstoppable sex.

Before being more explicit about this, I should acknowledge that the argument I wish to make is a highly speculative one, based primarily on the exclusion of the evidence that supports it. An important lesson to be learned from a study of the representation of AIDS is that the messages most likely to reach their destination are messages already there. Or, to put this in other terms, representations of AIDS have to be X-rayed for their fantasmatic logic; they document the comparative irrelevance of information in communication. Thus the expert medical opinions about how the virus cannot be transmitted (information that the college-educated mayor of Arcadia and his college-educated wife have heard and refer to) is at once rationally discussed and occulted. SueEllen Smith, the Arcadia mayor's wife, makes the unobjectionable comment that "there are too many unanswered questions about this disease," only to conclude that "if you are intelligent and listen and read about AIDS you get scared when it involves your own children, because you realize all the assurances are not based on solid evidence." In strictly rational terms, this can of course be easily answered: there are indeed "many unanswered questions" about AIDS, but the assurances given by medical authorities that there is no risk of the HIV virus being transmitted through casual contact among schoolchildren is in fact based on "solid evidence." But what interests me most about the *New York Times* interview with the Smiths from which I am quoting (they are a genial, even disarming couple: "I know I must sound like a country jerk saying this," remarks Mr. Smith, who really never does sound like a country bumpkin) is the evidence that they have in fact received and thoroughly assimilated quite different messages about AIDS. The mayor said that "a lot of local people, including himself, believed that powerful interests, principally the national gay leaders, had pressured the Government into refraining from taking legitimate steps to help contain the spread of AIDS."[12] Let's ignore the charming illusion that "national gay leaders" are powerful enough to pressure the federal government into doing anything at all, and focus on the really extraordinary assumption that those belonging to the group hit most heavily by AIDS want nothing more intensely than to see it spread unchecked. In other words, those being killed are killers. Watney cites other versions of this idea of gay men as killers (their behavior is seen as the cause and source of AIDS), and he speaks of "a displaced desire to kill them all — the teeming deviant millions" (p. 82). Perhaps; but the presumed original desire to kill gays may itself be understandable only in terms of the fantasy for which it is offered as an explanation: homosexuals are killers. But what is it, exactly, that makes them killers?

The public discourse about homosexuals since the AIDS crisis began has a startling resemblance (which Watney notes in passing) to the representation of female prostitutes in the nineteenth century "as contaminated vessels, conveyancing 'female' venereal diseases to 'innocent' men" (pp. 33–34).[13] Some more light is retroactively thrown on those representations by the association of gay men's murderousness with what might be called the specific sexual heroics of their promiscuity. The accounts of Professor Narayan and Judge Wallach of gay men having sex twenty to thirty times a night, or once a minute, are much less descriptive of even the most promiscuous male sexuality than they are reminiscent of male fantasies about women's multiple orgasms. The Victorian representation of prostitutes may explicitly criminalize what is merely a consequence of a more profound or original guilt. Promiscuity is the social correlative of a sexuality physiologically grounded in the menacing phenomenon of the nonclimactic climax. Prostitutes publicize (indeed, sell) the inherent aptitude of women for uninterrupted sex. Conversely, the similarities between representations of female prostitutes and male homosexuals

---

12. Jon Nordheimer, "To Neighbors of Shunned Family AIDS Fear Outweighs Sympathy," *New York Times*, August 31, 1987, p. A1.

13. Charles Bernheimer's excellent study of the representation of prostitution in nineteenth-century France will be published by Harvard University Press in 1988.

should help us to specify the exact form of sexual behavior being targeted, in representations of AIDS, as the criminal, fatal, and irresistibly repeated act. This is of course anal sex (with the potential for multiple orgasms having spread from the insertee to the insertor, who, in any case, may always switch roles and be the insertee for ten or fifteen of those thirty nightly encounters), and we must of course take into account the widespread confusion in hetero-sexual *and* homosexual men between fantasies of anal and vaginal sex. The realities of syphilis in the nineteenth century and of AIDS today "legitimate" a fantasy of female sexuality as intrinsically diseased; and promiscuity in this fantasy, far from merely increasing the risk of infection, is the *sign of infec-tion.* Women and gay men spread their legs with an unquenchable appetite for destruction.[14] This is an image with extraordinary power; and if the good citizens of Arcadia, Florida, could chase from their midst an average, law-abiding family, it is, I would suggest, because in looking at three hemophiliac children they may have seen — that is, unconsciously represented — the infi-nitely more seductive and intolerable image of a grown man, legs high in the air, unable to refuse the suicidal ecstasy of being a woman.

But why "suicidal"? Recent studies have emphasized that even in societies in which, as John Boswell writes, "standards of beauty are often predicated on male archetypes" (he cites ancient Greece and the Muslim world) and, even more strikingly, in cultures that do not regard sexual relations between men as unnatural or sinful, the line is drawn at "passive" anal sex. In me-dieval Islam, for all its emphasis on homosexual eroticism, "the position of the 'insertee' is regarded as bizarre or even pathological," and while for the ancient Romans, "the distinction between roles approved for male citizens and others appears to center on the giving of seed (as opposed to the receiv-ing of it) rather than on the more familiar modern active-passive division," to be anally penetrated was no less judged to be an "indecorous role for citizen males."[15] And in Volume II of *The History of Sexuality,* Michel Foucault has amply documented the acceptance (even glorification) *and* profound suspicion of homosexuality in ancient Greece. A general ethical polarity in Greek thought of self-domination and a helpless indulgence of appetites has, as one of its results, a structuring of sexual behavior in terms of activity and passivity, with a correlative rejection of the so-called passive role in sex. What

14. The fact that the rectum and the vagina, as far as the sexual transmission of the HIV virus is concerned, are privileged loci of infection is of course a major factor in this legitimizing process, but it hardly explains the fantasmatic force of the representations I have been discussing.

15. John Boswell, "Revolutions, Universals and Sexual Categories," *Salmagundi,* nos. 58–59 (Fall 1982–Winter 1983), pp. 107, 102, and 110. See also Boswell's *Christianity, Social Tolerance and Homo-sexuality,* Chicago, University of Chicago Press, 1980.

the Athenians find hard to accept, Foucault writes, is the authority of a leader who as an adolescent was an "object of pleasure" for other men; there is a legal and moral incompatibility between sexual passivity and civic authority. The only "honorable" sexual behavior "consists in being active, in dominating, in penetrating, and in thereby exercising one's authority."[16]

In other words, the moral taboo on "passive" anal sex in ancient Athens is primarily formulated as a kind of hygienics of social power. *To be penetrated is to abdicate power.* I find it interesting that an almost identical argument — from, to be sure, a wholly different moral perspective — is being made today by certain feminists. In an interview published a few years ago in *Salmagundi*, Foucault said, "Men think that women can only experience pleasure in recognizing men as masters"[17] — a sentence one could easily take as coming from the pens of Catharine MacKinnon and Andrea Dworkin. These are unlikely bedfellows. In the same interview from which I have just quoted, Foucault more or less openly praises sado-masochistic practices for helping homosexual men (many of whom share heterosexual men's fear of losing their authority by "being under another man in the act of love") to "alleviate" the "problem" of feeling "that the passive role is in some way demeaning."[18] MacKinnon and Dworkin, on the other hand, are of course not interested in making women feel comfortable about lying under men, but in changing the distribution of power both signified and constituted by men's insistence on being on top. They have had quite a bit of bad press, but I think that they make some very important points, points that — rather unexpectedly — can help us to understand the homophobic rage unleashed by AIDS. MacKinnon, for example, argues convincingly against the liberal distinction between violence and sex in rape and pornography, a distinction that, in addition to denying what should be the obvious fact that violence *is* sex for the rapist, has helped to make pornography sound merely sexy, and therefore to protect it. If she and Dworkin use the word *violence* to describe pornography that would normally be classified as nonviolent (for example, porno films with no explicit sado-masochism or scenes of rape), it is because they define as violent the power relation that they see inscribed in the sex acts pornography represents. Pornography, MacKinnon writes, "eroticizes hierarchy"; it "makes inequality into sex, which makes it enjoyable, and into gender, which makes it seem natural." Not too differently from Foucault (except,

---

16. Michel Foucault, *The Use of Pleasure*, trans. Robert Hurley, New York, Pantheon, 1985. This argument is made in chapter 4.

17. "Sexual Choice, Sexual Act: An Interview with Michel Foucault," *Salmagundi*, nos. 58–59 (Fall 1982–Winter 1983), p. 21.

18. Ibid.

of course, for the rhetorical escalation), MacKinnon speaks of "the male supremacist definition of female sexuality as lust for self-annihilation." Pornography "institutionalizes the sexuality of male supremacy, fusing the eroticization of dominance and submission with the social construction of male and female."[19] It has been argued that even if such descriptions of pornography are accurate, they exaggerate its importance: MacKinnon and Dworkin see pornography as playing a major role in constructing a social reality of which it is really only a marginal reflection. In a sense — and especially if we consider the size of the steady audience for hard-core pornography — this is true. But the objection is also something of a cop-out, because if it is agreed that pornography eroticizes — and thereby celebrates — the violence of inequality itself (and the inequality doesn't have to be enforced with whips to be violent: the denial to blacks of equal seating privileges on public busses was rightly seen as a form of racial violence), then legal pornography is legalized violence.

Not only that: MacKinnon and Dworkin are really making a claim for the realism of pornography. That is, whether or not we think of it as constitutive (rather than merely reflective) of an eroticizing of the violence of inequality, pornography would be the most accurate description and the most effective promotion of that inequality. Pornography can't be dismissed as less significant socially than other more pervasive expressions of gender inequality (such as the abominable and innumerable TV ads in which, as part of a sales pitch for cough medicine and bran cereals, women are portrayed as slaves to the normal functioning of their men's bronchial tubes and large intestines), because only pornography tells us why the bran ad is effective: the slavishness of women is erotically thrilling. The ultimate logic of MacKinnon's and Dworkin's critique of pornography — and, however parodistic this may sound, I really don't mean it as a parody of their views — would be *the criminalization of sex itself until it has been reinvented.* For their most radical claim is not that pornography has a pernicious effect on otherwise nonpernicious sexual relations, but rather that so-called normal sexuality is already pornographic. "When violence against women is eroticized as it is in this culture," MacKinnon writes, "it is very difficult to say that there is a major distinction in the level of sex involved between being assaulted by a penis and being assaulted by a fist, especially when the perpetrator is a man."[20] Dworkin has taken this position to its logical extreme: the rejection of intercourse itself.

19. Catharine A. MacKinnon, *Feminism Unmodified: Discourses on Life and Law,* Cambridge, Massachusetts, and London, England, Harvard University Press, 1987, pp. 3 and 172.
20. Ibid., p. 92.

If, as she argues, "there is a relationship between intercourse per se and the low-status of women," and if intercourse itself "is immune to reform," then there must be no more penetration. Dworkin announces: "In a world of male power — penile power — fucking is the essential sexual experience of power and potency and possession; fucking by mortal men, regular guys."[21] Almost everybody reading such sentences will find them crazy, although in a sense they merely develop the implicit *moral* logic of Foucault's more detached and therefore more respectable formulation: "Men think that women can only experience pleasure in recognizing men as masters." MacKinnon, Dworkin, and Foucault are all saying that a man lying on top of a woman assumes that what excites her is the idea of her body being invaded by a phallic master.

The argument against pornography remains, we could say, a liberal argument as long as it is assumed that pornography violates the natural conjunction of sex with tenderness and love. It becomes a much more disturbingly radical argument when the indictment against pornography is identified with an indictment against sex itself. This step is usually avoided by the positing of pornography's violence as either a sign of certain fantasies only marginally connected with an otherwise essentially healthy (caring, loving) form of human behavior, or the symptomatic by-product of social inequalities (more specifically, of the violence intrinsic to a phallocentric culture). In the first case, pornography can be defended as a therapeutic or at least cathartic outlet for those perhaps inescapable but happily marginal fantasies, and in the second case pornography becomes more or less irrelevant to a political struggle against more pervasive social structures of inequality (for once the latter are dismantled, their pornographic derivatives will have lost their raison d'être). MacKinnon and Dworkin, on the other hand, rightly assume the immense power of sexual images to orient our imagination of how political power can and should be distributed and enjoyed, and, it seems to me, they just as rightly mistrust a certain intellectual sloppiness in the catharsis argument, a sloppiness that consists in avoiding the question of how a center of presumably wholesome sexuality ever produced those unsavory margins in the first place. Given the public discourse around the center of sexuality (a discourse obviously not unmotivated by a prescriptive ideology about sex), the margins may be the only place where the center becomes visible.

Furthermore, although their strategies and practical recommendations are unique, MacKinnon's and Dworkin's work could be inscribed within

---

21. Andrea Dworkin, *Intercourse*, New York, The Free Press, 1987, pp. 124, 137, 79.

a more general enterprise, one which I will call the *redemptive reinvention of sex*. This enterprise cuts across the usual lines on the battlefield of sexual politics, and it includes not only the panicky denial of childhood sexuality, which is being "dignified" these days as a nearly psychotic anxiety about child abuse, but also the activities of such prominent lesbian proponents of S & M sex as Gayle Rubin and Pat Califia, neither of whom, to put it mildly, share the political agenda of MacKinnon and Dworkin. The immense body of contemporary discourse that argues for a radically revised imagination of the body's capacity for pleasure — a discursive project to which Foucault, Weeks, and Watney belong — has as its very condition of possibility a certain refusal of sex as we know it, and a frequently hidden agreement about sexuality as being, in its essence, less disturbing, less socially abrasive, less violent, more respectful of "personhood" than it has been in a male-dominated, phallocentric culture. The mystifications in gay activist discourse on gay male machismo belong to this enterprise; I will return to other signs of the gay participation in the redemptive sex project. For the moment, I want to argue, first of all, that MacKinnon and Dworkin have at least had the courage to be explicit about the profound *moral revulsion* with sex that inspires the entire project, whether its specific program be antipornography laws, a return to the arcadian mobilities of childhood polysexuality, the S & M battering of the body in order to multiply or redistribute its loci of pleasure, or, as we shall see, the comparatively anodine agenda (sponsored by Weeks and Watney) of sexual pluralism. Most of these programs have the slightly questionable virtue of being indubitably saner than Dworkin's lyrical tribute to the militant pastoralism of Joan of Arc's virginity, but the pastoral impulse lies behind them all. What bothers me about MacKinnon and Dworkin is not their analysis of sexuality, but rather the pastoralizing, redemptive intentions that support the analysis. That is — and this is the second, major point I wish to argue — they have given us the reasons why pornography must be multiplied and not abandoned, and, more profoundly, the reasons for defending, for cherishing the very sex they find so hateful. Their indictment of sex — their refusal to prettify it, to romanticize it, to maintain that fucking has anything to do with community or love — has had the immensely desirable effect of publicizing, of lucidly laying out for us, the inestimable value of sex as — at least in certain of its ineradicable aspects — anticommunal, antiegalitarian, antinurturing, antiloving.

Let's begin with some anatomical considerations. Human bodies are constructed in such a way that it is, or at least has been, almost impossible not to associate mastery and subordination with the experience of our most intense

pleasures. This is first of all a question of positioning. If the penetration necessary (until recently . . .) for the reproduction of the species has most generally
been accomplished by the man's getting on top of the woman, it is also true
that being on top can never be just a question of a physical position — either
for the person on top or for the one on the bottom. (And for the woman
to get on top is just a way of letting her play the game of power for awhile,
although — as the images of porn movies illustrate quite effectively — even
on the bottom, the man can still concentrate his deceptively renounced aggressiveness in the thrusting movement of his penis.)[22] And, as this suggests,
there is also, alas, the question of the penis. Unfortunately, the dismissal of
penis envy as a male fantasy rather than a psychological truth about women
doesn't really do anything to change the assumptions behind that fantasy.
For the idea of penis envy describes how men feel about having one, and,
as long as there are sexual relations between men and women, this can't
help but be an important fact *for women*. In short, the social structures from
which it is often said that the eroticizing of mastery and subordination derive
are perhaps themselves derivations (and sublimations) of the indissociable
nature of sexual pleasure and the exercise or loss of power. To say this is not to
propose an "essentialist" view of sexuality. A reflection on the fantasmatic potential of the human body — the fantasies engendered by its sexual anatomy
and the specific moves it makes in taking sexual pleasure — is not the same
thing as an a priori, ideologically motivated, and prescriptive description
of the essence of sexuality. Rather, I am saying that those effects of power
which, as Foucault has argued, are inherent in the relational itself (they are
immediately produced by "the divisions, inequalities and disequilibriums"
inescapably present "in every relation from one point to another")[23] can perhaps most easily be exacerbated, and polarized into relations of mastery and
subordination, in sex, and that this potential may be grounded in the shifting
experience that every human being has of his or her body's capacity, or failure, to control and to manipulate the world beyond the self.

Needless to say, the ideological exploitations of this fantasmatic potential
have a long and inglorious history. It is mainly a history of male power, and
by now it has been richly documented by others. I want to approach this
subject from a quite different angle, and to argue that a gravely dysfunctional

22. The idea of intercourse without thrusting was proposed by Shere Hite in *The Hite Report*,
New York, Macmillan, 1976. Hite envisaged "a mutual lying together in pleasure, penis-in-vagina,
vagina-covering-penis, with female orgasm providing much of the stimulation necessary for male
orgasm" (p. 141).

23. Michel Foucault, *The History of Sexuality, vol. 1, An Introduction*, trans. Robert Hurley, New
York, Vintage Books, 1980, pp. 93–94.

aspect of what is, after all, the healthy pleasure we take in the operation of a coordinated and strong physical organism is the temptation to deny the perhaps equally strong appeal of powerlessness, of the loss of control. Phallocentrism is exactly that: not primarily the denial of power to women (although it has obviously also led to that, everywhere and at all times), but above all the denial of the *value* of powerlessness in both men and women. I don't mean the value of gentleness, or nonaggressiveness, or even of passivity, but rather of a more radical disintegration and humiliation of the self. For there is finally, beyond the fantasies of bodily power and subordination that I have just discussed, a transgressing of that very polarity which, as Georges Bataille has proposed, may be the profound sense of both certain mystical experiences and of human sexuality. In making this suggestion I'm also thinking of Freud's somewhat reluctant speculation, especially in the *Three Essays on the Theory of Sexuality*, that sexual pleasure occurs whenever a certain threshold of intensity is reached, when the organization of the self is momentarily disturbed by sensations or affective processes somehow "beyond" those connected with psychic organization. Reluctant because, as I have argued elsewhere, this definition removes the sexual from the intersubjective, thereby depriving the teleological argument of the *Three Essays* of much of its weight. For on the one hand Freud outlines a normative sexual development that finds its natural goal in the post-Oedipal, genitally centered desire for someone of the opposite sex, while on the other hand he suggests not only the irrelevance of the object in sexuality but also, and even more radically, a shattering of the psychic structures themselves that are the precondition for the very establishment of a relation to others. In that curiously insistent, if intermittent, attempt to get at the "essence" of sexual pleasure — an attempt that punctuates and interrupts the more secure narrative outline of the history of desire in the *Three Essays* — Freud keeps returning to a line of speculation in which the opposition between pleasure and pain becomes irrelevant, in which the sexual emerges as the *jouissance* of exploded limits, as the ecstatic suffering into which the human organism momentarily plunges when it is "pressed" beyond a certain threshold of endurance. Sexuality, at least in the mode in which it is constituted, may be a tautology for masochism. In *The Freudian Body*, I proposed that this sexually constitutive masochism could even be thought of as an evolutionary conquest in the sense that it allows the infant to survive, indeed to find pleasure in, the painful and characteristically human period during which infants are shattered with stimuli for which they have not yet developed defensive or integrative ego structures. Masochism would be the psychical strategy that partially defeats a biologically dysfunctional process of maturation.[24] From this Freudian perspective, we might say that Bataille reformulates this self-shattering into the sexual as a kind of nonanecdotal self-debasement, as a masochism to which the melancholy of the post-Oedipal superego's moral masochism is wholly alien, and in which, so to speak, the self is exuberantly discarded.[25]

The relevance of these speculations to the present discussion should be clear: the self which the sexual shatters provides the basis on which sexuality is associated with power. It is possible to think of the sexual as, precisely, moving between a hyperbolic sense of self and a loss of all consciousness of self. But sex as self-hyperbole is perhaps a repression of sex as self-abolition. It inaccurately replicates self-shattering as self-swelling, as psychic tumescence. If, as these words suggest, men are especially apt to "choose" this version of sexual pleasure, because their sexual equipment appears to invite by analogy, or at least to facilitate, the phallicizing of the ego, neither sex has exclusive rights to the practice of sex as self-hyperbole. For it is perhaps primarily *the degeneration of the sexual into a relationship that condemns sexuality to becoming a struggle for power.* As soon as persons are posited, the war begins. It is the self that swells with excitement at the idea of being on top, the self that makes of the inevitable play of thrusts and relinquishments in sex an argument for the natural authority of one sex over the other.

Far from apologizing for their promiscuity as a failure to maintain a loving relationship, far from welcoming the return to monogamy as a beneficent consequence of the horror of AIDS,[26] gay men should ceaselessly lament the practical necessity, now, of such relationships, should resist being drawn into mimicking the unrelenting warfare between men and women, which nothing has ever changed. Even among the most critical historians of sexuality and the most angry activists, there has been a good deal of defensiveness about what it means to be gay. Thus for Jeffrey Weeks the most distinctive aspect of gay life is its "radical pluralism."[27] Gayle Rubin echoes and extends

24. See Leo Bersani, *The Freudian Body: Psychoanalysis and Art*, New York, Columbia University Press, 1986, chapter II, especially pp. 38–39.

25. Bataille called this experience "communication," in the sense that it breaks down the barriers that define individual organisms and keep them separate from one another. At the same time, however, like Freud he seems to be describing an experience in which the very terms of a communication are abolished. The term thus lends itself to a dangerous confusion if we allow it to keep any of its ordinary connotations.

26. It might be pointed out that, unless you met your lover many, many years ago and neither you nor he has had sex with anyone else since then, monogamy is not that safe anyway. Unsafe sex a few times a week with someone carrying the HIV virus is undoubtedly like having unsafe sex with several HIV positive strangers over the same period of time.

27. Weeks, p. 218.

this idea by arguing for a "theoretical as well as a sexual pluralism."[28] Watney repeats this theme with, it is true, some important nuances. He sees that the "new gay identity was constructed through multiple encounters, shifts of sexual identification, actings out, cultural reinforcements, and a plurality of opportunity (at least in large urban areas) for desublimating the inherited sexual guilt of a grotesquely homophobic society," and therefore laments the "wholesale de-sexualisation of gay culture and experience" encouraged by the AIDS crisis (p. 18). He nonetheless dilutes what I take to be the specific menace of gay sex for that "grotesquely homophobic society" by insisting on the assertion of "the diversity of human sexuality in *all* its variant forms" as "perhaps the most radical aspect of gay culture" (p. 25). *Diversity* is the key word in his discussions of homosexuality, which he defines as "a fluctuating field of sexual desires and behaviour" (p. 103); it maximizes "the mutual erotic possibilities of the body, and that is why it is taboo" (p. 127).[29]

Much of this derives of course from the rhetoric of sexual liberation in the '60s and '70s, a rhetoric that received its most prestigious intellectual justification from Foucault's call — especially in the first volume of his *History of Sexuality* — for a reinventing of the body as a surface of multiple sources of pleasure. Such calls, for all their redemptive appeal, are, however, unnecessarily and even dangerously tame. The argument for diversity has the strategic advantage of making gays seem like passionate defenders of one of the primary values of mainstream liberal culture, but to make that argument is, it seems to me, to be disingenuous about the relation between homosexual behavior and the revulsion it inspires. The revulsion, it turns out, is all a big mistake: what we're really up to is pluralism and diversity, and getting buggered is just one moment in the practice of those laudable humanistic virtues. Foucault could be especially perverse about all this: challenging, provoking, and yet, in spite of his radical intentions, somewhat appeasing in his emphases. Thus in the *Salmagundi* interview to which I have already referred, after announcing that he will not "make use of a position of authority while [he is] being interviewed to traffic in opinions," he delivers himself

28. Gayle Rubin, "Thinking Sex: Notes for a Radical Theory of the Politics of Sexuality," in Carole Vance, ed., *Pleasure and Danger: Exploring Female Sexuality*, Boston, London, Melbourne, and Henley, Routledge & Kegan Paul, 1984, p. 309.

29. A frequently referred to study of gay men and women by the Institute for Sex Research founded by Alfred C. Kinsey concluded that "homosexual adults are a remarkably diverse group." See Alan P. Bell and Martin S. Weinberg, *Homosexualities: A Study of Diversity among Men and Women*, New York, Simon and Schuster, 1978, p. 217. One can hardly be unhappy with that conclusion in an "official" sociological study, but, needless to say, it tells us very little — and the tables about gay sexual preferences in the same study aren't much help here either — concerning fantasies of and about homosexuals.

of the highly idiosyncratic opinions, first of all, that "for a homosexual, the best moment of love is likely to be when the lover leaves in the taxi" ("the homosexual imagination is for the most part concerned with reminiscing about the act rather than anticipating [or, presumably, enjoying] it") and, secondly, that the rituals of gay S & M are "the counterpart of the medieval courts where strict rules of proprietary courtship were defined."[30] The first opinion is somewhat embarrassing; the second has a certain campy appeal. Both turn our attention away from the body — from the acts in which it engages, from the pain it inflicts and begs for — and directs our attention to the romances of memory and the idealizations of the presexual, the courting imagination. That turning away from sex is then projected onto heterosexuals as an explanation for their hostility. "I think that what most bothers those who are not gay about gayness is the gay life-style, not sex acts themselves," and, "It is the prospect that gays will create as yet unforseen kinds of relationships that many people cannot tolerate."[31] But what is *the* gay life-style? Is there one? Was Foucault's life-style the same as Rock Hudson's? More importantly, can a nonrepresentable form of relationship really be more threatening than the representation of a particular sexual act — especially when the sexual act is associated with women but performed by men and, as I have suggested, has the terrifying appeal of a loss of the ego, of a self-debasement?

We have been studying examples of what might be called a frenzied epic of displacements in the discourse on sexuality and on AIDS. The government talks more about testing than it does about research and treatment; it is more interested in those who may eventually be threatened by AIDS than in those already stricken with it. There are hospitals in which concern for the safety of those patients who have not been exposed to HIV takes precedence over caring for those suffering from an AIDS-related disease. Attention is turned away from the kinds of sex people practice to a moralistic discourse about promiscuity. The impulse to kill gays comes out as a rage against gay killers deliberately spreading a deadly virus among the "general public." The temptation of incest has become a national obsession with child abuse by day-care workers and teachers. Among intellectuals, the penis has been sanitized and sublimated into the phallus as the originary signifier; the body is to be read as a language. (Such distancing techniques, for which intellectuals have a natural aptitude, are of course not only sexual: the national disgrace of economic discrimination against blacks is buried in the self-righteous call for sanctions against Pretoria.) The wild excitement of fascistic S & M becomes

30. "Sexual Choice, Sexual Act," pp. 11, 20.
31. Ibid., p. 22.

a parody of fascism; gay males' idolatry of the cock is "raised" to the political dignity of "semiotic guerrilla warfare." The phallocentrism of gay cruising becomes diversity and pluralism; representation is displaced from the concrete practice of fellatio and sodomy to the melancholy charms of erotic memories and the cerebral tensions of courtship. There has even been the displacement of displacement itself. While it is undeniably right to speak — as, among others, Foucault, Weeks, and MacKinnon have spoken — of the ideologically organizing force of sexuality, it is quite another thing to suggest — as these writers also suggest — that sexual inequalities are predominantly, perhaps exclusively, displaced social inequalities. Weeks, for example, speaks of erotic tensions as a displacement of politically enforced positions of power and subordination,[32] as if the sexual — involving as it does the source and locus of every individual's original experience of power (and of powerlessness) in the world: the human body — could somehow be conceived of apart from all relations of power, were, so to speak, belatedly contaminated by power from elsewhere.

Displacement is endemic to sexuality. I have written, especially in *Baudelaire and Freud*, about the mobility of desire, arguing that sexual desire initiates, indeed can be recognized by, an agitated fantasmatic activity in which original (but, from the start, unlocatable) objects of desire get lost in the images they generate. Desire, by its very nature, turns us away from its objects. If I refer critically to what I take to be a certain refusal to speak frankly about gay sex, it is not because I believe either that gay sex is reducible to one form of sexual activity or that the sexual itself is a stable, easily observable, or easily definable function. Rather, I have been trying to account for the murderous representations of homosexuals unleashed and "legitimized" by AIDS, and in so doing I have been struck by what might be called the aversion-displacements characteristic of both those representations and the gay responses to them. Watney is acutely aware of the displacements operative in "cases of extreme verbal or physical violence towards lesbians and gay men and, by extension, the whole topic of AIDS"; he speaks, for example, of "displaced misogyny," of "a hatred of what is projected as 'passive' and therefore female, sanctioned by the subject's heterosexual drives" (p. 50). But, as I argued earlier, implicit in both the violence toward gay men (and toward women, both gay and straight) *and* the rethinking among gays (and among women) of what being gay (and what being a woman) means is a certain agreement about what sex should be. The pastoralizing project

32. See Weeks, p. 44.

could be thought of as informing even the most oppressive demonstrations of power. If, for example, we assume that the oppression of women disguises a fearful male response to the seductiveness of an image of sexual powerlessness, then the most brutal machismo is really part of a domesticating, even sanitizing project. The ambition of performing sex as *only* power is a salvational project, one designed to preserve us from a nightmare of ontological obscenity, from the prospect of a breakdown of the human itself in sexual intensities, from a kind of selfless communication with "lower" orders of being. The panic about child abuse is the most transparent case of this compulsion to rewrite sex. Adult sexuality is split in two: at once redeemed by its retroactive metamorphosis into the purity of an asexual childhood, and yet preserved in its most sinister forms by being projected onto the image of the criminal seducer of children. "Purity" is crucial here: behind the brutalities against gays, against women, and, in the denial of their very nature and autonomy, against children lies the pastoralizing, the idealizing, the redemptive project I have been speaking of. More exactly, the brutality is identical to the idealization.

The participation of the powerless themselves in this project is particularly disheartening. Gays and women must of course fight the violence directed against them, and I am certainly not arguing for a complicity with misogynist and homophobic fantasies. I am, however, arguing against that form of complicity that consists in accepting, even finding new ways to defend, our culture's lies about sexuality. As if in secret agreement with the values that support misogynist images of female sexuality, women call for a permanent closing of the thighs in the name of chimerically nonviolent ideals of tenderness and nurturing; gays suddenly rediscover their lost bathhouses as laboratories of ethical liberalism, places where a culture's ill-practiced ideals of community and diversity are authentically put into practice. But what if we said, for example, not that it is wrong to think of so-called passive sex as "demeaning," but rather that *the value of sexuality itself is to demean the seriousness of efforts to redeem it?* "AIDS," Watney writes, "offers a new sign for the symbolic machinery of repression, making the rectum a grave" (p. 126). But if the rectum is the grave in which the masculine ideal (an ideal shared — differently — by men *and* women) of proud subjectivity is buried, then it should be celebrated for its very potential for death. Tragically, AIDS has literalized that potential as the certainty of biological death, and has therefore reinforced the heterosexual association of anal sex with a self-annihilation originally and primarily identified with the fantasmatic mystery of an insatiable, unstoppable female sexuality. It may, finally, be in the gay man's rectum that he demolishes his own perhaps otherwise uncontrollable identification with a murderous judgment against him.

That judgment, as I have been suggesting, is grounded in the sacrosanct value of selfhood, a value that accounts for human beings' extraordinary willingness to kill in order to protect the seriousness of their statements. The self is a practical convenience; promoted to the status of an ethical ideal, it is a sanction for violence.[33] If sexuality is socially dysfunctional in that it brings people together only to plunge them into a self-shattering and solipsistic *jouissance* that drives them apart, it could also be thought of as our primary hygienic practice of nonviolence. Gay men's "obsession" with sex, far from being denied, should be celebrated — not because of its communal virtues, not because of its subversive potential for parodies of machismo, not because it offers a model of genuine pluralism to a society that at once celebrates and punishes pluralism, but rather because it never stops re-presenting the internalized phallic male as an infinitely loved object of sacrifice. Male homosexuality advertises the risk of the sexual itself as the risk of self-dismissal, of *losing sight* of the self, and in so doing it proposes and dangerously represents *jouissance* as a mode of ascesis.

33. This sentence could be rephrased, and elaborated, in Freudian terms, as the difference between the ego's function of "reality-testing" and the superego's moral violence (against the ego).

2

Is There a Gay Art?

In speaking of gay film — or, more generally, gay art today — we tend to mean films or novels with gay topics, most often made or written by gay and lesbian filmmakers or novelists. That is, for all the anti-identitarian rhetoric of current queer theory, what we mean by gay and lesbian art would seem to be inseparable from notions of gay authorship, gay audiences, and gay subjects. I want to propose a notion of gay art — more exactly, a homo-esthetic — to which homosexual desire is essential, but which, precisely and paradoxically because of this, can dispense with the concept of homosexual identity.

The current interest in gay and lesbian culture coincided with a new, or renewed, sense of a gay community, one that was precipitated, or strengthened, by a specific event or crisis, such as Stonewall or AIDS. This raises interesting and difficult questions. Is the community mobilized by a specific crisis destined to disappear with the end of the crisis? Or is its historically precise formation the opportunity to define a gay culture perhaps already there but that might have remained invisible if there hadn't been a community to make it more visible? And if there is a culture, there must be, so the deduction might continue, a sensibility, and if there is a sensibility, how can it help but express itself in art? And so we have gay and lesbian film festivals and cultural studies. The latter takes many forms. There is, for example, a gay and lesbian history of which many of us were not aware until recent studies brought aspects of that history to our attention. Part of this history brings to light more or less underground gay communities in Europe and the United States before the

Unpublished lecture given in London, 1996.

modern period, communities in which we see rudimentary forms of what we would call a gay or lesbian culture. I will pass over for the moment the relation of this field of studies to the claim that the homosexual did not exist as a person — that there was only same-sex behavior — before he or she was invented in the mid-nineteenth century, a claim that might be thought of as erasing a whole area of gay studies. The latter discovers a premodern gay culture, one aware of itself as having a personality related to its sexual preferences, although obviously not one conforming to the terminology of modern sexology, psychiatry and psychoanalysis. It is also true — and this accounts for some of the best work in contemporary gay and lesbian studies — that "gay writing" has generally been a function of the writing that officially excluded it. It developed in an oppositional relation to the textual ideologies available to it. Thus Michael Warner (in *The Letters of the Republic*) and Chris Lane (in *The Ruling Passion*) have shown, respectively, how an imagination of intimate relations among men is encoded within such official heterosexual ideologies as the Puritan theological writing in precolonial America, and the literature celebrating British imperialism at the beginning of this century. Such studies point to the historical specificity and relativity of anything we might wish to call gay textuality: it resists the codes that would leave no place for it by different maneuvers that (to use terms developed by Judith Butler) subversively or parodistically resignify those terms. In Wilde, for example, a gay sensibility could be thought of as encoded within a systematic perverse reversal of dominant intellectual values. His famous maxim "It is only shallow people who do not judge by appearances" is a paradigmatic example of what we would call today queer writing — a designation that would avoid the essentializing traps set by the notion of gay writing by broadening the category to a sexually nonspecific resistance to the dominant culture. We can even have it both ways (specific and general). D. A. Miller, for example, speaks in *Bringing Out Roland Barthes*, of gay people having long recognized Roland Barthes's gayness in what he calls Barthes's gravitating toward "faggy topics — women's fashions, transvestism, Sade, wrestling, Proust," as well as in an aggressively mannered way of writing implicitly defiant of the straight reader with its unashamed cultivation of just those qualities of style stigmatized as homosexual by much straight criticism. At the same time, Miller praises Barthes for a less secretive, more explicit celebration of the perverse as a source of pleasure, a celebration that earns Barthes the distinction of being not only the imperfectly closeted gay man who was always giving himself away to us but also the hero of what Michael Warner has called critical "thinking against the grain of the normal."

What I take to be the fertile incoherence of gay and lesbian queer studies does not, then, really help us very much to come up with a definition of gay art. It's clear that we don't need such a definition, and that it might in fact narrow the reach and impoverish the content of invigoratingly centrifugal queer studies. And yet, at the risk of being thought an essentialist villain, I will now attempt to define a gay esthetic.

In the writers I study in *Homos*, identity is inseparable from specific positionings of the body in desire. Desire is depsychologized; a gay identity — I would prefer to say a gay specificity — would, as a result, not necessarily have to do with such psychic content as the difference between hetero- and homosexual shapings of Oedipal attachments and conflicts, but rather would be a direct inference from images of the body. Obviously I speak from the subject-position of gay male desire, but similar Inquiries could be done from lesbian perspectives. The male positioning is especially strong in the case of Genet. I emphasize a certain sexual positioning in his work *Funeral Rites*, a scene of two men fucking in which Genet opposes lovemaking face to face (which, he writes, would have confined them in a private, exclusionary oval) to one man standing behind the partner he is penetrating, both of them forming something like the prow of a boat, looking into the darkness as one "looks into the future." "Not loving one in the other," Genet continues, "they were escaping from themselves over the world, in full view of the world, in a gesture of victory." Victory, I would suggest, over the idea of sex as reinforcing an intimacy *à deux*, of using that oval to escape from the view of the world and of the future and to become instead absorbed by the always futile efforts to penetrate the other's secrets, that is, the other's desires. Sociality in Genet is something like a series of ejaculatory relays of the self through others, and an explosively narcissistic view of community that is, however, identical to a generous outpouring of the self. This homo-narcissism breaks down ego boundaries instead of reinforcing them. The renunciation of the couple's oval-like intimacy may be the precondition for a community in which relationality is a function of sameness rather than of hierarchical or antagonistic differences, a community in which we might be indifferent to difference, in which difference, instead of being the valued term, would be the nonthreatening supplement of sameness.

This would involve a kind of opportunistic appropriation on our part of some of the very categories that have been imposed on us. In particular we might welcome the somewhat abusive cultural reduction of sameness and difference to questions of sexual choice (that is, homosexuals pursue the same, heterosexuals desire and esteem difference). We might welcome the identification of homosexuality with sameness by insisting on the radical potential in that identification: the potential for our having a privileged role in demonstrating how a sort of impersonal narcissism can break down the defensive formation of the self-congratulatory ego, a breaking down that must take place if a fundamental restructuring of the social is ever to take place.

This is a privileged role but not one that is unique or even guaranteed. There is much self-identified gay writing in which the self-congratulatory ego reigns unchallenged. Conversely, we might wish to be attentive, in the productions of straight artists, not to the homoerotic impulse we have become so adept at ferreting out in their work, but rather to the currents of homo-ness, to those ego-dissolving self-extensions into the world that Ulysse Dutoit and I studied in Rothko's paintings and in Resnais' films in *Arts of Impoverishment*. Art, especially visual art, can manifest what Greil Marcus calls "the mystery of spectral connections" between phenomena separated by a conventional and restrictive perceptual syntax. The art I'm thinking of involves a massive and double negativity: the negation of relationality as we now know it, and an attack on the cult of difference that supports the dominant mode of relations. That negativity can be more prominent in canonical authors than in culturally marginal art. The latter frequently celebrates minority cultures, thus unwittingly supporting the differential barriers that the dominant culture is only too happy to see reinforced. The canonizing process in our culture, on the other hand, while explicitly seeking to immortalize art that affirms Western civilization, frequently and secretly makes into that civilization's required reading and viewing monuments of negativity that are the obverse, suicidal side of an exhaustingly defensive and self-congratulatory ego. Negativity in art attacks the myths of the dominant culture—the pastoral myth, for example, of sexuality as inherently loving and nurturing, of sexuality as continuous with harmonious community. Only by insisting on the bleakness, the love of power, even the violence perhaps inherent in human relations can we perhaps begin to redesign those relations in ways that will not require the use of culture to ennoble them. Or, put in other terms, how do we control the historical precipitates of a passion for violence without denying our intractable implication in that passion? An important function of art might be redefined as anticommunitarian, against (to the extent that this is possible) institutional assimilations of particular works. Beckett is exemplary here, as are, in gay writing, the novels of Dennis Cooper, where the Western ideal of intersubjective knowledge is ruthlessly desublimated and literalized into a cold and brutal ripping open of bodies as a means of knowing the other.

The disruption of differential relations can of course be figured in less literally violent ways. I think, for example, that Mallarmé knew that the violence he was doing to the syntax of normal sentences was a relational violence with implications beyond the aesthetic—a violence to language as the instrumentality of social understanding. In the visual arts, when, for example, painters as different as Da Vinci and Caravaggio at times juxtapose two figures, one of which seems to be growing out of the upper half of the other rather than to be fully drawn and distinctly separated from the other (figures that seem to be Siamese twins), we can see a rather uncanny invasion of the visual field by a relation of sameness or self-multiplication, a sameness that at once extends a figure and destroys its boundaries, its contained integrity.

In pursuit of this sort of inquiry, we make ourselves vulnerable to the attacks of those who want to know what their immediate political agenda should be, what they should fight for tomorrow. It can be difficult to recognize that art intervenes in political life at various distances from particular political issues. Even more: an attempt to reconfigure the relational field may be the precondition for durable political and social reorganizations. We can see how poignant that difficulty is by briefly looking in conclusion at that Italian Genet-type outlaw, Caravaggio. In *Caravaggio's Secrets*, Ulysse Dutoit and I paid particular attention to the painter's obsession with looking. There are the sexy looks of individual male figures provoking the viewer with an erotic visual tease; there is Caravaggio painting himself as the erotic tease so that he might perhaps contain and domesticate its sexual message within the self-protective, self-same oval of model and painter. There is, within several paintings, the spying on the enigmatic looks of others, as if visual codes could no longer be relied on in the setting up of relations. And there are, finally, the works where the looks of several figures are wildly divergent. Even when there is someone who should be thought of as centering looking, such as Christ, nearly everyone around that "central" figure seems to know, as Caravaggio did, that no one has the authority to center our gaze, to define its primary relation. That Caravaggio knew that, and principally painted religious subjects in which relational primacy could not by definition be questioned, is immensely moving. Almost nothing else was available to him, and so he truly was, even more than Genet, an outlaw, outside all the relational laws given to him. In painting, relationality is of course largely a question of visual attention. In Caravaggio, as the figures proliferate, frequently looking at some unidentifiable point beyond the painting, Caravaggio's aloneness becomes all the more visible. For his figures, like him, perhaps like us, know that it almost has to be started all over again, but for the moment they, he, we simply don't know where to look.

3

Gay Betrayals

With an imagination for surveillance that would have at once appalled and delighted Michel Foucault, some of the far-right groups in America sympathetic to the antigovernment fury apparently behind the 1995 bombing in Oklahoma City have come up with an amazing suggestion. According to them, the federal treasury has marked all the bills it issues in ways that make it possible for FBI agents to drive by anyone's home, point the appropriately attuned electronic device toward a front window, and immediately determine how much money, at that moment, is inside the house. The pecuniary inflection of this paranoid fantasy is perhaps characteristically American. We enjoy comparatively low income-tax rates, and yet a promise to lower taxes even more works like magic in an election campaign. It is therefore not unsurprising that few scenarios of panoptic surveillance evoke such dread as the daily monitoring of our cash assets. But the driving force behind this fantasy is not, or is not principally, economic insecurity. The invasion of financial privacy is, for the groups in question, only an especially ominous manifestation of another invasion: that of their identity. The federal government is the enemy of its people's particularities, whether these be religious, geographical, ethnic, racial, or class-determined. Put this way, the fantasy may strike many of us as not entirely mad, although the particular aberration of those fearful for the integrity of their dollar bills is to assert that sinister governmental monitoring is principally aimed at the white Christian majority. This could of course be

Revised version of "*Trahisons gay*," from a colloquium at the Centre Pompidou, Paris, June 23 and 27, 1997.

thought of as a triumph of the powerful right wing of the Republican Party, which has managed to convince a significant minority of Caucasian Americans that their grievances — often quite justified — are not caused by the Republican crippling of social services that only the federal government can provide, but are rather the result of federal activism, an activism motivated by a sinister identity-plot, a conspiracy at once Jewish, black and homosexual, designed to eradicate white, Christian, straight identity.

Identity-politics is far from dead. Today the notion of community — and now I'm by no means speaking only of the United State — is supported by, indeed often seems grounded in a terror, at times paranoid, at other times realistic enough, at the loss of an identity conferred by belonging to a community. Identity *is* communitarian. Politically reactionary Christian fundamentalism shares with other more seriously besieged minorities a conviction that the most precious values of life are definable in communitarian terms. Not only that: repression by the majority itself is identitarian. It's always my difference against your difference. In education, the defense of the Western artistic canon is just as much a defense of a cultural identity as, for example, the Chicano or gay studies programs against which, in American universities, such defenses are mounted. The value attributed to universalism, as we can see in France, can itself be a defining trait of a particular cultural identity, and when a society as culturally homogeneous as France is menaced by the heterogeneous, we see how easily a certain language of universalism becomes the defensive weapon against the proximity of a recalcitrant otherness. A universalist ideology lends itself to the imperialist promotion of a specific culture. Confrontation is inevitable, and irresolvable, as long as we debate the relative values of different cultural identities. Perhaps the only way to negotiate and ultimately end the conflict is through an effort for which few of us seem as yet prepared: the effort to rid ourselves not exactly of cultures (an impossible enterprise in any case), but rather of our belief in the inherent value of any cultural identity whatsoever. What if there were no sides to be taken in conflicts of cultural identity? There should perhaps be only a potentially explosive insistence that the value attached to such identities is nothing more than the disposable waste of their history.

These remarks could easily appear to be at odds with my principal argument in *Homos*. There I protest against the de-gaying of gayness, and the protest could be thought of as a way of reaffirming the value of a gay identity. Indeed, the book grew out of my perplexed sense that the unprecedented gay visibility of recent years has been accompanied by a willed invisibility on the part of those presumably most anxious to make themselves visible. A paradoxical relation to the notion of a gay or homosexual identity — at once proud and self-erasing — makes the cultural politics of gays and lesbians, or of queers, a particularly fertile ground in which to raise the issues of identity evoked a moment ago. In richly troubled fashion, queers have at once empowered and invalidated identitarian politics. And by simultaneously proclaiming pride in a gay and lesbian community and making that community essentially unidentifiable, queer thinkers have brought into sharper focus than ever before the problematic nature of what we nevertheless continue to take for granted: the very notion and value of community itself. And it is in doing that that queers should command the attention of straights — that is, not because we have anything to tell them about the value of relationships or community (something that might help to rescue them from what we glibly talk about as the hell of "compulsory" heterosexuality), but rather because of our exemplary confusion. Our implicit and involuntary message might be that we aren't sure of how we want to be social, and that we therefore invite straights to redefine with us the notions of community and sociality.

These issues were raised, in rather different ways, by Foucault, and to a large extent the arguments in *Homos* are an ambivalent response to some of his work. He has done more than any other modern writer to both enrich and confuse our thinking about homosexuality and how we might define and work toward a gay community. Chapter 3 of *Homos* begins with a discussion of remarks by Foucault that seductively and dangerously simplify the questions just raised. In a 1982 interview for the American magazine *Salmagundi*, Foucault said: "I think that what most bothers those who are not gay about gayness is the gay life-style, not sex acts themselves. . . . It is the prospect that gays will create as yet unforseen kinds of relationships that many people cannot tolerate." There are three assumptions in Foucault's claims that have been important in queer theory. First of all, homosexual sex is not what is threatening about homosexuality. Second, there is nothing to interpret in homosexual desire and, by implication, no homosexual character shaping such desire. Third, gays are more dangerous politically *without* an analyzable identity. It is the remarkable result of Foucault's argument that no one wants to be called a homosexual — an aversion most striking on the part of self-identified homosexual activists and theorists. Monique Wittig has claimed that "it would be incorrect to say that lesbians associate, make love, live with women"; for Judith Butler, the only thing lesbians have in common is a knowledge of how homophobia works against women; and Michael Warner argues that queerness is characterized by a determined "resistance to regimes of the normal." The extreme distrust of all self-identifying moves evidenced in such remarks is understandable. The elaborating of erotic preferences into a character — into a kind of erotically determined essence — is, as Foucault forcefully argues, inherently a disciplinary project. Panoptic vision depends on a successful immobilizing of the objects it surveys; only then can behavior be transformed into manipulatable characterological types.

And yet the way in which the Foucauldian suspicion of sexual essences has been picked up by queer theorists has made me almost nostalgic for those very essences. The principal critical argument of *Homos* is that gay men and lesbians have nearly disappeared into their sophisticated awareness of how they been culturally constructed as gay men and lesbians (which is not to deny the importance of cultural construction in the attribution to us of such things as a gay sensibility). And the consequence of self-erasure is . . . self-erasure, the elimination of gays — the principal aim of homophobia. An acceptance, a promotion of a certain homosexual specificity may be necessary in order for us to be as dangerous culturally, and ultimately politically, as many of us would like to be. Might same-sex desire be transgressive not simply of sexual customs, but, more radically, of the very notions of relationality in which such customs are grounded? Furthermore, the anti-identitarian critique needs to be qualified. It is not at all certain that modern typologies, genealogies, and schemes of desire are necessarily more essentializing than earlier sexual classifications on the basis of behavior alone (rather than some fixed inner disposition). The ancient Greek model, as both Foucault and David Halperin describe it, made for a brutal reduction of the person to his sexual behavior: phallic penetration of another's body not only expressed virility but also was a sign of social superiority, an expression of something we might call the (male) citizen-essence. This binary model is a striking example of the misogyny inherent in homophobia, even though it was not opposed to homosexuality per se. In a sense, the Greeks were so open about their revulsion to what they understood as female sexuality, and so untroubled in their thinking about the relation between power and phallic penetration, that they didn't need to pretend, as nineteenth-century sexologists did, that men who went to bed with other men were all secretly women. Only half of them were women, and that judgment had enormous social implications: the adult male citizen who allowed himself to be penetrated like women and slaves was politically disgraced. Even the crudest identity-mongering leaves us freer than that. To be a woman in a man's body can certainly be thought of as an imprisoning definition, but at least it leaves open the possibility of wondering, as Freud did, about the various desiring positions a woman might take. While psychoanalysis has played a major role in the essentializing of desire, it has also initiated an anti-essentializing inquiry into the nature of desire. There is no reason to be as suspicious of such inquiries as Foucault was, for they have helped us to see that the mobility of desire defeats the project of fixing identity by way of a science of desire. That mobility makes impossible correlations the Greeks found easy to make: most notably between on the one hand, penetrating or being penetrated by another person and, on the other, attributions of moral and political superiority and inferiority.

This, however, is not what I was principally interested in demonstrating in *Homos*. Important work has been done by others that shows, first, that psychoanalytic genealogies of desire may actually destroy rather than reinforce normative views of sexuality (the teleology according to which heterosexual genitality is the normal, mature end-point of sexual development) and, second, that the specificity of same-sex desire puts into question the very category of same-sex desire (because, precisely, of the gender-bending variety of desiring positions inherent in homosexual fantasy). In the context of the de-gaying—the gay and lesbian disappearing act—I began by examining, psychoanalysis proposes a mode of nonessentializing, always provisional psychic visibility. It suggests a specificity of both origin and movement in gay desire, a specificity quite different from the fixed identity constructed by disciplinary networks of power. However, given the necessarily uncertain nature of all etiological investigations of desire, and their tendency to harden into dogma (even presumably liberating dogma), I'm not interested in commiting myself to a stable definition of gay desire. Or, more exactly, such a definition is useful, perhaps even necessary, insofar as we investigate its relational implications—by which I mean the continuities between desire and community, between our sexuality and the ways in which we imagine sociality.

The psychoanalytic inquiry can be politicized in ways generally not allowed for by queer theorists. Like Eve Sedgwick, most of these thinkers feel that accounts of the origin of sexual preference and identity in individuals run counter to politically gay-affirmative work. The trouble is that gay affirmation has become a tame affair, which is perhaps inevitable when we are that suspicious of sexual identities. Queer rhetoric, as in Butler's definition of lesbians as people who know how homophobia operates against women, can be deliberately inflammatory, but in rejecting the sexual specificity of queerness we have become more and more inclined to define our communitarian goals in terms provided by the homophobic community. It seems at times as if we can no longer imagine anything more politically stimulating than to struggle for acceptance as good soldiers, good priests, and good parents. While I remain enough of a liberal to believe that we should defend people's rights to serve whatever worthy or unworthy cause inspires them, I'm more excited by some glorious precedents for thinking of homosexuality as truly disruptive — as a force not limited to the modest goal of tolerance for diverse lifestyles, but perhaps even mandating the choice of an outlaw existence. That choice (which I'll elaborate on in a moment) would be quite different from what currently passes for queer politics. Suspicious of any enforced identity, gays and lesbians play subversively — a word I've come to distrust, since it doesn't seem to mean much more than engaging in naughty parodies — with normative identities, attempting, for example, to resignify the family for communities that defy the usual assumptions about what constitutes a family. These efforts can have assimilative rather than subversive consequences; having de-gayed themselves, gays melt into the very culture they like to think of themselves as undermining. Or, having "realistically" abandoned what Steven Seidman, in his essay for *Fear of a Queer Planet*, calls a "millenial vision" of dominations's demise, we resign ourselves to the micropolitics of local struggles for participatory democracy and social justice — not shying away, as Seidman puts it, "from spelling out a vision of a better society in terms resonant to policy makers and activists." We thus reveal political ambitions about as stirring as those reflected on the bumper stickers that enjoin us to "think globally and act locally."

Curiously enough, the assimilative tendency seems to coexist quite comfortably with what might seem to exclude it: gay and lesbian self-identification in terms of other oppressed minorities. The aversion to homosexuality as an identity has made us into identity-floaters: we wish to both join the ranks of a heterosexual, family-oriented society and identify with the disenfranchised people truly marginalized by that society. In their yearning to be subversive, white middle-class gay men in particular have tended to either blur the differences between themselves and other groups demonstrably more oppressed than they are or suggest that those differences could be overcome by acts of political good faith. The relation of gay men to feminism, for example, and in particular to lesbian feminism, is bound to be more problematic than we like to admit. It's not simply that a white male, straight or gay, is more likely to enjoy privileges in our society than, say, a black lesbian. We're willing enough to admit that; what's more difficult to admit is our erotic complicity with the distributors of power, with the ways in which our society defines the sexiness of power. In "Is the Rectum a Grave?" I argued against a tendency among gay activists to ignore the connections between political sympathies and sexual fantasies and activities. There can be, I argued, a continuity between a sexual preference for rough and uniformed trade, a sentimentalizing of the armed forces, and right-wing politics. At the very least, our feminist sympathies will perhaps always be complicated by a narcissistic investment in the objects of our desire. In his desires, the gay man runs the risk of identifying with culturally dominant images of misogynistic maleness. A more or less secret sympathy with heterosexual male misogyny carries with it the narcissistically gratifying reward of confirming our membership in (and not simply our erotic appetite for) privileged male society. The fantasy underpinnings of gay men's feminism become particularly fraught when our feminist allies are lesbians. Indeed, it's not difficult to appreciate why "fantasy" has become, in certain activist circles, a politically suspect word. If we think of how remote lesbian desiring fantasies are, by definition, from gay male desiring fantasies, and if we acknowledge the influence of erotic investments on political choices, then the very notion of fantasy could easily seem like a heterosexist scheme to sow discord in the gay and lesbian community.

Queer critiques of homosexual identity have generally been desexualizing discourses. You would never know, from many of the works I discuss in *Homos*, that gay men, for all their diversity, share strong sexual interest in other human beings anatomically identifiable as male. Queer studies frequently takes the sex out of being queer. "Queer" is preferred to "gay," Michael Warner has suggested in *Fear of a Queer Planet*, in large part because of its sexually indeterminate reference; it becomes a universal political category, embracing every one who resists "regimes of the normal." (Since many gay men apparently feel quite comfortable with those regimes, would they, unlike many radical straights, be excluded from queerness?) At the same time, gay literary studies, for example, is tireless in its pursuit of what is called homoeroticism in an astonishing number of significant writers from the past. We end up with the implicit but no less extraordinary proposition that gays aren't homosexual but all straights are homoerotic. Given the terminological and epistemological confusion all this creates, it might not be a bad idea to drop the very category of homoeroticism, since it seems to me to be little more than a provokingly tendentious way of asserting a certain sexual indeterminacy in all human beings, a state of affairs hardly discovered by queer studies. The confusion and the denials are all the more unfortunate since queer studies does, as Warner emphasizes, set out to make sexuality "a primary category for social analysis." But, with a few exceptions, this has merely added another category to the analysis of social institutions (making explicit the prescriptive assumptions about sexuality embedded within institutions) rather than trying to trace the political productivity of the sexual. If queerness is to mean more than simply taking sexuality into account in our political analyses, if it means that modalities of desire are not only effects of social operations but are at the core of our very imagination of the political and the social, then something has to be said about how, in gay sexuality for example, erotic desire for the same might affect, even revolutionize, our understanding of how the human subject is, or might be, socially implicated.

It seems to me that the writers I discuss in *Homos*, especially Genet and Gide, address this question. I chose them not because they are relevant to specific policy issues that we might face today, but rather because they propose what are for the moment necessarily mythic reconfigurations of identity and sociality. Alongside the indispensable work, for example, that has been done in AIDS activism, we might also want to think about the ways in which a radical gay or queer politics might emerge not only from a horrendous episode in medical history in which we have been among the principal victims, but also from a gay specificity not dependent on such tragic contingencies. Queer politics has been mainly a micropolitics focused on particular issues which there is no reason to believe will ever be exhausted if the fundamental types of community and relationality out of which such issues spring are not in themselves questioned and redefined. And this activity has to be, at least for the moment, an activity of the intellectual imagination, one for which the micropoliticians often have no use or patience but which seems to me as indispensable, no more of a luxury, than our immediate and vital concrete struggles.

At his or her best, the homosexual is a failed subject, one that needs its identity to be cloned, or inaccurately replicated, outside of it. This is the strength, not the weakness, of homosexuality, for the fiction of an inviolable and unified subject has been an important source of human violence. Each monad-like subject—whether it be a personal, ethnic, national, or racial subject—feels obliged to arm itself against the difference embodied in other subjects equally determined to defend their "integrity" against the Other. It seems that the only way we can love the other or the external world is to find ourselves somehow in it. Only then might there be a nonviolent relation to the world that doesn't seek to exterminate difference. The homosexual, perhaps even the homosexual as a category (what I have called "homoness") rather than as a person (for very often the culturally elaborated differences between the sexes are reconstituted and played out between two men or between two women) might be the model for correspondences of being that are by no means limited to relations among persons. Indeed, the human itself has no ontological priority here. Homoness can first be experienced as a communication of forms, as a kind of universal solidarity not of identities but of positionings and configurations in space, a solidarity that ignores even the apparently most intractable identity-difference: between the human and the nonhuman. The apprenticeship for a relationality founded on sameness rather than on difference must perhaps first of all be a perceptual apprentice- ship (in which art can play a central role) in correspondences that participate in a single but vast family of forms in the universe. This may even involve (as it does explicitly in Genet) what appears to be a betrayal, a radical anti- relationality that may be the prerequisite negativity for an anti-identitarian community. In homosexual sociality, it is perhaps our antimonogamous pro- miscuity that best approximates this relational betrayal, a truly gay betrayal that frees us from some of the benefits of a social assimilation to which some of us understandably but no less sadly aspire.

4

Sociability and Cruising

Sociability is a form of relationality uncontaminated by desire.

I reformulate in this way — in this admittedly tendentious way — the argument made by Georg Simmel in his 1910 essay "The Sociology of Sociability." From Simmel's description, we could view sociability as a paradoxical effect of our socializing impulses. "The higher unity which one calls 'society,'" he writes, is motivated by "interests": "economic and ideal interests, warlike and erotic, religious and charitable." Such interests define the content of groups. "But above and beyond their special content, all . . . associations are accompanied by a feeling for, by a satisfaction in, the very fact that one is associated with others and that the solitariness of the individual is resolved into togetherness, a union with others." Indeed "a feeling for the worth of association as such" is involved in the very motives for association, and the "objective content which carries the particular association along" may, Simmel suggests, only later be called forth. The "special needs and interests" that account for the "special content" of groups may, then, provide an inadequate account of the very origin of groups. An initiating motive of social formations would be the impulse to develop the "special sociological structure" of sociability — which is to say, a structure without motive, a structure, Simmel argues, "corresponding to those of art and play, which draw their form from these realities [those of our life interests] but nevertheless leave the irreality behind them." Like art and play, sociability "takes its substance from numerous fundamental forms of serious relationships like among men," but

Originally published in *Umbr(a): A Journal of the Unconscious* no. 1 (2002): *Sameness*, 11–31.

it is precisely that substance which art, play and sociability leave behind, presenting only "the pure, abstract play of form," "a symbolically playing fulness of life."[1]

A pervasive theme in Simmel's writing is the sacrifice of individuality required by membership in groups. "The great problems placed before [the ethical forces of concrete society] are that the individual has to fit himself into a whole system and live for it: that, however, out of this system values and enhancement must flow back to him, that the life of the individual is but a means for the ends of the whole, the life of the whole but an instrument for the purposes of the individual." Because of "the seriousness, indeed the frequent tragedy of these requirements," sociability is all the more impressive in that, having carried these requirements "over into its shadow world, in which there is no friction," they can be replayed — in, for example, "the manner in which groups form and break up at parties," conversations get started and then break off without tragedy, allowing us to experience what Simmel strikingly calls "the freedom of bondage."[2] Thus sociability solves "the great problem of association": "that of the measure of significance and accent which belongs to the individual as such in and as against the social milieu."[3] The problematic nature of groups that must at once curb and serve individuality is resolved in sociability thanks to the particular pleasure gained from the restriction of the personal: the pleasure of the associative process itself, of a pure relationality which, beyond or before the satisfaction of particular needs or interests, may be at once the ground, the motive and the goal of all relations.

Simmel's essay more or less takes for granted the satisfaction inherent in the abstraction of the relational from concrete relations. But why, exactly, is pure relationality pleasurable? When Simmel speaks of "the pure, abstract play of form" characteristic of sociability,[4] he seems to mean a certain kind of rhythmical play. Rhythm is what remains when content is stripped away. Both the "objective qualities which gather about the personality" ("riches and social position, learning and fame, exceptional capacities and merits of the individual") and "the most personal things — character, mood, and fate"[5] — have no place in sociability, although the latter does keep what Simmel calls a symbolic relation to all this content. Without content sociability nonetheless imitates the rhythms of "real life." In conversation, for example,

1. G Simmel, *On Individuality and Social Forms*, DN Levine (ed), Chicago: The University of Chicago Press, 1971, pp 127–29.
2. Ibid., pp 137–38.   4. Ibid., p 129.
3. Ibid., p 130.   5. Ibid., pp 130–31.

it is the movement of arguments rather than their substance that excites us — such as "binding and loosening, conquering and being vanquished, giving and taking."[6] Similarly, coquetry "plays out the forms of eroticism"; it moves between "hinted consent and hinted denial," "swings between yes and no," stopping at neither pole, divesting sexuality of consequential decisions.[7] As these examples suggest, the fundamental rhythm of sociability is "association and separation."[8] The particular modes of sociable conduct — such as group formation, conversation, coquetry — imitate the movement of individuals toward and away from social systems which is for Simmel the principal object of sociological study.

Because the movement never stops, nothing essential is lost in sociability: neither the individual's selfhood nor the advantage of living in groups. But this very preservation is nonetheless predicated on sacrifice. We live rhythmically only if we renounce possession. We don't expect economic advantages from entering into a group at a party; the "free moving play"[9] of coquetry depends on the suspension of sexual demand; sociable conversation does not definitively settle arguments. We can escape "the solitariness of the individual" and enjoy "the pure essence of association"[10] only if we renounce, at least momentarily, the acquisitive impulses that draw us into groups. In this account, the pleasure of sociability can't help but refer — negatively, as it were — to the conflicts and pressures generated by those socializing impulses. Sociability gives us the pleasure of *relief* from "the frictional relations of real life."[11] But there are hints in Simmel's essay of a more radical view of the relation between pleasure and negativity. The pleasure of sociability would not be merely that of a restful interlude in social life. Instead, it would be the consequence of *our being less than what we really are.* Simmel speaks of a lady who, while avoiding "extreme *décolletage* in a really personal, intimate situation with one or two men," feels comfortable with it "in a large company." "For she is," he adds, "in the larger company, herself, to be sure, but not quite completely herself, since she is only an element in a formally constituted gathering."[12] It is as if there were a happiness inherent in not being entirely ourselves, in being "reduced" to an impersonal rhythm. Here such rational explanations as an escape from the solitariness of individual life, or the relief from conflicts with others, are no longer relevant. Neither, it seems to me, is any

6. Ibid., p 136.
7. Ibid., pp 134–35.
8. Ibid., p 138.
9. Ibid., p 135.

10. Ibid., p 128.
11. Ibid., p 129.
12. Ibid., p 131.

psychoanalytic account that would trace the pleasure of sociability either to intersubjective desires or to a lost (if fantasmatic) *jouissance*. Perhaps because as a sociologist Simmel is less interested in the genealogy of pleasure than in its social nature and function, his account of the satisfaction sociability gives is at once somewhat unsatisfying and free of the assumptions governing most psychoanalytic thought. Simmel calls the pleasure of sociability an "excitement,"[13] and he seems to be positing a nonsexual excitement, one that would be a function of a subject without personality, of a partially dismantled subject. Considering all the interests and passions we lay aside in order to enjoy sociability, we might speak of sociability as an ascetic conduct. It is a self-disciplining that yields pleasure, or excitement. It is not the disciplining itself that is felt as pleasure, so it would be a mistake to speak of sociability as a form of masochism. Indeed, if there is a pleasure accompanying the shedding of our interests, it is the nonmasochistic one of escaping from the frictions, the pain, even the tragedy endemic to social life. Once stripped of those interests, we discover a new type of being, as well as a new type of pleasure. The pleasure does not serve an interest, satisfy a passion, or fulfill a desire. It is an intransitive pleasure intrinsic to a certain mode of existence, to self-subtracted being. A willingness to be less — a certain kind of ascetic disposition — introduces us (perhaps reintroduces us) to the pleasure of rhythmed being.

Most profoundly, the pleasure of sociability is the pleasure of existing, of concretely existing, at the abstract level of pure being. There is no other explanation for that pleasure. It doesn't satisfy conscious or unconscious desires; instead, it testifies to the seductiveness of the ceaseless movement toward and away from things without which there would be no particular desires for *any* thing, a seductiveness that is the ontological ground of the desirability of all things. Simmel ends his essay by proposing the ubiquity of phenomena that, like sociability, represent what he calls the fundamental reality of being. The play, the movement, the rhythm of that fundamental reality inaccurately replicates itself in the multiple spectacles and conducts of the phenomenal world. From the awe-inspiring rising and receding of the ocean's waves to the superficial chatter of the *salon*, being ceaselessly unveils and plays itself in creation. That a phenomenon as commonplace as sociability should be one of the bearers of this metaphysical weight perhaps suggests the lightness of the burden itself, the kind of playful, impersonal narcissism circulating within the proliferations of being. Sociability, as the great sociolo-

---

13. Ibid., p 136.

gist discovered, is the one social structure that owes nothing, in its essence, to the sociology of groups.

"It seems certain," Freud writes in *Group Psychology and the Analysis of the Ego*, "that homosexual love is far more compatible (than hetero-sexual love) with group ties, even when it takes the shape of uninhibited sexual impulses — a remarkable fact, the explanation of which might carry us far."[14]

How far? And in what direction?

Freud never fully answers these questions, although *Group Psychology* is not the only place in his work where he proposes a marked compatibility between sociality and homosexuality. Ten years earlier, in his account of Dr. Schreber's paranoia, he had spoken of the persistence of homosexual tendencies "after the stage of heterosexual object-choice has been reached." " . . . Merely deflected from their sexual aim . . . , they now combine with portions of the ego-instincts and . . . help to constitute the social instincts, thus contributing an erotic factor to friendship and comradeship, to *esprit de corps* and to the love of mankind in general."[15] Not only that: the "social instincts" are even more finely developed in those who have failed to reach the stage of heterosexual object-choice: " . . . It is not irrelevant to note," Freud concludes, "that it is precisely manifest homosexuals, and among them again precisely those that struggle against an indulgence in sensual acts [the passage quoted from *Group Psychology* modifies this by suggesting the compatibility of "uninhibited" homosexual impulses with a special aptitude for group ties], who distinguish themselves by taking a particularly active share in the general interests of humanity — interests which have themselves sprung from a sublimation of erotic interests."[16] Finally, in the short paper "Some Neurotic Mechanisms in Jealousy, Paranoia and Homosexuality," written early in 1921, just before he began the final version of *Group Psychology and the Analysis of the Ego*, Freud writes: "It is well known that a good number of homosexuals are characterized by a special development of their social instinctual impulses and by their devotion to the interests of the community."[17]

14. S. Freud, *Group Psychology and the Analysis of the Ego* (1921), trans. J Strachey, New York: WW Norton, 1959, p 95.

15. S Freud, "Psychoanalytic Notes Upon an Autobiographical Account of a Case of Paranoia (Dementia Paranoides)" (1911), in *The Standard Edition of the Complete Psychological Works of Sigmund Freud*, J Strachey (ed), 24 vols, London: Hogarth, 1953–1974, 12:61.

16. Ibid., p 61.

17. S Freud, "Some Neurotic Mechanisms in Jealousy, Paranoia and Homosexuality" (1921), in *The Standard Edition*, 18:232.

What Freud means by social feeling is more general than sociability. It includes all those "interests"—the play of frequently conflicting passions and ambitions—that are, for Simmel, suspended, at least ideally, during the sociable gathering. The value of Simmel's analysis nonetheless seems to me to lie in the possibility of sociability as he defines it pointing, paradoxically, to something beyond itself. That possibility has frequently been examined in literary texts—in, for example, texts as different from one another as Stendhal's *La Chartreuse de Parme* and Molière's *Le Misanthrope*. In *La Chartreuse*, Stendhal proposes the *salon* as a social, even a political model, thus suggesting the relevance of sociability to sociality itself. In maintaining the special aptitude of homosexuals for social feeling, Freud appears to be arguing—fleetingly, to be sure—that a "devotion to the interests of the community" might be inherent in a particular mode of sexual desire. It is as if Freud were reserving a certain area of sexuality for a successfully civilized relationality—a prospect absent (forgotten?) in the fierce antagonism spelled out in *Civilization and Its Discontents* between individual happiness and the interests of society. Nothing would be more surprising than to find psychoanalysis granting this privilege to homosexuals. In contemporary adventures—both straight and gay—of reimagining sociality and community, psychoanalysis is notably absent, as a helpful source or reference, from efforts to conceptualize a sociality no longer imprisoned within identitarian ideologies. Not only that: for most queer theorists, psychoanalysis, even if it were to be seen as welcoming such efforts, would necessarily exclude from them what it considers as the "perversion" of homosexual desire. Can a regression, even when it is no longer labeled a neurosis, have a place within a utopic imagination? It will therefore be exceedingly strange to discover, at the very origin of psychoanalysis, the outline of a conceptualising of queer desire as somehow exempt from the destructive sociality of straight desire.

This is by no means the same thing as saying that gay and lesbian communities, as they are currently constituted, offer persuasive evidence for the speculative argument I will be making. Indeed, they rather confirm the Foucaldian injunction to which I have already appealed: we must *learn* to be gay. Psychoanalysis was not a place Foucault would have turned to in order to find new relational modes, and I have myself recently specified what seem to me the constitutive limitations of psychoanalytic thinking for any such enterprise. That thought nonetheless remains indispensable not only because it reminds us, as I have argued elsewhere, of the dangers attached to the pastoralizing of any form of sexual relation, but also because it points—hesitatingly, even unwillingly—to a sociality no longer governed by

the unavoidable aggressiveness accompanying what Lacan has analyzed as
the subject's impossible and intractable demand for a sexual relation. Already
in Freud, however, a certain reflection on the sexual opens the way to a dissolving of the sexual *in* that impossible relation, and in so doing it encourages reconfigurations of the social far more radical than those contemporary
queer attempts to present as revolutionary, as seriously threatening to the
dominant social order, such reformist, harmless, and familiar "innovations"
as gay marriage, public sex, or the corporate charities that have arisen in response to the AIDS epidemic. Nothing we have imagined so far sufficiently
betrays the relational orders under which much of humanity continues to be
oppressed. While it has certainly served those orders in its emphasis on normative sexuality, psychoanalysis has from the beginning been subversive of
the dogmas thanks to which it became, in a relatively short period of time, a
respectable social institution. Specifically, Freud's theoretical flirtation with
the idea of homosexuality as conducive to a "special development" of social
impulses can, so to speak, itself be speculatively flirted with to the point, as
we will now see, of yielding an astonishing yet plausible argument for a truly
sociable sexuality.

It's true that the "particularly active share in the general interests of
humanity" which presumably characterizes homosexuals is, for Freud,
simply a more visible manifestation of the role of homosexuality in *all*
social feelings. In heterosexuals (as well, we might presume, as in those
homosexuals who "struggle against an indulgence in sexual acts"), homosexual tendencies are sublimated into friendship and *esprit de corps*.
Freud succinctly summarizes this view in "Some Neurotic Mechanisms": "In the light of psychoanalysis we are accustomed to regard social feeling as a sublimation of homosexual attitudes towards objects."[18]
Furthermore, diverted from their original aims, these tendencies, no
longer capable of "really complete satisfaction," Freud notes in *Group
Psychology*, are more likely "to create permanent ties" than if they had
remained uninhibited (and subject to the loss of energy consequent
upon the satisfaction of a directly sexual desire).[19] And yet: Freud suggests that the compatibility of homosexual tendencies with social feelings
does not depend on the mere availability of sexual energy from a stage
of desire that has, in the majority of cases, been left behind. Remember
that, according to the passage from *Group Psychology*, sociality is especially pronounced even when homosexual impulses have *not* been left

18. Ibid., 231.
19. S Freud, *Group Psychology and the Analysis of the Ego* (1921), p 91.

behind, remain uninhibited. There must be a specificity to the desire itself that accounts for its socializing aptitude, even when the desire can no longer be recognised in the cohesion and activities of groups.

"Some Neurotic Mechanisms" ends with the apparently casual observation that "in the homosexuals with marked social interests, it would seem that the detachment of social feeling from object-choice has not been fully carried through."[20] This thunderously obvious fact would have been an unnecessary (and flat) conclusion to the preceding speculations of this essay if it did not resonate — in ways Freud leaves unexamined — with both one of Freud's earlier etiologies of homosexual desire *and* the conceptually troubled distinction put forward in *Group Psychology and the Analysis of the Ego* between object-choice and identification. As his title indicates, in order to explain "group psychology" — and, more specifically, "the libidinal constitution of groups"[21] — Freud finds it necessary to go back to "the analysis of the ego" with which readers of his earlier papers "On Narcissism: An Introduction" (1914) and "Mourning and Melancholia" (1917) would be familiar. The study of melancholia in particular, Freud recalls, had revealed "an ego divided, fallen apart into two pieces, one of which rages against the second." Here is Freud's description of the first ego-piece, a description most fully and most famously elaborated a few years later in the discussion of the superego in *The Ego and the Id* (1924): "It [the part of the ego that 'rages against the second'] comprises the conscience, a critical agency within the ego, which even in normal times takes up a critical attitude towards the ego, though never so relentlessly and so unjustifiably."[22]

As it has frequently been observed in the literature devoted to the Freudian notion of the ego ideal, the latter is at once loved as a source of narcissistic satisfaction (it possesses "the perfections which we have striven to reach for our own ego"[23]), and feared as a source of rageful moral (frequently moralistic) demands made upon the ego. Most interestingly, the ego ideal allows Freud to make a somewhat tortuous distinction between object-love and identification. In an extraordinary paragraph in which Freud abandons and reinvents his analytical arguments and terms as he goes along, that distinction is at once affirmed and questioned. In attempting "to define the difference between identification and such extreme developments of being in love as may be described as 'fascination' or 'bondage,'" Freud finally settles

20. S Freud, "Some Neurotic Mechanisms in Jealousy, Paranoia and Homosexuality" (1921), in *The Standard Edition*, 18:232.

21. S Freud, *Group Psychology and the Analysis of the Ego* (1921), p 60.

22. Ibid., p 52.

23. Ibid., p 56.

on a distinction between an object that has been lost with which the ego then identifies and, in the "bondage" of love, a hypercathexis of the retained object at the expense of the ego. But then he brings up yet another difficulty: "Is it quite certain that identification presupposes that object-cathexis has been given up? Can there be no identification while the object is retained?" The question, Freud notes, is a "delicate" one, although he fails to embark upon a discussion of it. Instead, he concludes with another alternative that, happily, "embraces the real essence of the matter, namely, *whether the object is put in the place of the ego or of the ego ideal.*"[24] It is as if the question of whether the object must be lost or given up before identification can take place — in other words, the question of whether identification and object-cathexis can coexist — no longer needs to be answered if a "place" in the mind is invented where the loved object can exist without being identified with. The ego ideal comes to the rescue here: it is both an internalized otherness and an alienated interiority, the loved object at an uncrossable distance from the ego within the ego as well as the originally self-sufficient ego of primary narcissism torn away from the ego and assimilated to a foreign body inhabiting an ego it observes and judges.

It is the invention of the ego ideal, of a "differentiating grade in the ego" (as Freud calls it in the title of *Group Psychology*'s final chapter) that has allowed Freud to elude the possibility of (a nonpathological) object-love as self-love. Identification in the official Freudian scheme is either the most primitive of emotional ties to an object, or, regressively, a substitute for a lost object-tie. It can, Freud maintains in *Group Psychology*, involve recognition of "a common quality shared with some other person" only if that person "is not an object of the sexual instinct."[25] What is inconceivable in the Freudian scheme is *identification as libidinal recognition.* But this is not quite accurate; it is conceived of within the Freudian scheme, but only as a perversion. And it is of course the perversion of homosexuality. In his study of Leonardo da Vinci, Freud proposes an account of male homosexual desire which he refers to in both "Some Neurotic Mechanisms" and *Group Psychology.* After a long and intense fixation upon his mother, the budding homosexual does not abandon her at the end of puberty but rather "identifies himself with her; he transforms himself into her, and now looks about for objects which can replace his ego for him, and on which he can bestow such love and care as he has experienced from his mother."[26] The renunciation of women as love-objects means that "all rivalry with [the father] (or with all men who may

24. Ibid., p 58.
25. Ibid., p 50.

26. Ibid., p 51.

take his place) is avoided." Freud adds that "the retiring in favor of the father . . . may be ascribed to the castration complex."[27] This is of course a very familiar psychoanalytic "reduction" of homosexuality, and it is one that most self-respecting queers find both obsolete and offensive. There is, however, as we say today, a gay-friendly way of reading this account, one that in fact turns it against itself. First of all, the relevance of that reference to the castration complex is by no means certain. Freud's hypothetical homosexual has after all really not abandoned his mother, but neither has he fantasmatically struggled with his father in order to have her. The Oedipal rivalry — which "should" end with the boy giving up his passionate attachment to his mother in order to avoid threatened castration at the hands of the father — has simply been bypassed by an identification that is neither a loss nor object-love in the usual sense.

Lacan would say that perversion denies castration — but even the Lacanian promotion of castration from an Oedipal fantasy to the meta-genital status of a lost plenitude of being does not prove the necessity of *any* type of "deniable" castration for a theory of desire. Castration from a retroactively fantasised fullness of being from which our entry into language severed us is perhaps itself the fantasy of a fantasy. This conceptual meta-fanstasy may be dictated by a heterosexual inability to think of desire other than as lack or loss. It is the final step in a generalizing of privation consequent upon the dependence of male heterosexual desire on a rivalry that one has not exactly overcome but which has more simply and more catastrophically ended in defeat. All heterosexual desire, according to the terms of that very discipline that has argued for the psychic (not to mention moral) superiority of heterosexual desire, can't help but be to some degree conditioned by the memory, or the fantasy, of that defeat. The heterosexual male's rageful resentment at the victorious father must, in what are hardly negligible aftereffects, find expression not only in the antagonism toward other men which, according to Freud himself, makes heterosexual social feeling less developed than homosexual social feeling, but also in a misogynous aggressiveness toward all those women who, to some degree, can't help but be seen as mere substitutes for an abandoned, irreplaceable, supreme object of love. It would, then, hardly be surprising if, far from being a secondary manifestation of a fall from Being, Oedipal castration were the source and the motivation for elaborations — satisfying to the psychanalytic ego — of an ontological cut or castration.

27. S Freud, "Some Neurotic Mechanisms in Jealousy, Paranoia and Homosexuality" (1921), in *The Standard Edition*, 18:231.

The psychoanalytically defined homosexual, on the other hand, in spite of psychoanalysis's best — or worst — intentions, is (at least insofar as he is exclusively homosexual, which of course he never is) a stranger to these murderous passions — perhaps, most fundamentally and most beneficently, to passion itself. He wanders in the world — cruises the world, we might almost say — in search of objects that will give him back to himself as a loved and cared for subject. Homosexual desire for others is, in this account, motivated by the wish to treat oneself lovingly. It gives an affirmative answer to the question Freud asks but finds unnecessary to answer in *Group Psychology and the Analysis of the Ego:* Can there be identification when the object of love is retained? The man Freud describes a few pages before asking this question chooses love-objects *because* he identifies with them. He has, it's true, lost himself when he identifies with his mother, and so he "looks about for objects which can replace his ego for him,"[28] but he will identify with those objects without introjecting them. Contrary to the usual Freudian sequence of a loss compensated for by fantasy-identification with the lost object, in the scenario of homosexual desire the subject has himself managed the loss (presumably by placing his mother in the position of his ego) and, most importantly, the loss is made up for not by another introjection but by *new relations with new love-objects.*

I am not anxious to defend the clinical truth of what might be called the Leonardo-factor in Freud's account of homosexual desire. Instead, let's consider that account as a myth analogous to (if less satisfying poetically than) Aristophanes' myth in the *Symposium.* Both stories emphasize what I have called in my discussion of Plato's dialogue our at-homeness in the world.[29] Every subject reoccurs differently everywhere. "Differently" is crucial: it is the recognizing and longing for sameness that allows us to relate lovingly to difference. A certain homosexualizing of heterosexual love can make this privilege universal. Just as homosexual desire can never be entirely free of "paternal" Law having rendered otherness unknowable, prohibited and intrinsically hostile, so heterosexual desire must contain — however much it seeks to occlude — the recognition that difference can be loved as the nonthreatening supplement of sameness. I would even go so far as to say that the homosexual way into this recognition is a *pis aller*, something like a second-best solution. Without in any way denying the immense range of differences that can be accommodated by homosexual love, we might

28. S Freud, *Group Psychology and the Analysis of the Ego* (1921), p 51.
29. See Leo Bersani, "Sociality and Sexuality," *Critical Inquiry*, vol 26, no 1 (Summer 2000), pp 641–56.

also acknowledge the even rarer opportunity in heterosexual love for a nonmurderous wonder at difference. While, as it has been vehemently argued in recent years, sexual difference has been prejudicially sanctified in our psychoanalytically oriented culture as the ground of all difference, it perhaps does have a unique epistemological function in human growth as an early and crucial model for structuring difference. The ego ideal is the psychoanalytic myth that reifies the traumatic component of sexual difference. It refers to the mental resource that allows the subject permanently to judge others as resistant to an identification based on recognition — and, correlatively, to stigmatize the external world as constitutively alien and hostile to the self. Hatred of the world, as Freud writes in "Instincts and Their Vicissitudes," "always remains in an intimate relation with the self-preservative instincts."[30] The impossible demand upon a world in which I am nowhere to be found, where self-recognition would always be a mistake, is that the world provide exact replications of myself, that in fact it be erased and replaced by the specular mirage of a universalized selfhood. But since those hated alien objects also elicit desire, since no human subject can survive walled in by a wholly narcissistic love, the subject loves and hates, desires and fears, the same object — a situation duplicated in Freud's description of the ego's relation to the ego ideal (or the superego). The latter eroticizes interdiction (which is perhaps itself merely the escape route from otherness, the subject's willed flight from traumatically different objects — a flight transformed into a command from the outside), and interdiction, the Law, becomes a privileged source of the very *jouissance* it forbids.

The ability to identify with the loved object — that which Freud sees as one of the sources of the "problem" of homosexuality — allows for a very different relation to the world. The subject's productive illusion of becoming one with a loved parental caregiver is the useful pretext for the subject to go searching for him- or herself in the world. The self-preservative hatred of objects, never entirely eradicated, can at least become secondary to an object-love identical to self-love. A self-love hospitable to difference: misrecognition here is not the fateful error of imaginary specularization, but rather both describes the accommodating of difference by sameness and becomes the motive for continuing the search. As in Aristophanes' myth, we can never find our "original nature," or, in Freud's terms, the ego we need to replace. Finally, however, both myths are somewhat diverting misrepresentations of

---

30. S Freud, "Instincts and Their Vicissitudes" (1915), *The Standard Edition*, 14:139.

our presence in the world. They divert us — I mean they turn us away from our presence *already there*. Plato and Freud narrativize that presence as a being we once had but have lost or given up. Thus the subject is — touchingly but erroneously — made the agent of its reoccurences outside itself. If, as I have been proposing here and elsewhere, we are in the world before we are born into it, this is not because we once — historically or mythically — possessed ourselves, but rather because it is impossible to take on a form — a being — to which the world does not have a response, with which it is not already in correspondence.

Cruising is sexual sociability. The danger associated with cruising is not that it reduces relations to promiscuous sex, but rather that the promiscuity may stop. Few things are more difficult than to block our interest in others, to prevent our connection to them from degenerating into a "relationship." In the model of cruising implicitly proposed by both the Freudian account of homosexual desire and Aristophanes' fable in the *Symposium*, the search for the self *out there* can only be beneficently fruitless. The boys Leonardo may love as his mother loved him are of course not exactly Leonardo, and Aristophanes notes, in what I take to be a tone of ironic resignation, " . . . the nearest approach to [our exactly identical other half] is best in present circumstances . . . Love does the best that can be done for the time being."[31] This erotic best is faithful to an ontological truth: the replications of being are always, however minutely, inaccurate replications.

In, however, an imperceptible but momentous shift of psychic registers, the object of desire can evoke not the loving mother but, instead, the impenetrable mother, the mother whose terrifying unintelligibility we domesticated by assimilating it into a narrative of paternal interdiction. The object of desire is now an object of fascination; he or she reactivates a world in which the subject is nowhere to be found, one of pure otherness. The world has become, again, what Laplanche has called the enigmatic signifier who sent us, who appears to be sending us once again, messages we can't process, or "metabolize."[32] The sign and consequence of this resurrection of the enigmatic signifier in an object of desire is sexual passion. In an extraordinary passage of *Un Amour de Swann*, Proust exactly dates the shift I'm speaking of in Swann's relation to Odette. It occurs when, having failed to appear at

31. Plato, The Symposium, trans. A Nehemas and P Woodruff, in *Complete Works*, JM Cooper (ed), Indianapolis: Hackett, 1997, p 476.

32. See J Laplanche, *Seduction, Translation, Drives*, J Fletcher and M Stanton (eds), London: Institute of Contemporary Arts, 1992.

a party where Swann had expected her, Odette is metamorphosed from an object of noninsistent sensual interest into an *être de fuite*, a creature whose inaccessibility has become her very essence. Searching for her throughout the night in the restaurants and on the streets of Paris, Swann brushes past the dim forms of other women, "as though among the phantoms of the dead, in the realms of darkness, he had been searching for a lost Eurydice."[33] He has indeed changed realms, or worlds — or, more exactly, it is Odette who has moved into a world that can be "known" only as a place where Swann is not. Thus his love becomes the constantly renewed epistemological defeat of, to adopt Lacan's term, the desire of/for her desire. Swann's sexual fascination, bizarrely yet logically, has little to do with Odette's body. Odette as enigmatic signifier can be "metabolized" not if she lets herself, to use a phrase Proust mocks, be possessed by him, but only if she allows her desire to be inhabited by Swann's consciousness. Constitutively, this is what she can't allow, for in the crisis of his nocturnal search for Odette, Swann himself disappeared, and Odette has become nothing more — and, more portentously, nothing less — than the place where he may be hidden, hidden, moreover, as unimaginable otherness. And it is in defining erotic desire as epistemological catastrophe that Proust himself becomes a novelist of heterosexual — or, at least, heteroized — love. The note of condescending acceptance towards Proust's homosexuality that enters into many admiring critical commentaries on *A la recherche du temps perdu* is wholly unnecessary. In its somber glamorizing of a desire grounded in the irreducible opposition between an empty subject and objects of desire that might but won't reveal and return the subject to himself, Proust masochistically celebrates difference as the very condition of desire, thus renouncing the privilege his homosexuality might have afforded him of recognizing, and loving, himself in an hospitably familiar otherness.

"What makes homosexuality 'disturbing,'" Foucault remarked in a 1981 interview, is "the homosexual mode of life, much more than the sexual act itself." He spoke of "a homosexual ascesis that would make us work on ourselves and invent — I don't say discover — a manner of being that is still improbable."[34] Ascesis — a central concept in Foucault's study of ancient Greek and Roman "practices of the self" in volumes 2 and 3 of the *History of Sexuality* — would be perhaps the principal strategy in any attempt "to become gay," which

33. M Proust, *Swann's Way/Remembrance of Things Past*, trans. CK Scott Moncrieff and T Kilmartin, New York: Vintage Books, Random House, 1989, p 252.

34. M Foucault, "Friendship as a Way of Life" (1981), in *Ethics/Subjectivity and Truth*, vol 1 of *Essential Works of Foucault 1954–1984*, P Rabinow (ed), New York: The New Press, 1997, pp 136–37.

Foucault understood as radically different from merely "being homosexual." In another interview, Foucault specified that he was taking ascesis "in a very general sense — in other words, not in the sense of a morality of renunciation but as an exercise of the self on the self by which one attempts to develop and transform oneself, and to attain to a certain mode of being."[35] While appearing to dismiss "the sexual act itself" as irrelevant to the elaboration of a new "mode of life" (as well as to the fear and hostility with which much of straight society responds to gays), Foucault also asked the interesting question: "How can a relational system be reached through sexual practices?"[36] Rather than think of sexuality as "the secret of the creative cultural life," he encouraged us "to create a view of cultural life underneath the ground of our sexual choices."[37] "The desexualization of pleasure" (we should perhaps specify: the degenitalizing of pleasure) Foucault found in gay S & M had, he seemed to think, important cultural or relational implications. S & M would help to undermine more general systems of domination modeled on a sexual ideology in which sexual passivity has been, as Foucault put it, "isomorphic" with social inferiority. S & M, Foucault claimed, has helped to "alleviate [the] problem" of men thinking of themselves as natural masters because and only if they are never on the bottom, always on top.[38]

In *Homos*, I expressed my skepticism about the viability of S & M — a practice constitutively committed, it seems to me, to the idolatry of power — for such major relational shifts. In cruising I'm proposing another sexual model — one in which a deliberate avoidance of relationships might be crucial in initiating, or at least clearing the ground for, a new relationality. Having criticized queer theorists for proposing such things as public sex or the nonmonogamous gay couple as examples of the new relational modes Foucault urged us to invent, I certainly don't mean to offer the centuries-old practice of cruising as a more authentic relational invention. Since we are not going to reinvent relationality *ex nihilo*, the point is to see how certain familiar practices — such as S & M, public sex, sexually unstable intimacies — have or do not have the potential for tracing what Foucault also called "new-alliances and. . . . unforseen lines of force."[39] The fact that the practices just referred to are generally condemned outside the circles that engage in them can hardly be said to certify their relational inventiveness.

35. M Foucault, "The Ethics of the Concern of the Self as a Practice of Freedom" (1984), in *Ethics*, p 282.
36. M Foucault, "Friendship" interview, in *Ethics*, p 137.
37. M Foucault, "Sex, Power, and the Politics of Identity" (1982), in *Ethics*, p 164.
38. M Foucault, "Sexual Choice, Sexual Act" (1982), in *Ethics*, p 152.
39. M Foucault, "Friendship" interview, in *Ethics*, p 136.

An understandable but unfortunate queer response to this condemnation has been, on the one hand, the untenable suggestion that these practices are something new and, on the other, that, contrary to what most people think, they are perfectly consistent with human decency, integrity and dignity. This second argument defeats the first; it brings us right back to values embraced (if obviously not invented) by homophobic "morality." In short, these defensive arguments insufficiently betray the relational modes sanctified by the dominant culture. Does cruising make us feel as, perhaps even more, worthy than a comfortably monogamous straight couple — in which case cruising becomes even less interesting than marriage — or does it help us to at least glimpse the possibility of dismissing moral worthiness itself, of constructing human subjects whom such moral categories would fail to "cover"? In other words, it is not a question of demonstrating that certain outrageous practices are really taking place within the parameters of a traditional ethics, but rather of specifying the ways in which those practices may or may not require us to elaborate new ethical vocabularies.

Cruising, like sociability, can be a training in impersonal intimacy. The particularity that distinguishes it from sociability is, of course, that it brings bodies together. It is as if the game of coquetry described by Simmel moved into a sexual relation — but one to which Simmel's description of a nonsexual coquetry would still apply. Simmel, we remember, speaks of the coquette not being quite herself. She is, as we all are when we are sociable according to Simmel, somewhat less than herself; the game goes on only if her passions and practical interests stay out of the game. Similarly, in cruising — at lest in ideal cruising — we leave our selves behind. The gay bathhouse is especially favorable to ideal cruising because, in addition to the opportunity anonymous sex offers its practitioners of shedding much of the personality that individuates them psychologically, the common bathhouse uniform — a towel — communicates very little (although there are of course ways of wearing a towel . . .) about our social personality (economic privilege, class status, taste).

Most important, the intimacy of bodies no longer embellished or impoverished, protected or exposed, by the "clothing" of both dress and character is an exceptional experience of the infinite distance that separates us from all otherness. Psychological and social difference forecloses this naked (in more than one sense) perception of otherness. Differences traumatize and fascinate us; they inspire our aggressiveness but also our tolerance; they are never *totally nonnegotiable*. It seems to me useful to distinguish between these differences and the more than physical distance — the metaphysical distance — that always, and irremediably, separates the subject from otherness. The otherness I refer to is one that cannot be erased or even reduced by the inaccurate replications that, by inviting multiple and diverse self-recognitions, make of the world a hospitable space in which the subject ceaselessly, and always partially, reoccurs. Outside, even where I am again, is, simply by virtue of its being outside, infinitely distant. The intimacy with an unknown body is the revelation of that distance at the very moment we appear to be crossing an uncrossable interval. Otherness, unlocatable within differences that can be known and enumerated, is made concrete in the eroticized touching of a body without attributes. A nonmasochistic *jouissance* (one that owes nothing to the death drive) is the sign of that nameless, identity-free contact — contact with an object I don't know and certainly don't love and which has, unknowingly, agreed to be momentarily the incarnated shock of otherness. In that moment we relate to that which transcends all relations.

For me, this illuminates the connection I have previously made, and which has always remained somewhat mysterious to me, between *jouissance* and ascesis. The *jouissance* of otherness has as its precondition the stripping away of the self, a loss of all that gives us pleasure and pain in our negotiable exchanges with the world. In the *jouissance* of otherness, an entire category of exchange is erased: the category of intersubjectivity. This erasure is an ascetic (not a masochistic) practice — a "practice of the self," to use Foucault's term, but not in his sense of "an intensification of subjectivity," nor for the sake of self-domination or the domination of others. In ascetic erotic contact, we lose much that is presumed to be "good" in sex (especially, it is said, the heightened awareness of another person), but the nonattributable intensity I'm attempting to evoke also makes impossible that envy of the other's *different jouissance* which nourishes homophobia and misogyny. In "Is the Rectum a Grave?" I speculated on the fantasy, in heterosexual men, of an intolerably alien ecstasy inherent in female sexuality and in gay male sexuality. I now think that the hateful envy of that ecstasy is the envy of a certain kind of death. The association of sex with death is familiar; I suggest that this association is made when we feel that we can't profit from it. More specifically, it is the association of sex not with death but with dying. The envied sexuality is the *lived jouissance* of dying, as if we thought we might "consent" to death if we could enter it orgasmically.

The sexual sociability of cruising facilitates the move into what can only be referred to by the oxymoron of metaphysical sociability. The inadequate subjectivity that sociability requires — the self-subtraction — is, by definition, the absence of those psychic, sexual and social differences in which sex becomes secondary to the anguished dream of plotting our own dying. Our task now might be to see how viable the relationality we have uncovered in activities apparently so removed from — even antagonistic to — each other as sociability and cruising might be for other types of connectedness. Foucault wrote that "after Descartes, we have a nonascetic subject of knowledge."[40] Might the diffusion of certain ascetic practices threaten the security of that "subject of knowledge" — and in particular the hyperbolic ego's destructive illusion of power over the objects of knowledge? In attempting to answer these questions, we would of course be elaborating a new ethics. Let's call this an ecological ethics, one in which the subject, having willed its own lessness, can live less invasively in the world. If our psychic center can finally seem less seductive than our innumerable and imperfect reappearances outside, it should then seem not only imperative but natural to treat the outside as we would a home.

40. M Foucault, "On the Genealogy of Ethics: An Overview of Work in Progress" (1983), in *Ethics*, p 279.

5

Aggression, Gay Shame, and Almodóvar's Art

Nothing is more absurd, Freud asserts in *Civilization and Its Discontents* (1930), than what is perhaps the most cherished biblical commandment: "Thou shalt love thy neighbor as thyself." This commandment, revered as "one of the ideal demands" of civilized society, is "really justified by the fact that nothing else runs so strongly counter to the original nature of man," which, Freud claims, dictates not that we love our neighbors, but rather that we exploit them, rob them, rape them, murder them." Much of Jacques Lacan's 1959–60 seminar, "The Ethics of Psychoanalysis," and in particular the March 20 lesson entitled "Love of one's neighbor," is a gloss on Freud's profoundly disabused view of the moral law that enjoins us to love others. The way in which Freud confronts this commandment is, for Lacan, the very heart of *Civilization and Its Discontents:* ". . . that is where he begins, where he remains throughout, and where he ends up. He talks of nothing but that."

"That," for the Lacan of the ethics seminar, is the problem of evil as an intractable murderousness constitutive of the human itself. If we dismiss — as it seems to me we should — the more or less optimistic psychoanalytic theories between Freud and Lacan, theories that would make us more or less happy by way of such things as adaptation to the real and genital normalcy, then we may judge the great achievement of psychoanalysis to be its attempt to account for our inability to love others, and ourselves. The promises of adaptive balance and sexual maturity undoubtedly explain the phenomenal appeal of psychoanalysis as therapy, but its greatness may lie in its insistence on a

Translation (by the author) of a lecture given to the Ecole lacanienne in Strasbourg, France, in 2003. The discussion beginning on p. 76 was written in collaboration with Ulysse Dutoit.

human destructiveness resistant to any therapeutic endeavors whatsoever. This has little to do with sex, and we can distinguish between the practices normally identified as sex and a permanent, irreducibly destructive disposition which such great figures of psychoanalytic theory as Freud, Laplanche and Lacan more or less explicitly define as sexuality. In Freud, the connection between the destructive and the sexual is most apparent in *Civilization and Its Discontents*, which, in all likelihood, explains the appeal of that work for the Lacan of the ethics seminar. While insisting on the nonerotic character of the aggressiveness presumably opposed to love, Freud at the same time undermines his own resolutely embraced dualism by recognizing the "extraordinarily high degree of narcissistic enjoyment" that accompanies satisfied aggression. Sex becomes sexuality when the pleasure of "losing ourselves" in sex is interpretively remembered as a sign and a promise of the painful ecstasy once gained from the shattering of consciousness and the devastation of the world in the sexualized aggressiveness of infantile fantasy. There is, then, a certain continuity between the pleasures of sex and the even greater pleasure of a massive aggressiveness. But the latter is a sexual pleasure which sex can't give, to which sex is irrelevant.

Both the continuity and the incommensurability are simply and profoundly designated by Lacan's use of the word *jouissance*. *Jouir* is the French word for coming, for having an orgasm. Lacanian *jouissance* unavoidably evokes orgasmic pleasure, but it pushes pleasure beyond itself, to the point of becoming the enemy of pleasure, that which lies "beyond the pleasure principle." " . . . My neighbor's *jouissance*," Lacan states in the March 20 Lesson of the Ethics Seminar, "his harmful, malignant *jouissance*, is that which poses a problem for my love"—the insurmountable problem of an ecstasy dependent (for both my neighbor and myself) on my being destroyed. *Jouissance* accompanies the "unfathomable aggressivity" that I find at the heart of both the other's love for me and my love for the other—an aggressivity which, as Freud demonstrates in *Civilization and Its Discontents*, can become even more ferociously destructive of the (internalized) other when the subject turns it against himself. The other as prohibitive Law becomes permanently available as both an object of vengeful attack and the moral voice that at once thwarts and nourishes forbidden desires. With the reign of the superego, sexuality is, as it were, born again as psychic violence; desire is satisfied as rage, from which it can become inseparable. To follow Freud in *Civilization and Its Discontents* is, as Lacan claims, to conclude that "we cannot avoid the formula that *jouissance* is evil."

With the notion of *jouissance*—in fact, already with the Freudian notion of the "extraordinarily high degree of narcissistic enjoyment" that (Freud acknowledges in *Civilization and Its Discontents*) is at once the sadistic and masochistic benefit of "the blindest destructive fury"—psychoanalysis formulates an irreducible "evil" in the human psyche. Individual histories are irrelevant to this destructiveness, as is perhaps history *tout court*; it is not determined or fundamentally affected by gender differences or by differences of sexual preference. It is postulated as a universal property of the human psyche, something as species-specific as the human aptitude for verbal language. The immense psychological edifice of psychoanalytic theory (the stages of sexual maturation, the shapes and outcomes of the Oedipus complex, the interpretation of dreams, the analysis of symptoms, the classifications of neuroses and psychoses, the mechanisms of repression and sublimation, the illuminations and subterfuges of memory) is, from the point of view of the intractable human impulse to destroy, merely a distraction, a Pascalian *divertissement* that nourishes therapeutic commerce. In telling us that the greatest human happiness is exactly identical to the greatest human unhappiness, psychoanalysis at once "explains" a violence that no individual or social transformations would eliminate and renders superfluous any further explanations. The *jouissance* inherent in that violence is the final cause of our desires, the cause (in Lacanian terms) to which no object of our desires ever corresponds.

There may, however, be a "beyond *jouissance*." By this I do not mean that we can be "cured" of the drive that continuously threatens individuals and civilization, that it can somehow be done away with. Rather, just as the death drive does not eliminate the pleasure principle in Freud, what I have in mind would not erase *jouissance* but might play to the side of it, supplement it with a pleasure at once less intense and more seductive. But the effectiveness of this other seduction first of all depends on a painful acknowledgment of *jouissance* as perhaps our most cherished property. It is only by thinking psychoanalytically that we will be able to experience the limits of psychoanalytic thought. If, however, we consider the death drive as crucial to psychoanalysis's self-discovery—that is, the articulation of its own specificity—then it is doubtful that psychoanalysis can help us to define an other order of pleasure. How, then, might we best approach the mode of being that makes that pleasure available to us?

It is doubtful that queer theory will be helpful in this enterprise. The most striking aspect in the evolution of this theory has been a somewhat troubled reflection on the question of sexual identity. *Homos* was largely a reaction to the first phase of this reflection. Inspired by Foucault (or claiming to be inspired by Foucault), several of the early texts of the queer movement defiantly challenged the ways in which a dominantly heterosexual culture has defined and categorized homosexuality. But the anti-identitarian politics of queer theory risked erasing the specificity of homosexual desire by defining as "queer" that which resists the regime of the normal. This criterion, while accepting a large number of heterosexuals as queer, implicitly denied that privilege to quite a few gays and lesbians. Recently, however, there have been some interesting attempts to trace a gay subjectivity, attempts that inevitably give some psychic density to the polemical definition of queer as resistance to normativity. On the one hand, given my criticism of queer theory in *Homos*, I can only applaud this development. When such eminent queer thinkers as Didier Eribon and David Halperin set out to investigate the contours of a gay subjectivity, I'm surprised and delighted to find a similarity, however general it may be, to my own efforts to define a gay specificity. Furthermore, we agree in our emphasis on the difference between this subjectivity or specificity and an essentialist identity.

But the agreement stops there, and "there" is first of all the point where psychoanalysis is called upon — or not called upon — to play a role. The gay mistrust of psychoanalysis was for a long time, and still is to a certain extent, wholly justified. Queer critics have had no trouble finding evidence of a homophobia perhaps made inevitable by the normative bias of psychoanalysis. (In their *Dictionary of Psychoanalysis*, Jean Laplanche and Jean-Bertrand Pontalis note that Freud and all the psychoanalysts who have followed him have spoken of a "normal" sexuality, since "the very notion of development presupposes a norm.") But things have changed somewhat, thanks in large measure to the attempts of the Ecole lacanienne, and of Jean Allouch in particular, to establish a positive moral and intellectual connection between psychoanalysis and all those associated with gay and lesbian studies in France, and perhaps especially in the United States. Given this development, the persistent hostility of queer thinkers toward psychoanalysis is all the more surprising. I of course don't mean that the sympathy of certain analysts in itself justifies giving up a healthily suspicious approach to psychoanalysis. It's possible to participate in a dialogue with psychoanalysis — Didier Eribon is the best example of this — and remain convinced that psychoanalysis is constitutively unable to imagine a dynamically viable gay subjectivity, and in particular, as I will argue in my discussion of Almodóvar, the relation of homosexuality to the cultivation of an aesthetic subject. But we may be perplexed by the antipsychoanalytic virulence of many queers (evident in two 2003 American colloquia, on gay shame, at the University of Michigan, and on queer sexuality, at Northwestern University). A flagrant example of this hostility was the uncritical acceptance of the suggestion made by one of the colloquia participants that that the death drive is a psychoanalytic invention that easily, perhaps even intrinsically, lends itself to homophobic intentions. That such a proposal could be received almost as if it were a truism is astonishing enough; even more stupefying is the apparent compatibility, in the most eminent queer circles, of the rejection of psychoanalysis with a marked interest in an especially flat version of ego psychology. It's as if certain thinkers had made the apparently surprising discovery that it's very difficult to banish all references to the operations of the psyche when we speak of subjectivity. But since many queer intellectuals have decided to reduce those operations to the ways in which individual subjects receive social messages (either identifying with them or resisting them), to be a subject is conceived of as determined entirely by intersubjectivity. My subjectivity is the messages others send me; my self-image is the image I receive from them. In the case of an oppressed minority subjectivity, the self can hardly avoid being contaminated by a paranoid mistrust of those specular others who possess its alienated identity. To study the mechanisms by which the subject receives, and acknowledges, this imposed identity (as well as the alienating strategies themselves) would be the first step in resisting the imaginary subjectivities elaborated by the dominant culture.

The queer thinkers who would embrace this account of subjectivity have quite logically found in the originator of Affect Theory, Silvan Tomkins, a major intellectual inspiration. This psychological theorist, who has been highly praised by Eve Sedgwick and whose thought has been important for recent work by Michael Warner, makes a sharp distinction between affects and drives. Indifferent to drives, he has devoted himself to exhaustive studies of the various manifestations on the human face of the entire range of emotions. Our eyes, he teaches us, receive and send messages from all the affects (divided between "good" and "bad" affects). Shame, by virtue of its heightening the face's visibility, nearly has the status of the ideal emotion for Affect Theory. In shame, he writes in volume 2 of *Affect Imagery Consciousness* (1963), the eyes turn away from the object and are, so to speak, directed back to the subject's own face: full of ambivalence, he looks at himself being looked at. Tomkins's work monumentally celebrates the visibility of the human subject's depths. Affect Theory is a catalogue of the expressive vicissitudes of intersubjectivity. It derives from the staggeringly banal observation that "all human beings inevitably have interpersonal experiences in which others express the primary affects and in which these are activated in the self. This is the basis for the construction of a whole series of Images in which the other is excited, or smiling, or ashamed, or contemptuous, or angry and afraid of crying and in which the self is made to feel one or another of these primary affects."

How can we explain the interest of such eminent thinkers as Eve Sedgwick and Michael Warner in such platitudes? Let's first of all note what is excluded by this psychologism. Drives, first of all, as Tomkins himself points out. His theory assumes that my field of action is reactive — a response to the invasive images that would constitute my subjectivity. There is no place, most notably, for a destructive movement (toward the other or toward myself) that might take place outside the intersubjective field, that would not be determined and justified by the emotions transmitted to me. Or, in other terms, there would be no place for a *jouissance* produced by the destructiveness at once promised and remembered as inherent in that *jouissance*. Significantly, queer theory expresses great interest in shame — not in guilt, but in shame. Shame is an eminently social emotion; others make me feel it. Consequently, shame is accompanied by innocence; we might even say that it is a sign of innocence. Nothing would be more foreign, and disagreeable, to Tomkins's admirers than Freud's claim in *Civilization and Its Discontents* that the sense of guilt does not depend on our being blamed, or praised, by others for our desires and actions. The great appeal of Tomkins's thought is, it seems to me, that it relieves the subject — and in particular the gay subject — from all guilt. The unsaid implication of the argument that psychoanalysis has used the death drive to further a homophobic plot is that the death drive doesn't exist in homosexuals. Unlike guilt, shame is in perfect symmetry with the external world. Shame has nothing to do with my own drives, with my own secret pleasures; it is entirely what others make me feel. Shame therefore fully justifies an aggressiveness toward a hateful world intent on destroying me, and the only question raised by shame is, as Sedgwick says, how it can be transformed into a sense of the subject's value, or dignity. With a little work on our part, shame can mutate into pride. Militant queer groups in San Francisco and New York have chosen to call themselves Gay Shame. Reproaching the Gay Pride movement for an assimilationist mania that has led it to demand little more from a heterosexist and homophobic society than its recognition of gays as good husbands, good priests, and good soldiers, Gay Shame proudly chooses the counterslogan "Fuck Gay Pride." Thus gays proudly accept the very insults meant to reduce them to silence and, ideally, invisibility.

The situation is of course a delicate one. It's true that a heterosexist culture seeks to overwhelm homosexuals with shame, and, as the Gay Shame militants affirm, there are certainly better ways of fighting shame than to eagerly embrace the norms of the dominant culture. But we will never participate in the invention of what Foucault called "new relational modes" if we merely assert the dignity of a self we have been told to be ashamed of. Instead, we might begin by recognizing an abject destructiveness irreducible to intersubjective power plays, a destructive drive from which no human subject is entirely free. The gay specificity I spoke of in *Homos* is based on the assumption that a desire for sameness, while it is always vulnerable to a hyperbolizing of an image of the self, can also initiate the subject to a seductive self-dissolution, or, more exactly, to his or her partial, fugitive, and mobile extensions or reappearances in the external world. Only a subject aware of living within these multiple correspondences with an otherness that both replicates and exceeds the subject can experience a sensual pleasure which, while it may be unable to eliminate the drive to erase all otherness, can at least be a kind of therapeutic or civilizing supplement to that drive. I associate this sensual pleasure with a new relational mode that might be the result of an aesthetic subjectification. "The loss of the self," Marcel Jouhandeau wrote in his 1939 book *De l'abjection*, "is the concern of all being," which is to say that self-loss is an ontological imperative. But it does not have to be a question, as it was for Jouhandeau, of losing oneself in God, but rather of the subject losing himself in order to find himself again (but now unidentifiable) disseminated among the appearances of the visible world.

In a 2002 essay entitled "Sociability and Cruising," I spoke of sexual cruising as an ascesis. Cruising can be an apprenticeship in impersonal intimacy. Like the sociability described by Georg Simmel, the anonymity and the multiplicity of sexual partners involve a certain self-subtraction, a diminishing of our subjectivity — or, in other terms, a suspension of the psychological, social, and professional interests that constitute a person's individuality. The connection between this reduction of the subject and anonymous promiscuity can be seen very clearly in Catherine Millet's remarkable book *The Sexual Life of Catherine M.* (English-language edition published in 2002). For Catherine M., self-reduction is also an expansion, one that depends, however, on the loss of that which constitutes an individual identity. If Catherine M. enjoys above all being fucked by several men in total darkness, it is because of the pleasure she feels being engulfed in "an undifferentiated sheet of flesh." In sex, Catherine M. loses all awareness of herself as a body circumscribed in space ("the body's frontiers are dissolved," she writes) — that is to say, as a visible "representative" of the ego which, according to Freud, is itself a mental projection of the body's surface. She speaks of her "great joy" experienced "when bodies, pressed together, have the sensation of unfolding." Fucking outdoors ("*en plein air*"), Catherine M. discovers the literal accuracy of the expression "*s'envoyer en l'air*" (to get off sexually; literally: "to be sent in the air"): terraces, a roadside, country fields are places where "I find it good to be, like them, open." She distances herself from herself in order to open out into the entire visible field; her bodily dwelling expands beyond all boundaries ("*l'habitacle corporel se dilate à l'infini*").

In sex, Catherine M. discovers a profound truth: lessness is the condition of allness. Finally, it seems to me significant that Catherine M., like her double Catherine Millet, is an art critic. She sees very clearly (without putting it exactly in these terms) that her sexual promiscuity transforms her from a psychological subject into an aesthetic subject. Sex allows Catherine M. to play a game with space (she speaks of opening and closing space) that she also finds in the paintings of Barnett Newman, Yves Klein, and Alain Jacquet. The aesthetic is not confined to works of art; sex can also be one of the modalities of the aesthetic. Finally, if *The Sexual Life of Catherine M.* also gives us the curious impression of being the document of a prolonged ascetic exercise, it is undoubtedly because, as Catherine M. specifies, "to have sexual relations and to feel desire were almost two separate activities." Sexual surrender can be experienced not as sensual gratification, but rather as a discipline in anonymity, one that helps us to escape from what Lacan has called "the hell of desire"—the hellish desire that is the sign, or perhaps we should say the symptom, of our psychological individuality.

It may seem strange that I have chosen a heterosexual woman as the model for what I have associated (especially in *Homos*) with homosexual desire: its aptitude for transforming itself into "homoness." The desiring individual is erased in order to become a site of correspondences with the world. According to this argument, homosexuality finds its specificity when it is dissolved as an identity. Thus my astonishment, and my disappointment, when I read recent queer theory, which seems to be redefining itself as a new identitarianism. In the sector of queer theory inspired by Sedgwick and the psychologism she has promoted, the self, far from being challenged as a stable individualizing entity, is fortified as such an entity by identifying itself with the claims of the ego. There is perhaps nothing surprising about this, given the centrality of the penis in gay male desire, and of the ease with which the penis can be elevated (or degraded) into the phallus, the emblem of mastery and of a hyperbolized ego. But let's not lose all hope: a gay cinematographer, Pedro

Almodóvar, will give us a very agreeable lesson on the dephallicizing of the penis, although this may involve, for him, the elimination of the desiring homosexual subject.

Early in Pedro Almodóvar's 2000 film, *All About My Mother*, Esteban (Eloy Azorín) and his mother, Manuela (Cecilia Roth), are sitting on a couch having dinner and watching a dubbed version of Joseph Mankiewicz's 1950 film *All About Eve*. Esteban, whose ambition is to be a writer, and who has begun writing about his mother for a competition, complains to Manuela that the Spanish version of Mankeiwicz's title, *Eva al desnudo*, is all wrong: the proper title, he claims, is *Todo sobre Eva*. Immediately after this, we see Esteban beginning to write in his notebook what will presumably be the title of the piece he has just referred to. He forms the word "Todo," and then the title of Almodóvar's film appears on the screen for the first time, in red and white block letters, in the space between the seated Esteban and his mother.

What is interesting about Esteban's correction is that it is picked up, as it were, by Almodóvar. More exactly, Almodóvar has chosen to present his choice of his own film's title (and its possible source in the title of Mankiewicz's film) as his copying of his character's choice. The film has been without a title for its first few minutes; it is only when Esteban writes "todo" as the first word of his own composition that *Todo sobre mi madre* appears on the screen as the title for Almodóvar's finished film. The effect of this juxtaposition is to encourage us to identify Almodóvar with Esteban, or rather to identify the boy with a younger Almodóvar, an Almodóvar without accomplishments, with, for example, only a project for a piece of writing to be called *Todo sobre mi madre* (and not a work finished more than thirty years later in his — whose? — life, a film this time, with the same title).

The serious problem with this identification is that Almodóvar the writer and filmmaker does away with Esteban a few minutes after the scene we have been discussing. The boy is run over by a car on his seventeenth birthday (after attending, with his mother, a performance of *A Streetcar Named Desire*), and what will interest us most about his mother will take place after his death. Almodóvar and Esteban have important things in common: their artistic vocation and their devotion to their mother. To say that is to suggest, according to popular psychoanalytic wisdom, that they have something else in common: homosexuality. Remember also that, at least in English, a gay man might refer, perhaps ironically, to that "wisdom" by saying about the origins of his homosexuality: "Of course, it's all about my mother . . . " Esteban, it's true, is not portrayed as a homosexual; he is coded as one. As if his artistic sensibility, his father's absence, and his great love for his mother were not enough, his aesthetic tastes leave no doubt, for a public even minimally trained in such codes, about his gay sensibility: Bette Davis, Truman Capote, and Blanche DuBois. We may begin to suspect that in plotting the death of his young double, Almodóvar is also doing away, at least aesthetically, with his — with their — homosexuality. The presumed gay sensibility does not, however, disappear. A *Streetcar Named Desire* will play a major role in the rest of the film, and Almodóvar appears to be at least as devoted to the great campy actresses, and to his mother, as Esteban is (among those to whom Almodóvar dedicates his film are actresses who play actresses — Bette Davis is one of those mentioned — and Almodóvar's mother).

There is also a dedication to men who act and become women, which could be taken as a tender joke on poor Esteban. It more or less describes his father, also named Esteban, about whom the boy knows nothing. He does, however, very much want to know about his father, and Manuela promises, a moment before he is struck down running after a taxi to get an autograph from the actress he has just seen in the role of Blanche DuBois, to tell him all when they return home later that evening. Curiously, Esteban's homosexuality is neither established nor denied; it is heavily coded, and ignored. The identification between Almodóvar and Esteban has been made, the gay sensibility has been, and will be, embraced, but homosexuality as a sexual preference is irrelevant both to Esteban as a character in the film and, correlatively, to Almodóvar's identification with him. What is relevant to Esteban's character is his obsessive curiosity about his father. It is as if the gay coding were put into place as the perhaps secret logic of that curiosity and, primarily, in order to be separated, liberated, from that curiosity. Esteban is insistently anguished about the paternal gap in his life, a gap that has been just as insistently maintained by Manuela. He begs her to talk to him about his father and when, much later, she finds Esteban's father in Barcelona, she shows him passages from their son's notebook in which Esteban had expressed his grief at finding photos from Manuela's youth from which half of the image had been cut away. It was, he wrote, as if half of his own life had been taken from him; to be whole, he needs that missing image, which would mean knowing about his father. Almodóvar's film may be "all about my mother," but the story his surrogate self wants to hear would be, and he says exactly these words, "todo sobre mi padre."

Almodóvar tells, and refuses to tell, that story. In a sense, the entire film is a search for the father, at first on the part of Esteban, and then on the part of Manuela, who leaves Madrid for Barcelona after Esteban's death in order to find his father and tell him about his son. But the story Almodóvar has to tell about the father is a startling subversion of paternal identity. It is a story that might have seriously compromised, even while satisfying, Esteban's longing for a father, and it ultimately dismisses whatever attributes — of power, of justice, of legality — we might "normally" associate with the paternal function. It turns out that half of the missing half in Esteban's life is identical to the half he already knows. The young lovers Manuela and Esteban (the father) had come from Argentina to Spain. Esteban left to work in Paris, and returned to Barcelona as Lola two years later. He returned, more precisely, half transsexualized, with his male genitals intact and with breasts larger than his wife's. It is with this partial copy of herself that Manuela conceived her son. Unhappy with her more or less newly gendered mate — not, as far as we can tell, because of his new anatomical makeup but rather because of a persistent machismo that led him/her to run after other women while forbidding Manuela to wear a miniskirt or a bikini on the beach — Manuela had fled to Madrid early in her pregnancy without telling Lola that he/she was soon to be a mother/father.

Back in Barcelona, Manuela eventually finds Lola, although she really hasn't spent much time searching for him/her. The Barcelona sequences are about Manuela's friendships with three other women. Soon after her arrival, Manuela runs into Agrado (Antonia San Juan), a former truck driver and friend from many years ago who, like Esteban, had had an incomplete sex change in Paris that had allowed her to return to Barcelona as a prostitute specializing in oral sex. Somewhat less sexually ambiguous is the great actress Huma Rojo (Marisa Paredes), whose autograph the young Esteban had been pursuing when he was killed and who is now playing Blanche in Barcelona. Huma, who is having a troubled affair with the actress who plays Stella (Candela Pena) in *Streetcar*, hires Manuela as her personal assistant, and they become friends. Finally, Manuela takes in Rosa (Penelope Cruz), a nun who, in the course of her social work with prostitutes, has been seduced by Lola and is now carrying their child. In one of his conversations with Frédéric Strauss, Almodóvar remembers with affection an at once ordinary and highly suggestive scene from his childhood: that of women in his provincial village sitting together and talking. He has also said: "This vagueness, this walking about, of the female characters [in his first feature film, *Pepi, Luci, Bom, and Other Girls on the Heap*] interests me very much. Some one who is alone, who doesn't have any particular goal and who is always close to a state of crisis, is exceptionally available, anything can happen to her, and she is therefore an ideal character for telling a story [*c'est donc un personnage idéal pour raconter une histoire*]." The phrasing is somewhat ambiguous: ideal as the author of a story or as some one to tell stories about? Let's read the remark both ways; the essential point is that such women originate stories. Interestingly, Almodóvar has a very non-Proustian reaction to the spectacle of people speaking together, perhaps just far enough away so that he can't hear them. In Proust, such spectacles tend to set off paranoid mistrust: they must be saying something unflattering about him, or at the very least something they want to keep from him, a perhaps sinister secret. In Almodóvar's response to his ideal female character, the key word is availability (the person he describes is "*dans une situation de grande disponibilité*"). Like that character, the women sitting together in his home town (in *The Flower of My Secret*, Leo [Marisa Paredes] participates in such a scene when she returns to her native village) are evoked as a promise. They are remembered not exactly for the experience they have already shared, but rather for the impression they give him of experience yet to be, of a prospective sociability.

What might that sociability be like? *All About My Mother* comes as close as any of Almodóvar's films to answering that question, although it does so within a motivational structure that might have stifled any such project. Manuela returns to Barcelona in order to make those photographs whole again, to put the father back in the picture in the only way now possible, which is to give him a photo of his son. In other words, she returns in order to make the family whole. To find the first Esteban would be to close a circle; Manuela would be returning her son to his point of origin, and with that his — their — story would be over. But of course the point of origin has already made a trip outside the family circle — to Paris — and s/he returned from that trip with the signs of a more radical crossing: transsexualized, s/he has traveled from one sex to the other, although with each new seduction of women Lola makes an at least temporary return to the Esteban still appended to her body.

Long before we know all that, the film has trained us to expect and to enjoy diversified forms of traveling, of moving from one point to another. Not only will there be all sorts of movements or crossings throughout the film (from country to country, from city to city, from one sex to another, between different sons, among different mothers); the repetition of the trans-motif takes place within its first appearance. Rather than prefiguring the importance of the motif with just one version of it (the donation of Esteban's heart), Almodóvar juxtaposes three cases of the organ-transplant example. (The second of the three is a theatrical rehearsal of an aspect of organ transplant procedures.) Movement in *All About My Mother* will be inseparable from repetition. The point of arrest along lines or circuits of movement between places, psychic functions, or identities are not wholly heterogeneous; there is also a certain persistence or continuity within the trajectories of mobility. But it will be difficult to define both the content and mode of continuity. What exactly is repeated when a theatrical character or situation reoccurs, differently, in reality — a reality which is of course itself the aesthetic construction of Almodóvar's film?

We are beginning to suspect that there may be a type of construction very different from those constructed imperatives of desire, especially of sexual obsession, that had given both psychic and structural consistency to some of Almodovar's earlier work. Violent death brings together the heterosexual couple of *Matador*. Both Maria Cardenal (Assumpta Sema) and the retired matador Diego Montes (Nacho Martínez) kill their sexual partners during sex; the perfect sexual act, and the perfect act of violence, will be killing each other as they reach orgasm together. *The Law of Desire* homosexualizes this fantasy of sex and violence. Antonio (Antonio Banderas) becomes obsessively attached to the film director Pablo Quintero (Eusebio Poncela) after having with Pablo his first homosexual experience. Antonio kills the young man Pablo loves and, after keeping the police at bay long enough to make love once more with Pablo, he shoots himself. *The Law Of Desire* both centers this obsessive sexuality and distances itself from it. The film opens with a young man acting in a sequence from a porno film. He masturbates with his back turned to us, his buttocks raised, repeating "Fuck me!" The words are instructions given to him by two middle-aged men directing the scene, who seem more turned on by it than the actor, who refuses to cry "Fuck me!" until he is assured that no one will take up the invitation. Once the scene is over, he picks up his money, with a more authentic expression of pleasure, from the table next to the bed where the pseudo-action has taken place. Soon after this we see Antonio alone in a toilet stall, voicing the same request but really turned on by the prospect of its being satisfied. Pablo accommodates him shortly thereafter in a scene whose nonpornographic realism is emphasized by Antonio's obvious discomfort as he is being penetrated for the first time. The film moves toward its sexual seriousness; it's as if that seriousness were anticipated, and put into question, in a version of sex as pure construction. We see it both as an unexciting construction for the porno actor and as an exciting one for Antonio in the toilet stall before sexual demand becomes the film's deadly serious subject. The suggestion of desire as artifact is made even stronger by the solipsistic nature of Pablo's love for Juan (Miguel Molina). As if he were writing a scenario for one of his films, Pablo sends himself letters in which "Juan" tells him how much he loves him. Desire is construction, and law. The porno sequence makes the connection very clear: the two older men dictate — order — the scenario of mounting desire to the compliant (and indifferent) actor. Antonio's subsequent real excitement is just as constructed. His excited demand to be fucked, delivered to no one and inspired by the porno sequence he has just seen, can be addressed only to his own desire; it formulates the laws of a desire he will then actualize with Pablo.

The laws of desire conceal its imaginary nature; they can perhaps be undone only if the being of the subjects to whom they are applied becomes uncertain. The laws of desire will collapse with the disappearance of the subjects of desire. In Almodóvar's work, repetition, far from certifying the reality of what is repeated, undermines the very category of the real (at the very least, as a category to which the imaginary might be confidently opposed). The relation between the imaginary and the real will be one of exchange, not of opposition. Identities in *All About My Mother* are dissipated as they are being repeated.

To whom does the "my" refer in the film's title? Manuela begins her new life in Barcelona by taking care of Agrado, who has been beaten up by one of her tricks; she will take in Rosa and care for her during her pregnancy; her job with Huma seems to consist mainly of watching over the drug-addicted Nina; and she will become the new Esteban's mother after Rosa's death. Manuela more or less becomes everyone's mother (including other mothers: Rosa and to a certain extent even Rosa's mother), although it seems somewhat reductive of the richness of those relations to fit them all into a familiar maternal mold. Furthermore, the original family model is kept intact — we might even say protected — at the same time that Manuela is continuously stepping outside that model. By insisting on the first son's uniqueness, Almodóvar reveals a reluctance merely to repeat the category of "the mother" with different figures filling in for "my." Manuela's grief persists. And it persists not only because young Esteban can never be simply replaced by anyone else, but also because Manuela's move into new relational modes requires a certain mourning for the relationality left behind. Lola had already wrought havoc with the myth of unambiguous family identities, but in fleeing from him/her and in destroying his/her image on her photographs, Manuela has worked to preserve that myth. Eliminated as a presence, paternal identity and paternal prestige might be, and nearly were, permanently secured. The security is, however, threatened by the same move designed to reconfirm it: the search for the person who might fill the gap. In sobbing over the loss of her son, Manuela also grieves over the loss of the principal guardian of the paternal myth. And it is undoubtedly right that she should do so: to lose the father's absence, or the paternal function at once dependent upon and incommensurable with any real father, is to lose the Law that governs and stabilizes the attributing of identities. Manuela's move outside the family circle is, most profoundly, a dismissal of legitimating symbolic systems, an implicit claim that social presence and social viability do not necessarily depend on symbolic authorizations.

The symbolic cannot be seriously contested. The film does not, so to speak, take on the paternal phallus directly; instead, it dismisses that constitutively unlocatable fantasy product with numerous lighthearted evocations of the penis. During their dinner in front of the TV screen, Esteban, responding to his mother's joke that he should eat more because he might have to keep her one day, shocks her slightly by saying: "You don't need pounds for that, you need a big dick." His point is confirmed by Agrado, whose credentials in this matter are impeccable: she informs Nina that "clients like us pneumatic [with, she explains, "a pair of tits as hard as newly inflated tires"] and well hung." It was apparently a wise move on Agrado's part, given his/her intention of returning to Barcelona as a female prostitute, to keep his/her penis. In fact, nearly everyone is turned on by her male appendage, not exactly as an object of solemn desire, but as—what? Huma's lover Nina tries to feel Agrado's breasts and, not seeming to expect much of a response, presses her behind against Agrado's crotch. When the good-looking and rather dim-witted Mario (who is playing Stanley Kowalski in *Streetcar*) tells her that he has been feeling tense and sweetly asks for oral sex, he also shows an interest in her penis. Agrado, somewhat exasperated by all this highly focused attention, asks Mario if men ask him to suck their cocks because he also has one. And, during the wonderful sequence in Manuela's apartment when she, Rosa, Agrado and Huma improvise a party of drinks, ice cream, and talk, the general good humor builds up to hilarity on the subject of the penis. Agrado describes herself as "a model of discretion, even when I suck a cock," to which Huma responds: "It's been ages since I sucked one." Rosa the pregnant nun, to the laughter of the others, cries out with mock naughtiness: "I love the word cock—and prick!" as she joyfully bounces on the sofa. The penis does, then, get a great deal of attention, which, far from highlighting its sexual appeal, makes it an object of fun. Not exactly something to be made fun of, but rather something to have fun with. Not quite neutralized, the penis is, let's say, naturalized. Unlike the absent father and the fantasmatic phallus, the Almodovarian penis is present even where, in principle, it should not be:

on the bodies of such (at least self-proclaimed) women as Agrado and Lola. The penis's many reoccurrences help to dephallicize it. Lola's penis, it's true, is at once an anomaly and a menace (she is, as Manuela says, not a person but an epidemic), but she can scarcely be said to represent phallic power and authority. And Agrado is anything but a phallic woman; rather, she embodies the agreeable (as her name suggests) perspective on the penis as an attractive object of sensual and social interest, detaching it from fixed ideas of male and female identities. And it is perhaps this possibility of the penis lending itself to a noncastrating detachment that accounts for its presence as an enlivening, civilized and nonobsessive topic of interest — a passing topic of interest — at the little party Almodóvar's four women throw for themselves in Manuela's apartment.

All About My Mother invites and dismisses several serious attempts to get an identification right. Who is the real mother? Who is the real child? Who is the real woman? We are seduced into these questions mainly to be educated in the techniques by which they may be ignored. Crucial to this double enterprise is the movement within the film between "reality" and art, and between theater and film. One of the film's several dedications is to actresses who play actresses, and this includes not only the actresses Almodóvar mentions, but also figures from his own film. Marisa Paredes, Cecilia Roth, and Candela Pena all play actresses in *All About My Mother*. Paredes repeats herself, differently, as Huma, who repeats herself as Blanche. Such repetitions place the imaginary at the heart of the film's realism: Huma playing Blanche reminds us that Huma herself is a role, that she is both the actress playing such roles as Blanche and a role being played by Paredes. Curiously, the scenes chosen from *All About Eve* and especially *A Streetcar Named Desire,* as well as the sequence of Huma rehearsing lines from Lorca's *Blood Wedding,* assume the status of the film's narrative raw material, the already given texts which "life" in *All About My Mother* mysteriously imitates. But it is of course not quite a question of life imitating art, but rather of art (this film) imitating, or repeating, art — although, because the film does distinguish what is meant to be real from the film, the play, and the poem it inaccurately replicates, Almodóvar is in fact constructing a much more interesting comment about the tenuous nature of any such distinctions. He constructs, not derivations (such as life from art), but rather exchanges within a vast realm of possibility. Long after Manuela goes to Coruna in pursuit of her son's heart, a scene from *Streetcar* is performed in which a distraught Blanche searches for what she calls her heart (which, Stella explains, is the heart-shaped case in which she keeps her jewelry). It is a curious repetition: occurring long after the episode it revives (although as part of a play written long before that episode, at once preceding it and, as a text, contemporaneous with it), and vastly different in its terms of reference (a jewel box rather than a son's transplanted organ), it nonetheless confirms the finitude and the formal unity of a linguistically designated world—a world made familiar, not by inherent attributes of being, but by inevitable reoccurrences within our descriptions of it.

The fascination of such works as *All About Eve* and *A Streetcar Named Desire* most probably derives from the skill with which they, like so many other plays and films labeled as realistic, reformulate psychological fantasy as a given, irrevocably realized world. Lacan has spoken of the defensive function of desire. The fantasy scenarios of desire are imperative constructions, made imperative by the drives that must at all costs remain hidden. Desire's scenarios are fantasmatic fortresses, and their strength depends on the finality of their plots, the strength with which they resist being potentialized. Desire presents itself not only as a law but also as a fatality. Since desire constitutively mistakes its object for its cause (this is the truth desiring fantasy hides from us), the failure of those objects to satisfy desire is interpreted as a gap or hole in the objects themselves. Lack is judged to be omnipresent: what desire lacks is also missing in the world, not as something lost but, more tragically, as something that was never, that never could be, in the world. This does not mean that objects that might satisfy the repressed drives could ever be found in the world. Those objects (the partial body-objects aggressively incorporated and expelled by infantile fantasies?) constitute by their very nature a rejection of the real world. To satisfy the drives we must die to the world; the "death instinct" pursues a fantasy-ecstasy given by fantasy-objects, and in so doing it removes us from life itself. The death drive can be satisfied only by the violence that annihilates it.

If these psychic depths have entered our discourse, it is thanks, most notably, to Freud's meta-psychological speculations, the identification by Melanie Klein of the very being of the human subject with fantasy-objects, and the line of reflection in Lacan that would lead him to assert not only that "there is no sexual relation," but also, perhaps even more radically, that object-investment is something of a miracle. These are the great moments of psychoanalysis, and, as Lacan never tired of proclaiming, they have nothing to do with a supposed cure presumed to help us adapt more happily to reality. The failure to adapt—which Freud traced in *Civilization and Its Discontents* to the incomparable *jouissance* of a self-destructive and world-destructive aggressiveness—constitutes the psychoanalytic subject. And it accounts for, among other things, the perennially unsatisfied (and therefore productive) nature of desire and the melancholy attached to what can only be the second-ary, derived, and always misaimed scenarios of desire. If *A Streetcar Named Desire* is such an important foil in *All About My Mother* against which the Almodovarian world will be constructed, it is perhaps because Almodóvar recognized in Williams's play an ideally transparent version of the failures and the melancholy inherent in desire. Blanche DuBois is a glamorously pathetic caricature of the psychoanalytic subject's absence from the world.

To say this, however, is also to say that the psychoanalytic subject, and psychoanalysis, have little to say to us about possible exchanges with the world (exchanges which would not be projections or incorporations or adap-tive techniques). *All About My Mother* shows us such exchanges working out of, and against, desire and its fantasies. More precisely, it implicitly makes an argument for an aesthetic subject, one for whom a relationality that in-cludes the real world (and not merely our fantasy-inscriptions on the world) is born not from a dismissal of the real but rather from an elaboration of the real as always in the process of being realized. By inaccurately replicating them in his own film, Almodóvar appears to be suggesting that the characters from *Streetcar* and *All About Eve* are insufficiently aestheticized. His many repetitions — both intertextual and intratextual — are ways of reinitiating iden-tities and situations rather than emphatically reconfirming them. As a result, the film becomes a massive deconstruction of its title. "All About" is mere epistemological fantasy. There is no single (or proprietary) subject to support "My" (Esteban? which one? Rosa? Almodóvar?). and "Mother" has no clearly identifiable referent (Almodóvar's mother? What is the relation between the mother of the title and the mother of the dedication? Can "mother" include all the ways Manuela cares for others?) "Mother" is both present and already lost everywhere; its presence is its lostness, the unlocatable and unsettled na-ture of its referent and its attributes. Repeatable being — being that continu-ously fails to be unique — creates a hospitable world of correspondences, one in which relations, no longer blocked by difference, multiply as networks of similitudes. It is as if the reappearance of identities were antecedent to their realization; we could even say that nothing is ever even about to be because imminence is always preempted by the power to persist inherent in purely potential being.

Almodóvar's aesthetic references in *All About My Mother* are to works that are fantasmatically heavy and deficient in the imaginary. The movement in the film between these works and the diegetically defined real is nonetheless crucial to Almodóvar's elaboration of the imaginary. They serve on the one hand to make the important point that the imaginary as a mode of potentialized being is not to be restricted, and sequestered, within the category of "art." The retreat from being is not a particularity of the aesthetic narrowly conceived; it is an ethical duty coextensive with life itself.

All About My Mother is a performative reflection on the possibility of a nonfantasmatic imaginary. It proposes an answer to a question of great consequence: how might the imaginary be separated from the defensive functions of fantasy? Almodóvar's very early films lightheartedly answer this question without, as it were, taking the trouble to acknowledge its difficulty. *All About My Mother* is of necessity less exuberantly wild than *Pepi, Luci, Bom . . .* and *Labyrinth of Passion*: the exhilarating lightness of the imaginary is, in Almodóvar's more recent film, in frictional and possibly dangerous contact with the seriousness of settled identities and established being. The threat comes from two directions: from the rigid fantasy-structures of the very works that seem to inspire Almodóvar's version, in this film, of a nonfantasmatic imaginary, and from the family structure that unravels even as Manuela awaits the meeting that might consolidate it. Almodóvar's nonfantasmatic imaginary in *All About My Mother* seems to depend on the extinction of desire, an extinction signaled by the absence of the father as the legislator of desire and the death of the (author-)son as the possible subject of desire. Homosexual desire is, however, obliquely referred to by nearly everyone's very unsolemn interest in the penis. The male organ, we have suggested, is naturalized. It is by no means excluded as an erotic object, but it has become an erotic object dephallicized and depsychologized, thereby at least raising the possibility of a gay (and straight) desire for the male body that would no longer be burdened by fantasy-illusions of power and castration. Furthermore, the dispersal and repetition of identities in the film point to a solidarity or homo-ness of being, the partial reoccurrences of all subjects elsewhere. Identities are never individual; homosexual desire would be the erotic expression of a homo-ness that vastly exceeds it, a reaching out toward an other sameness.

Finally, the erasure of any relations at all between men in *All About My Mother* clears the field for an extraordinary reworking of the absence of desire for women. Far from being the more or less willing participants in a nonerotic gay sociability, women are given the space not only to reinvent themselves, but, more radically, to refashion relationality itself. Almodóvar's women, unlike those in the work of Tennessee Williams, are not fantasy-constructions of a repressed, distorted, and vengeful heterosexual desire. Such elaborations are undoubtedly — however reluctant many of us may be to agree with this — one fate of heterosexual desire when, at least as far as conscious sexual preferences go, it has been completely occluded by homosexual desire. It is perhaps Almodóvar's desexualizing and depsychologizing of homosexuality that make possible a very different version of sexual indifference toward women. In a discussion of *All About My Mother* with Frédéric Strauss, Amodóvar has said: " . . . the fact that a group of women are speaking together constitutes the basis of fiction, the origin of all stories." But what stories will they tell? We take it as a sign of Almodóvar's generosity that he does not simply identify those fictions with his own stories about women. If his work suggests that he is not quite sure what those stories will be, what forms the talk will take, it may be because his talk, like everyone's talk, can't help but be inspired and nourished by our culture's richly significant narratives of desire and psychic complexity. In a new relational regime, what will there be to talk about? Almodovarian sociability is remarkably less constrained by that richness than sociability usually is, but perhaps because he has come very close to escaping from "the laws of desire," he is all the more anxious (eager — and a little worried?) about what exceeds them. There is, at any rate, the exhilarating freshness of that modest party in Manuela's apartment, and there is the great and touching modesty of Almodóvar himself moving his camera out of hearing range as Pepa and Marisa, who have not yet spoken together, begin to converse on Pepa's terrace at the end of *Women on the Verge of a Nervous Breakdown*. As if his characters were about to speak of things that he, Almodóvar, has not yet been able to imagine.

PART
2
Toward an Aesthetic Subject

6

Against Monogamy

Psychoanalytically speaking, monogamy is cognitively inconceivable and morally indefensible.

This severe truth bears emphasis at a time when monogamy appears to be enjoying — often in the most unexpected places — a new lease on life. In the current celebration of family values in the United States, for example, the value placed on monogamy and on the institution that (at least officially) mandates it — marriage — by conservative religious groups was to be expected; somewhat more surprising is the conjugal furor manifested by many individuals who, having often been more or less brutally excluded from the comforts and reinforcements of family life, might have been expected to continue marching under a Gidean banner defiantly proclaiming: *Famille, je vous hais!* I refer to all those European and American gay men and lesbians who have recently been demanding for homosexual couples legal rights and benefits similar to those enjoyed by married heterosexual couples. I mention this not to question the legitimacy of these demands (they are entirely just demands), but rather to note that a community that has been at times notorious in its embrace of sexual promiscuity has, during the past decade or so, made an unprecedented attempt to persuade what is curiously called the general population of the gay commitment to the ideal of the monogamous couple. The AIDS epidemic can certainly be held partially accountable for this rush to respectability, although, since we seem anxious to demonstrate that we can be not only good husbands and wives but equally good

[margin note: Edelman-esque. Using "negative" terms, claiming them]

Originally published in *Oxford Literary Review* 20 (1998): 3–21.

clergymen and soldiers, the drive behind the defense of monogamy can probably not be wholly explained as a private and public health strategy. Foucault's hope that gays might be in the vanguard of efforts to imagine what he
called "new ways of being together" appears, for a large number of gay people
today, to be considerably less inspiring than the hope that we will be allowed
fully to participate in the old ways of being and of coming together.

And yet, if the monogamous model seems more firmly established than
ever before as the hegemonic model of sexual relations, the very publicity it
has been enjoying suggests that its hegemony has been subjected to perhaps
unprecedented strains. It's not simply the fragility attested to by such things as
high divorce rates, large numbers of single parents, and the surprisingly large
group of heterosexual men and women apparently untempted by married
life, although this surely accounts for much of the defensive praise of family
values. More interestingly, monogamy has become a *subject of reflection* — a
reflection that is a minor but crucial aspect of a more widespread problematiz-
ing of the nature and value of community, of the relation between community
and identity, and, most profoundly, of the nature of sociality itself. With the
fracturing of our world into frequently antagonistic communities — national,
racial, religious, ethnic, sexual — a troubled reflection about the relation
between community and identity (more exactly, about identity as communitarian) was perhaps inevitable. Identity-politics is far from dead. Indeed,
with the collapse of communism it practically defines our entire political
life. We know that, in practice, communism was inseparable from nationalist ambitions; in its universal revolutionary aspirations, however, it was an
anti-identitarian ideology, a global social project independent of substantive
local identities. Those identities, as the hostilities in the former Yugoslavia
and among the republics of the former USSR dramatically illustrate, immediately filled the void left by the collapse of communist regimes. To this must
be added the new confrontations in Western European nations between the
dominant groups and the vast numbers of political refugees and immigrant
workers from Eastern Europe or from Africa, and, in the United States, confrontations between established powers (generally white, male, heterosexual,
and Christian) and the various minority cultures demanding social spaces for
their communities, social recognition for *their* particular identities.

Such demands, it seems to me, can't help but raise questions about their
premises. What relations exist, or should exist, between the various communities in which we live, most notably between minority communities and
the dominant culture? Are communitarian identities necessary, or even desirable? Does sociality depend on such identities? To what extent do antago-

nistic confrontations between different communities derive not merely from particular historical and sociological conditions but, more profoundly, from the very value attributed to communitarian identities? Doesn't this valorizing of particular communitarian — and cultural — identities in turn privilege difference over sameness in human relations, thus condemning the social to repeated efforts to overcome the trauma of difference as well as to a dependence on such weak cohesive virtues as a mere tolerance for diversity? Might there, finally, be another way to think of the social, a view of relationality as grounded in the extensibility of the human subject, that is, grounded in sameness rather than in prejudicial hierarchies of difference? And might this refiguring of the relational help us to elaborate modes of being-in-the-world to which the concept of identity itself might be irrelevant?

In short, we are in a time of relational crisis, of a dangerous but also potentially beneficial confusion about modes of connectedness, about the ways in which who or what or how we *are* depend on how we connect. I will be speaking primarily of social relationality, although it is also important to address (as Ulysse Dutoit and I have begun to do in our recent work on Caravaggio, Rothko, and Resnais) perceptual orders that design some of the multitudinous relations between the human and the nonhuman. If there is no moment at which human connectedness has not already been initiated, we might nonetheless posit, largely for heuristic purposes, different plateaux of relationality. The isolating of such plateaux implicitly sets up a structural successiveness — from the simple to the complex, from spatial connections to intersubjectivity — within the various orders of the relational. Such analytic moves obviously have a certain artificiality since we live those orders simultaneously. They can, however, help us to redirect our relational attention; they can serve as a cognitive prelude to what I will be putting forth as an ethical imperative to readjust or to reorient our extensions. I will illustrate this by examining what we might think of as a threshold between two relational plateaux: that of the intimately conjoined couple (and this will return us to the subject of monogamy) and that of the subject's nonintimate connections to the multitudinous points of disseminated sociality.

B ut why psychoanalysis? Psychoanalysis — and especially Freud — provides the most significant account we have of how human beings initiate, sustain, repudiate, and redirect affective and social ties with one another. Specifically, Freud's work is a profound — and profoundly troubled — reflection on the passage from the sociality of the couple to the sociality of the group. In Freud's thought, the prohibition of an incestuous monogamous passion is given as the precondition of an exogamous monogamy later on. The little boy, for example, renounces desire for one particular woman in order to desire other particular women, and especially, in marriage, one other particular woman. However, the Freudian description of the Oedipus complex — the crucial moment of passage from the family to the social — provides some reason to think of it as the structural occasion on which the child (male or female) renounces an exclusive desire for *any* particular person.

Oedipal love is an ambiguous model for adult monogamy. In Chapter III of *The Ego and the Id*, Freud complicates his theory of the "simple positive Oedipus complex in a boy" in ways that nearly destroy its descriptive usefulness. It consists, most simply, in "an ambivalent attitude to [the boy's] father and an object relation of a solely affectionate kind to his mother"; the necessary demolition of this complex involves the boy's giving up his object-cathexis of his mother and internalizing his rival-father as conscience, or superego. This is the 'normal' outcome of the Oedipus complex, and it both permits "the affectionate relation to the mother to be in a measure retained" and "consolidate[s] the masculinity in a boy's character." But, first of all, as Freud recognizes, this is not what we should have expected: he has claimed a few pages earlier that when we are forced to abandon a love-object we introduce it into the ego, identifying with it. Indeed, on the basis of this more familiar psychoanalytic rule Jean Laplanche has argued that the positive Oedipus complex in a boy leads to homosexuality (he has internalized the desired Oedipal mother *and* her desires), while the negative Oedipus complex in a boy (in which the boy's love for the father was the dominant attachment) will lead to a heterosexual object choice modeled on the desires of the father whom the heterosexual man has taken, permanently, into himself. Freud himself doesn't draw these conclusions; he simply notes, in passing, that "this alternative outcome [of introducing the abandoned object into the ego] may also occur," although here identification, instead of explaining how we manage to give up an object of love without really giving it up, will depend, for both sexes, on "the relative strength of the masculine and feminine sexual dispositions." By identifying with the lost father object instead of with the rival-mother, for example, the little girl will "bring her masculinity into prominence."

Now something quite new has entered the picture. Identification with the parent of the other sex may not be the resolution of Oedipal rivalry (a resolution that, drawing on the affectionate component of an original ambivalence toward that parent, also guarantees the continuing strength of the rival's prohibition by internalizing it) but may instead be largely due to our

constitutional bisexuality. Having mentioned this possibility, Freud immediately goes on to give bisexuality a much more important role in Oedipal
desires. It suddenly benefits from a remarkable promotion: no longer simply
a factor that may, for example, explain a boy's exceptional identification, in
the simple positive complex, with his mother instead of his father (the exceptional nature of which is, in any case, curious since it obeys, as we have seen,
the more general psychoanalytic law of identification with lost love-objects),
bisexuality now determines an Oedipal structure in which the simple positive
complex is nothing more than "a simplification or schematization" justified, "to be sure," by "practical purposes." Everyone lives both the positive
and the negative Oedipus complex. This means that in the little boy there
is one desiring subject that takes the mother as the primary object of love
and will end by identifying with a father originally (pre-Oedipally) loved
but then perceived as a rival, and another subject that desires the father and
will identify with the rival mother. Rather conveniently, "analytic experience
. . . shows that in a number of cases one or the other constituent disappears,
except for barely distinguishable traces." Nonetheless, "at the dissolution of
the Oedipus complex the four trends of which it consists [both an object
relation and an identification with both parents] will group themselves in
such a way as to produce a father-identification and a mother-identification,"
and "the relative intensity of the two identifications in any individual will re-
flect the preponderance in him of one or other of the two sexual dispositions
[masculine and feminine]."

A lot has come to depend on those "two dispositions." The stability of the
"official" end-point of each version of the Oedipus Complex depends on
the strength of the masculine or feminine disposition that determines which
parent—the rival or the love-object—the child will identify with. Sexual
preference depends not on whom we loved in our Oedipal drama, but on
whom we identified with, which may mean that there can be a homosexual *or*
a heterosexual consequence of *both* the "normal positive" and the "inverted
negative" complexes. Furthermore, the appeal to sexual disposition changes
the motivating force behind identifications. In the Oedipus complex, we
identify with the lost love-object only if we have the same sexual disposition
as that object. We become again that which we are already. This is particularly surprising given Freud's frequently reiterated skepticism about the validity of the masculinity-femininity distinction. Even in the passage I have been
discussing, he qualifies his confident statement that the little girl's identifying
with her lost loved father "will clearly depend" on the strength of her masculine disposition by adding: "whatever that may consist in." And in the long

note to the final sentence of Chapter 4 in *Civilization and Its Discontents,* Freud simultaneously reasserts the importance of bisexuality for psychoanalytic theory and acknowledges that sex "is hard to grasp psychologically." We may have thought that sex is exactly what psychoanalysis sets out to 'grasp,' but to the extent that understanding sex would mean understanding maleness and femaleness, psychology, unlike anatomy, Freud writes, cannot define those terms with any precision. "For psychology the contrast between the sexes fades away into one between activity and passivity, in which we far too readily identify activity with maleness and passivity with femaleness, a view which is by no means universally confirmed in the animal kingdom." Bisexuality, a theory "surrounded by many obscurities," is nonetheless brought in to explain the most momentous consequences of the Oedipus complex. The theory depends on the existence of sexual dispositions which, Freud suggests, may be meaningless (or, at the very least, whose meaning we have yet to grasp), and yet apparently nothing is more important than "the relative strength of the masculine and feminine sexual dispositions" in each of us, in the determination of our lifelong sexual identity.

The notion of bisexuality, which has been welcomed by many defenders of psychoanalysis as proof that Freud himself disputed the claim that heterosexuality is more "natural" than homosexuality, is in reality a murky and even somewhat treacherous concept, one that contravenes the very plurality of desire it would appear to confirm. It is not only that bisexuality in Freud is nothing more than heterosexuality doubled. Since, as Judith Butler has pointed out, it is in desiring with his "feminine disposition" that a boy sees his father as an object of sexual love, bisexuality is simply "the coincidence of two heterosexual desires [that of the masculine boy for his mother, that of the feminine boy for his father] within a single psyche." Even more: bisexuality doubles the Oedipal couple, making of the very agent that disrupts copulative intimacy the occasion for repeating that intimacy. Indeed, its function as a concept may be to account for that repetition by disguising it. A presumably natural, and universal, bisexual disposition would be somehow more acceptable, more respectable, than the child's efforts *to stay within the family on any terms,* and to do so by initiating an intimate relation of desire with the very parent trying to break up such a relation. To see the child's so-called bisexual impulses as his or her most refined strategy for remaining within the family would be for Freud to acknowledge his own reluctance to imagine how we ever move beyond familial desires, his reluctance to imagine that move within the very situation — the Oedipus complex — which psychoanalysis proposes as an account, precisely, of how we become social beings and not merely familial beings.

An authentic breaking away from the family within psychoanalysis's own account of the Oedipus complex does, however, take place; it is enabled by the multiple partners necessitated by the child's so-called bisexuality. This is a less acceptable exit from Oedipal ties than the father's — the Law's — terrifying prohibitions, for it suggests that post-Oedipal desire may owe very little to the structures of Oedipal family desires, and any such failure to preserve and repeat those desires — I will return to this — is what Freud is incapable of entertaining and of conceptualizing, even when he has himself provided the material for such conceptualizing. The Oedipal situation, as Freud describes it, is, after all, an agitated movement among various couples: the male child with the beloved mother, the male child with the father who must be internalized as Law, the feminine male child with the loved father, the feminine male child with the rival mother. The Oedipal triangle is a misnomer; it always contains at least four people, and this doesn't even take into account the shifts in the parents' identities as a result of the shifting sexual dispositions — masculine and feminine — that model the child's relations to them. There are not only the masculine boy and feminine boy; there are also the desired father and the law-giving father, as well as the desired mother and the threatening mother, which gives us six Oedipal identies. In a famous letter to Fliess, Freud wrote: "Bisexuality! I am sure you are right about it. And I am accustoming myself to regarding every sexual act as an event between four individuals." By this he presumably meant that in heterosexual intimacy, there is a repetition of the bisexuality already governing Oedipal relations — that is, a fantasmatic desiring woman within the man and a fantasmatic desiring man within the woman. But since this creates, for the man, a male partner instead of a female partner, and, for the woman, a female partner instead of a male partner, we need two more shadow partners for the bisexual scenario. (It's true that a certain economy of identities might be managed by superimposing the fantasy man created in the woman by the real man's homosexuality [that is, according to Freud, his feminine self] on the woman's masculine [or, again according to Freud, homosexual] self, since both these fantasy figures are males desiring females. The verification of any such economy of fantasmatic moves is, to say the least, somewhat problematic . . .) Furthermore, to the extent that our sexual behaviour always includes a motivating memory of our Oedipal fantasies of sexual intimacy (includes, that is, the memory of a presence summoning us away from that intimacy), each partner sees the other not only as two desired objects (male and female) but also as two possibilities of interdiction and identification.

With ten figures, the "memory" of the Oedipal triangle in our adult intimacies becomes a fantasmatic orgy. This is, it could of course be argued, a reductio ad absurdum of what Freud himself characterizes as object choices and identifications so complex as to make it nearly impossible "to describe them intelligibly." Our fantasy calculus does, however, have the advantage of highlighting the instability of the psychoanalytically conceived couple. The fantasy-relation that would be the most important antecedent for the adult drive toward monogamy — the phallic drive toward the Oedipal parent — turns out to have been but one in a whirlwind of desiring mobility. Monogamy disciplines the orgies of childhood. In constantly renewing our fidelity to that early loved object, we just as constantly betray the polygamous conditions in which we loved it. If it is true that bisexuality in Freud perversely reinforces the heterosexual couple, it also institutes a mobility of desiring positions and a multiplicity of identities that make of the couple itself a unit in continuous dissolution. Psychoanalytically, monogamy is inconceivable except as something that blocks circuits of desire. A particular couple with particular identities begins to be traced when one relational line holds us with what is probably a paranoid fascination — when the desired other has become what Jean Laplanche calls an enigmatic signifier imagined to be in possession of, and to be wilfully withholding, the secret of our being. Monogamy perhaps thrives on this at once narcissistic and paranoid fascination with the secrets of the other as *our* secrets. Monogamy is nourished by an impoverished narcissism; it is the arrested deployment of desire's appetites and curiosities.

From Freud to Lacan, psychoanalytic therapy has been vastly more conservative than psychoanalytic theory. While thrillingly dismantling received psychoanalytic wisdom about, most notably, castration, the ego, the death instinct, and the very possibility of that which appeared to be the psychoanalytic object par excellence: a sexual relation, the most radical theorists have for the most part remained remarkably silent — or at best vague and inconclusive — about the relevance of their theoretical subversions to a possible questioning of the couple — especially, but by no means only, the heterosexual couple — as a normative model for psychoanalytic therapy. Given this disjunction between sexual theory and sexual politics, it is hardly surprising that psychoanalysts, from Freud to the present, have been somewhat incoherent not only about the social function and value of monogamy but even about its psychic genealogy, about precisely those continuities between childhood and adult life that have for the most part been psychoanalysis' self-defined specialty. Freud, for example, while never treating the topic exhaustively, touches upon it in a series of comments that make for anything but a unified point of view. The remark in the *Three Essays on the Theory of Sexuality* to the effect that in finding a love object we are refinding it appears to ground monogamous impulse in the memory of an infinitely satisfying (if only in fantasy) infantile relation to the mother. From this perspective, monogamy would be a relation indifferent, even hostile, to the needs of larger social orders. Indeed, in *Civilization and Its Discontents*, libidinal bonds uniting a couple contribute to the antagonism between civilization and sexuality. Civilization uses "every means" to bind "the members of the community together in a libidinal way," an aim that sexual love between two individuals resists. "A pair of lovers are sufficient to themselves, and do not even need the child they have in common to make them happy"; a love-relationship at its height leaves "no room . . . for any interest in the environment." Four pages earlier, however, such love-relationships, institutionalized in marriage, are just what society requires in order to rein in our naturally promiscuous bent. It is a kind of concession to the antisocial drive toward sexual pleasure: "Present-day civilization makes it plain that it will only permit sexual relationships on the basis of a solitary, indissoluble bond between one man and one woman, and that it does not like sexuality as a source of pleasure in its own right and is only prepared to tolerate it because there is so far no substitute for it as a means of propagating the human race." An even more disabused interpretation of monogamy is suggested in the passing remark, in the 1918 piece on "The Taboo of Virginity," that "the right to exclusive possession of a woman . . . forms the essence of monogamy." Far from having profound roots in the history of each individual's sexuality, monogamy would be the intimate arrangement most consistent with the more general social right to private property.

An analogous interpretive mobility can be found in Adam Phillips's reflections on the subject in his recent book, *Monogamy*. The couple, Phillips writes, is "home": "Because we begin our lives in a couple, and are born of a couple, when we talk about couples we are telling the story of our lives." And: "Our survival at the very beginning of our lives involves us in something like monogamy." "The stuff of which monogamy will be made" are the "inklings" the child has, in relation to his or her mother, "of privilege and privacy, of ownership and belonging." And yet, "One of the most striking things about reading stories to young children is the ruthless promiscuity of their attention." Children's "curiosity is not monogamous. It ranges." In growing up, we lose, Phillips writes in one of his most striking formulas, "the primitive art of losing interest in things or people" — and that art may be "the best thing we can learn from children." On the one hand, a revival of the form of our first passion; on the other, a betrayal of the healthy promiscuity of childhood desire. (We might think of this promiscuous curiosity as a socialized version of Freud's scenario of mobile Oedipal desires.) Finally, the psychoanalyst Christopher Bollas expresses most forcefully the view of monogamy — and of marriage — as a regression to infantile securities. In the chapter "Why Oedipus?" from the 1992 *Being a Character,* Bollas writes that we need to retreat from both the anguishing "complexity born of having a mind to oneself" as well as from "the distresses of group life" which, with its competing points of view that never cohere into a unified social identity, "often operates according to psychotic principles." In order to survive both within groups and within our individual consciousness, we regress, and this regression "has been so essential to human life that it has become an unanalyzed convention, part of the religion of everyday life. We call this regression 'marriage' or 'partnership,' in which the person becomes part of a mutually interdependent couple that evokes and sustains the bodies of the mother and the father, the warmth of the pre-Oedipal vision of life, before the solitary recognition of subjectivity grips the child." Thus monogamy, for Freud, Phillips, and Bollas, turns out to be nearly all things: a civilized necessity that represses desire and betrays the promiscuous curiosity of childhood, a self-sufficient arrangement that, on its own, would never open out into community life and is therefore threatening to civilization, a denial of the mobility inherent in what was only superficially monogamous desire during the Oedipal stage, and a retreat to the comforting immobility of childhood ties and away from the multitudinous and wildly scattered "subjectivities competing for selfhood" in both mature consciousness and social groups.

The psychoanalytic content of the Oedipus Complex (incestuous desire, parricidal impulses, the derivation of a superego from parental authority, bisexuality) distorts a much simpler and, I believe, more consequential drama to which the identity and the sex of the agents are irrelevant. The major function of the figure Freud speaks of as the rival father is not to be either a sexual rival or a parent, but rather to redirect the child's attention, to suggest that there are other modes of extension into the world. It doesn't matter if the agent doing that is a real father in the traditional nuclear family, or another woman, or indeed another man when the desired adult is also a man or, finally, the several agents that may compete for the child's interest, redirect its curiosity, in the single-parent family. The crucial thing is to get the child out of the family, although such a reading may appear to be forestalled by Freud's relegating of that function to the father.

Sophocles' tragedy points less ambiguously to this reading of the Oedipal myth than Freud's appropriation of it. First of all, *Oedipus Rex* is not about Oedipal desires. There is no evidence that Oedipus, having killed his father and married his mother, has fantasies of incest and parricide, whereas the psychoanalytic version of the myth is about nothing if not the determinant role in our psychic lives of incestuous and parricidal fantasies. What Oedipus comes to realize in Sophocles' play is the failure of efforts to remove him from the site of Oedipal fantasies, of the Oedipus complex. After hearing the oracle's prophecy of Laius's death at the hands of their son, Laius and Jocasta literally throw the child into the world, hoping he will die on the "barren, trackless mountains" on which a servant is ordered to abandon him. But thanks to the good—or bad—services of another shepherd, Oedipus is taken in by another family, this time the royal family of Corinth. When he himself hears Apollo cry to him that he will kill his father and couple with his mother he flees his adoptive home and, as everyone knows, after his murderous encounter with Laius lands right back in his real home. Oedipus is catapulted from home to home—as if there were no way to escape from the terrible intimacies of the Oedipal family. The play does, however, recognize the urgency (as well as the tragic futility) of the attempted escape; it projects a defeated dream of pure, orphaned being in the world. But it also represents this being-in-the-world as a violent fate: the probable death of the child abandoned in nature, the extraordinary violence of Oedipus's encounter with Laius and his retinue (he kills all of them). It is at a meeting of three roads that the three lives of son, mother and father begin tragically to intersect. Not only does Oedipus leave home only to circle back to it; the father moves in the world as a familial menace, guaranteeing that whatever the son finds in the world will be, as Freud might say, a refinding of scenes and structures from home.

And yet there is an ambiguity about the father's "place" in both Sophocles and Freud. In *Oedipus Rex* he is met after all *out there*, and the event of his murder—and especially the murder of those accompanying him—exceeds the prophecy of parricide. In Freud, the father's prohibition at once tears the child away from a familial intimacy and guarantees the permanent fantasmatic repetition of that intimacy. The crucial factor here is identification. On the one hand, the child's identifying with the father is a kind of internal monumentalizing of the most violent sides of the Oedipal conflict.

Unable to satisfy the revengeful aggressiveness toward the parent who thwarts its desire to have the other parent all to itself, the child, as Freud writes in *Civilization and Its Discontents*, "takes the unattackable authority into himself" where it both continues to play the father's threateningly prohibitive role and, very conveniently, can also be the defenseless object of the child's aggressiveness toward it. In this version of things, the Oedipus complex, far from being dissolved, is repressed, which means that it will be symptomatically repeated throughout the subject's life. As Freud also says in *Civilization and Its Discontents*, when human families expand into human communities, they repeat, in intensified form, the conflicts and the guilt of the past. "What began in relation to the father is completed in relation to the group." What we "re-find" in the erotic attachments of adult life are not only the warmth of pre-Oedipal intimacy but also the desires, the furious aggressiveness and the ineradicable guilt of the Oedipus complex.

But let's suppose that identification can be something quite different, that it can truly dissolve the fixity of Oedipal desires that are, paradoxically, at once monogamous and promiscuous. It can do this, I think, only if the child identifies with the other *as himself*. It is as if Freud obscurely realized this by making the exception, for the Oedipus complex, to his rule that we internalize lost love-objects. That is, it is as if he realized that at issue in the Oedipus complex is not how we preserve a relation to those objects, but rather, whether we will successfully, *and with pleasure*, move from away from, abandon love-objects. This can be done only if the rival father, or the rival mother, for both the little boy and the little girl, is no longer seen either as a rival or as a parent, but rather as a seductive summons. He or she intrudes upon familial intimacy with a promise (and not merely the prohibitive threat Freud emphasizes) — the promise that if the child leaves the family it will have the narcissistic pleasure of finding itself in the world.

From this perspective, the privileged position Freud gives to the so-called positive Oedipus complex can be understood, and justified, not because it is the structure that holds forth the prospect of a heterosexual resolution, but rather because it is the structure in which narcissistic identification with the other can best take place. And this is because within this structure, the other, the one disrupting the erotic Oedipal couple, is the parent of the same sex as the child. An alien world best exercises its seduction when it appears with the familiar aspect of sameness. It is true that here I am giving a great deal of importance to sexual difference and sameness as phenomenological indexes of all sameness and difference, a move for which queer theorists have sharply criticized our heterosexist (and psychoanalytically inspired) culture. I would forestall any such criticism of what I'm now proposing by pointing out that we are speaking of that particular moment in development when, as Bollas has put it, "in the course of 'answering' questions about the origins of their body's genital urges, [children] discover with what sex they are identified, therefore with what parent they are identified, and they realize their lineage." Bollas speaks of "a new psychic structure" arising out of the new libidinal position of "genital primacy." It is the self corresponding to this repositioning of bodily intensities that naturally sees in sexual difference the phenomenology of all difference, and this limited (even distorted) view of sameness and difference is immensely helpful in guiding the child away from the anxieties of Oedipal intimacy to what might otherwise be seen as a dangerous move away from home.

But the guiding away can be successful only if something is truly lost, or forgotten, and here we confront both a necessity and an opportunity alien to psychoanalytic thought. But what exactly is psychoanalytic thought, and how might answering this question help us to define what might be called the psychoanalytically constituted subject? One of the most curious aspects of *Civilization and Its Discontents* is Freud's reiterated self-reproach to the effect that he is not speaking psychoanalytically. The work was written in 1929, late in Freud's career, so it's not as if he hadn't had time to develop a distinctively psychoanalytic language. You would think that by now Freud would be "speaking psychoanalysis" fluently. But the complaints start in Chapter 3, where he laments that "so far we have discovered nothing that is not universally known," nothing, that is, that might not have been said without the help of psychoanalysis. Given the repetition of this complaint three more times in the work, we should be alert to anything that breaks the self-critical trend, to any moment when Freud might be saying: "This is it! Now I'm being profound, saying things that people didn't know before I said them! Now I'm speaking the language of psychoanalysis!" And indeed there is just such a moment. In the middle of Chapter 7, Freud announces an idea worthy of the founder of a new science, a new way of thinking about the human mind. "And here at last an idea comes in which belongs entirely to psychoanalysis and which is foreign to people's ordinary way of thinking."

What is that idea? It tells us, Freud continues, that while "conscience is indeed the cause of instinctual renunciation to begin with . . . later the relationship is reversed. Every renunciation of instinct now becomes a dynamic source of conscience and every fresh renunciation increases the latter's severity and intolerance." And Freud declares himself "tempted to defend the paradoxical statement that conscience is the result [rather than the cause] of instinctual renunciation." It would seem, then, that paradox is central to psychoanalytic thinking. There is, however, something troubling in the fact that *Civilization and Its Discontents* has been dealing in paradoxes long before Freud announced the arrival of an idea worthy of psychoanalysis. We have learned, for example, that the more virtuous a man is the more severe is his superego, and that he blames himself for misfortunes for which he is clearly not responsible. Such paradoxes may be at first puzzling, but they are resolvable. To renounce instinctual satisfaction is not to renounce instinctual desire; the frustration of desire increases its intensity, and so saints, Freud remarks, "are not so wrong" to call themselves sinners: frustrated temptations are inescapable temptations.

Freud moves on, however, to say something quite different: renunciation itself *produces* conscience. The more familiar view, Freud himself reminds us, is that "the original aggressiveness of conscience is a continuance of the severity of the external authority and therefore has nothing to do with renunciation." But internalization turns out to have two very different aspects. On the one hand, the authority becomes an internal watch-dog and is thereby able to continue to exercise its prohibitive functions. On the other hand, Freud tells us, it is internalized *in order to be attacked.* The authority's imagined aggression toward the desiring subject is taken over by the subject, not only to discipline desire but in order to attack the authority itself. The subject-ego is being punished for its guilty desires, but the punishing energy is taken from the subject's fury at the agent of punishment, who in fact also becomes its object. The child is showing the father what a good punishing father he, the child, would be, but since it is aggression toward the father which allows for this instructive demonstration, the object of it is bound to be the father, "degraded," as Freud says, to sitting in for or as the child in the punished ego. This ferociously severe conscience enacts the phenomenology of the renounced instinctual drives. We no longer have the paradox of virtue intensifying the reproaches of conscience, a paradox explained, and dissolved, by the role of secret desires compensating for the renounced behavior. Now we are not speaking of degrees of guilt or of moral severity but rather of an aggressiveness that accompanies renounced desires. The external authority's severe demands on the subject are, as it were, fused with the subject's vengeful anger at those demands, both of which constitute the subject's renunciation: the consequence, and the content, of renunciation are a doubly reinforced conscience.

This idea may be called distinctively psychoanalytic in that it describes a process in which the world has been sacrificed but *nothing has been lost*. The external authority now exists only as a function of the subject's fantasies: both as the reappropriated angry father originally projected onto the real father and as a carrier of the subject's revengeful aggressiveness toward the father. Psychoanalysis does not deny the world's existence, but it does document the procedures by which the mind dephenomenalizes the world, freezes it in a history of fantasmatic representations, or persistently resists the world with its fantasy of lost *jouissance*. To complain, for example, as critics have done, that Freud turned away from the real world and studied the seduction of children only as fantasy is like complaining about astronomers turning their analytic attention to the stars. Psychoanalysts are no more and no less capable than anyone else of recognizing such phenomena as real child abuse, but that recognition is irrelevant to what is 'psychoanalytic' in psychoanalysis. In fact psychoanalysis is hyperbolically aware of the world as different from the self—which is why it can so brilliantly describe all our techniques for erasing that difference, and why it is of so little help in constructing an epistemology and an ethics grounded in perceptions of sameness, an epistemology and an ethics that might allow us to build a nonviolent relation to the real.

In psychoanalysis, nothing is ever forgotten, given up, left behind. In Chapter 1 of *Civilization and Its Discontents* Freud claims that "in mental life nothing which has once been formed can perish," and, soon after this, "everything past is preserved." Everything persists; psychoanalysis classifies the modalities of persistence and return: conscious memory, slips-of-the-tongue, repression, symptomatic behavior, acting out, sublimation. *Civilization and Its Discontents* textually confirms this law. It wanders, and Freud appears to have trouble finding his subject (the function of religion, the conditions of happiness, the nature of civilization, erotic and nonerotic drives, the etiology of conscience.) And yet aggressiveness comes to include everything: it is accompanied by an intense erotic pleasure; like the oceanic feeeling discussed in Chapter 1, it breaks down the boundaries between the self and the world; it gives expression both to instinctual needs and, in the form of conscience, to the inhibiting energy of civilization. With the analysis of aggressiveness, the boundaries separating concepts are broken down; manifesting a kind of oceanic textuality, ideas flood together in a dense psychoanalytic mix that obliterates such cherished distinctions as those between Eros and nonerotic aggression, even between the individual and civilization (both are at once objects and sources of aggression.)

Distinctions between ideas are perhaps grounded in assumptions of a difference of being between the self and the world. In demonstrating the mind's resources for erasing that distinction, psychoanalysis understandably has difficulty articulating its concepts, keeping some space between them. For Freud, this meant holding on, for dear intellectual life, to dualisms he himself recognised as fragile. Their terms may constantly be collapsing into one another—sadism into masochism, the nonerotic into the erotic, even, as Jean Laplanche has demonstrated, the death drive into sexuality—and yet Freud continued to insist, to insist all the more tenaciously, on the validity of his dualisms. "Our views," he writes in *Beyond the Pleasure Principle*, "have from the very first been *dualistic*, and today they are even more definitely dualistic than before." The logical incoherence that results from the break-down of conceptual distinctions accurately represents the overdetermined mind described by psychoanalysis. For over-determination, far from being merely a characteristic of primary process thinking, defines the psychoana-lytic mind—that is, the mind that has renounced none of its interpretations of the real.

This also is an oceanic phenomenon—not exactly, however, the "limitless narcissism" of the self everywhere present in the world, but rather that of the world entirely reformulated as the self. The distinction, which may appear tenuous, is actually of the greatest importance, for what I take to be to be psychoanalysis's most serious limitation is precisely the difficulty it has imag-ining that we can find ourselves *already* in the world—there not as a result of our projections but as a sign of the natural extensibility of all being. This is the presence to which art—not psychoanalysis—alerts us. I have recently been interested—especially in the work done with Ulysse Dutoit—in tracing the communication of forms in art as the affirmation of a certain solidarity in the universe, a solidarity we must perhaps first of all see not as one of identi-ties but rather of positionings and configurations in space. The narcissistic pleasure of reaching toward our own 'form' *elsewhere* has little to do with the flood of an oceanic, limitless narcissism intent on elimating the world's differ-ence. Rather, it pleasurably confirms that we are inaccurately replicated ev-erywhere, a perception that may help us, ultimately, to see difference not as a trauma to be overcome but as the nonthreatening supplement to sameness. Psychoanalysis profoundly describes our aptitude for preserving the world as subjectivity. Even the metonymic excesses of desire in Lacan are not the result of self-accretion through what might be called the accurate perception of inaccurate self-replications. Rather, Lacanian desire's excess is a function of misregonition; constantly confusing the objects of our desires with their cause, we multiply desires in a hopeless effort to rejoin a retroactively fanta-sised lost "true" object of desire — thus remaining faithful, in an even more desperate version of fidelity to the past than the more literal Freudian one, to a lost nothingness. Art gives us a model of the world *as world*, one we 'know' as aesthetic subjects thrown outwards, 'defined' by relations that at once dis-solve, disperse and repeat us.

We move by forgetting — and no human faculty is more alien to psycho-analysis than that of forgetting. Freud initiated the systematic study of all the ways in which we remain faithful, the strategies by which we manage to go on loving and fearing our first fantasmatic objects. Psychoanalysis, with its obsessive concern with the difference between the self and the world, neces-sarily sees the latter as the repository of everything hostile to the self. It is a place to which, at best, we adapt and from which we retreat and regress to the imagined familial securities nourished by such privileged institutions as monogamy and marriage. The family is the psychoanalytic haven to which we regress, a regression that might be unnecessary if we had left it in the first place. If psychoanalysis, in its account of the extraordinary mobility of childhood and, more specifically, even Oedipal desires, has itself described for us the original inconceivability of a monogamous fixity of desire, and therefore of a stable sexual identity, monogamy nonetheless is the relational figure most congenial to what we might call the psychoanalytic fidelity of the self to the self, its indifference to signs of self that are not signs of inter-pretation, and, finally, its profoundly immoral rejection of our promiscuous humanity.

7

Sociality and Sexuality

Nothing, it would seem, is more difficult than to conceive, to elaborate, and to put into practice "new relational modes." Foucault used this expression to define what he thought of as our most urgent ethical project, one in which gays, according to him, were destined to play a privileged role. Indeed, in an interview published in 1981 in the French magazine *Gai pied*, he went so far as to argue — against what we might call psychoanalytic common sense — that what disturbs people about homosexuality is not "the sexual act itself" but rather "the homosexual mode of life," which Foucault associated with "the formation of new alliances and the tying together of unforeseen lines of force." Such alliances, such lines of force would somehow escape "the two readymade formulas" — both perfectly consistent with the normalizing coercions of the dominant culture — "of the pure sexual encounter and the lovers' fusion of identities." But we should remember that the "new ways of being together" — which, apparently, neither genital nor psychic intimacy would help us to imagine — are for the most part as yet "unforeseen." Foucault seems to have thought of cultural subversion and renewal as inherent in homosexuality, but, to a large extent, it is also something not yet realized. Homosexuality "is not a form of desire but something desirable. Therefore," he went on, "we have to work at becoming homosexuals." In so doing, we might, curiously and impressively, help to bring heterosexuals closer to what Foucault also called "a manner of being that is still improbable." "Homosexuality is a historic occasion to reopen affective and relational virtualities

---

Originally published in *Critical Inquiry* 26, no. 4 (Summer 2000): 641–56.

not so much through the intrinsic qualities of the homosexual but because
the 'slantwise' position of the latter, as it were, the diagonal lines he can lay
out in the social fabric allow these virtualities to come to light."[1]

I want to suggest that in order to imagine "a mode of life" that would, as
Foucault put it, "yield a culture and an ethics" we might momentarily bracket
some of the work that has been done in recent years and respond as if we
had just heard Foucault's challenge for the first time.[2] Let's start again, which
means taking a foundational approach to the question of relationality. Our
thinking about new ways of being together has been predominantly reactive,
against established relational modes. Thus the criticism of hierarchical relational structures — that posit difference in terms of superiority and inferiority,
of dominant groups and oppressed groups — has led not to a questioning of
the prioritizing of difference itself as a foundational relational structure but
rather to praiseworthy but somewhat ineffective pleas for the respect of difference and diversity. Predictably, the strongest work done so far has been
critical histories of hegemonies, histories that also frequently propose certain
transgressive reversals or antithetical reformulations of hegemonic categories.
In *Homos*, I contrasted this with an admittedly utopic form of revolt — one
I located principally in Genet — that would seek to escape transgressive relationality itself and might contest given categories and values by failing to
relate to them either adaptively *or* transgressively. But how do we get to such
a "place"? I would like to move back from Genet's confident performance
of antirelationality in *Funeral Rites* and hypothesize a genealogy of the relational, more specifically, a certain threshold of entry into the relational. I am
of course not referring to a historically locatable moment, one at which each
human subject — and not only human subjects — might have the option of
not moving, of *not* connecting. Such beginnings are both inexistent — there
was never any moment when we were not already in relation — and structurally necessary: it is perhaps only by positing them that we can make existent
relations intelligible. Or, more exactly, it is only through the figuration of
such beginnings that we can see the being of relations, a being that at once
grounds and is obscured by the complicated contingency of all relations.
This is the enabling assumption of much of Beckett's fiction — of *Company*,
for example, in which a life that is nearly over remembers itself *essentially*
by remembering (which is to say, by inventing) its relational origins. The

1. Michel Foucault, "Friendship as a Way of Life," interview by R. de Ceccaty, J. Danet, and J. Le
Bitoux, trans. John Johnston, *Ethics: Subjectivity and Truth*, vol. 1 of *The Essential Works of Foucault*,
ed. Paul Rabinow (New York, 1997), pp. 136, 137, 138.
2. Ibid, p. 138.

Beckettian narrator goes back to a place where he never was as the only way to account for his being anywhere, for it was from "there" that he was summoned into relations, called up from the immobility of perfect self-adequation to be displaced within a language that, before meaning anything, operates as a directional motor, an agent of spatial dispersion.

Because the representation of the birth of relations requires a figure of nonrelationality, the danger inherent in any such representation is the erasure of figurality itself. Nothing is more haunting in the work of artists otherwise so different from one another as Turner and Rothko than their reduction of the canvas to the wholly undifferentiated origins of the canvas's work. In the nearly unpunctuated whiteness of Turner's late paintings, in the blankets of dark sameness on the panels of the Rothko Chapel in Houston, we come as close as we can to suffering the truly rare privilege of seeing nothing — as if the lines of movement in space that art represents could, as it were, be ontologically illuminated only as they almost disappear within a representation of their emergence from nothing. If art is the principal site/sight (both place and view) of being as emergence into connectedness, then the metaphysical dimension of the aesthetic — which may also be its aesthetically distinguishing dimension — is an erosion of aesthetic form. Origination is designated by figures of its perhaps not taking place; the coming-to-be of relationality, which is our birth into being, can only be retroactively enacted, and it is enacted largely as a rubbing out of formal relations. Perhaps traditional associations of art with form-giving or form-revealing activities are at least partly a denial of such formal disappearance in art. If art celebrates an originating extensibility of all objects and creatures into space — and therefore our connectedness to the universe — it does so by also inscribing within connectedness the possibility of its not happening. Relationality is itself related to its own absence. Emphatically present forms designate nonaesthetic functions and registers of being. Brutally authoritative interventions in space — presences secure in their legitimation — violate the ecological ethic for which art trains us.

The notion of an immobility before relations is a heuristic device designed to help us see the invisible rhythms of appearance and disappearance in all being. There is a further question: why extend at all? Why do objects and living beings even begin to move? Again, there is no beginning of movement; nonetheless, relational movement requires an account of a foundational motor — in the case of human subjects, a fundamental motivation for all movement. "Requires" in the sense that all particular motivations of all particular movements share a founding structure of desire, by which

I mean a structure that accounts for the *will to be* in all things. Somewhat unexpectedly, psychoanalysis, which has presented itself as the most finely elaborated theory of desire in the history of human thought, will not be of much help here. It has elaborated extremely tendentious accounts of desire, accounts that make of the world we live in a place inherently alien to any subject's desire. Psychoanalysis has conceptualized desire as the mistaken reaction to a loss; it has been unable to think desire as the confirmation of a community of being.

"At the very beginning, it seems," Freud writes in the 1915 essay "Instincts and Their Vicissitudes," "the external world, objects, and what is hated are identical." Not only at the very beginning: "As an expression of the reaction of unpleasure evoked by objects," he goes on, hate "always remains in an intimate relation with the self-preservative instincts."[3] Given the (perceived) fundamental hostility of the world to the self, the very possibility of object relations depends on a certain mode of appropriation of the object. That appropriating mode is identification, which plays a major role in the psychoanalytic theory of self-constitution. The different internal agencies described in *The Ego and the Id* are sediments of object relationships, the result of the subject's having composed its multiple identificatory acts into a psychically individuating design. The identificatory appropriation of the other is especially striking in the Freudian account of love where, as Freud writes in *Group Psychology and the Analysis of the Ego*, the object often "serves as a substitute for some unattained ego ideal of our own. We love it on account of the perfections which we have striven to reach for our own ego, and which we should now like to procure in this roundabout way as a means of satisfying our narcissism."[4]

"Roundabout" indeed: in this account the external world would have to be invented if it didn't already exist in order for the subject to suppress it. We need it in order to love ourselves, to have the illusorily objectified self-confirmation of a mirror. Freud famously — or infamously — associated narcissistic love with women and, as he writes in the essay "On Narcissism," "people whose libidinal development has suffered some disturbance, such as perverts or homosexuals."[5] But those of us who belong to one — or more — of those unfortunate categories can perhaps take some solace from the fact that Freud saw object love in the most privileged, the most happily developed

3. Sigmund Freud, "Instincts and Their Vicissitudes" (1915), *The Standard Edition of the Complete Works of Sigmund Freud*, trans. and ed. James Strachey, 24 vols. (London, 1953–74), 14:136, 139.

4. Freud, *Group Psychology and the Analysis of the Ego* (1921), *Standard Edition*, 18:112–13.

5. Freud, "On Narcissism: An Introduction" (1914), *Standard Edition*. 14:88.

group—heterosexual men—as also motivated to some degree by a nostalgia for the narcissism they have presumably given up. With this view of the straight man yearning to be the self-contained, self-sufficient woman he loves, the turning away from the other inherent in the Freudian account of sexual love is nearly universalized, although it is a turning away identical to an intense concentration on the other. Because what the man must appropriate as his is the woman's exclusion of him, he can narcissistically suppress her only by an intense, mimetic attention to her self-absorption, her utterly private pleasure in her own image.

I have used the word *appropriate* several times. The relational mechanisms studied most thoroughly by psychoanalysis—identification, projection, introjection—could perhaps only have been theorized in a civilization that has privileged an appropriative relation of the self to the world, one that assumes a secure and fundamentally antagonistic distinction between subject and object. While psychoanalysis has certainly demystified the subject's disinterested pursuit of truth, it has had great difficulty positioning the subject in a nonantagonistic, nonappropriative relation to the world. Indeed, in dramatically desublimating the entire epistemological project in which knowledge is the key to power, to mastery of the real, Freud did not free us from that project; rather, he transformed it into a psychic fate. Psychoanalysis has psychoanalyzed the subject's need to master otherness, and, in so doing, it has exposed that need as the inescapable consequence of the equally inescapable dysfunctionality in the human subject's efforts to negotiate the world's difference.

In the Lacanian Imaginary, difference is denied before there is even an ego to oppose itself to difference. The jubilation with which the infant, in the mirror stage, anticipates a unifying ego in the specular mirage of itself as a unified physical form becomes, in the reenactments of Imaginary relationality, the subject's paranoid suspicion that the other is deliberately withholding the subject's being. In his seminar *Freud's Papers on Technique*, Lacan emphasizes both the distinction and the correlation between physical and psychological maturation. The subject's imaginary mastery over its own body in the mirror stage is also, Lacan writes, an anticipation of psychological mastery, one that "will leave its mark [*donner son style*] on every subsequent exercise of effective motor mastery." But much more than an effect on physical mastery is involved. Lacan goes on to say that the anticipated mastery of the mirror stage is "the original adventure through which man, for the first time, has the experience of seeing himself, of reflecting on himself and conceiving of himself as other than he is—an essential dimension of the human, which entirely structures his fantasy life."[6] By giving such enormous importance (and in spite of the possibility, indeed the necessity, of other relational registers to which I'll return in a moment) to this originating self-(mis)recognition, Lacan suggests that the subject's relation to the world will always bear traces of (Lacan actually speaks of our entire fantasmatic life being structured by) an original self-identification taking place before there is a self, or more exactly a conscious ego, to be identified.

Psychoanalytic accounts of a dysfunctional relation between perception and self-constitution can't help but legitimize — in the sense of demonstrating their necessity — projects of mastery, since they ground all such projects in a biologically determined history of self-apprehension. Indeed, they endow power, or the impulse to master, with a certain pathos because mastery turns out always to bear the mark of that "original adventure" in which we celebrated our capacity for mastery (our bodily coordination and unity) by locating it where it was not. That pathetically misconceived celebration was bound to become a ferocious antagonism toward a world that prevents me from joining my own being. The repetition of an original anticipation of psychological mastery necessarily takes the form of a sense of loss, of theft. A happy expectation is, retroactively, transformed into a hateful resentment.

Interestingly, Laplanche's recently elaborated theory of the enigmatic signifier provides yet another psychoanalytic version of relationality as initiated by misapprehension, by a failure to relate. Laplanche's concept of the enigmatic signifier refers to an original and unavoidable seduction of the child by the mother, a seduction inherent in the very nurturing of the child. The seduction is not intentional; simply by her care, the parent implants in the child the "unconscious and sexual significations" with which the adult world is infiltrated and that are received in the form of an enigmatic signifier, that is, a message by which the child is seduced but which he or she cannot read.[7] Laplanche speaks of this seductive address as an account of the structural formation of the unconscious: primal repression would be the making unconscious of those elements in the enigmatic signifier that infants can't "metabolize," that they are incapable of understanding through some form of symbolization. The implication here is that we are originally seduced into a relation by messages we can't read, enigmatic messages that are perhaps inevitably interpreted as secrets. The result of this original seduction

6. Jacques Lacan, *Freud's Papers on Technique, 1953–1954,* vol. 1 of *The Seminar of Jacques Lacan,* trans. John Forrester, ed. Jacques-Alain Miller (New York, 1991), p. 79.

7. Jean Laplanche, *Seduction, Translation, Drives,* trans. Martin Stanton, ed. John Fletcher and Stanton (London, 1992), p. 188.

would be a tendency to structure all relations on the basis of an eroticizing mystification. If we feel not only, as Freud proposed, that others threaten the stability the ego must defend for its very survival, but also, more dangerously, that we can be seduced by such threats — in Laplanchian terms, "shattered" into an ego-shattering sexuality — then it is reasonable to confront others with paranoid mistrust. The enigmatic signifier becomes a knowledge they are at once willfully withholding from me and using in order to invade my being. But this invasive secret can, in the final analysis, only be *about me*: the enigmatic signifier seduces me because it "knows" me, because it contains in me that which can be seduced, the very formula of a desire of which I myself am ignorant. It is Proust who, with his usual psychoanalytic profundity, both anticipates Laplanche's notion and explicitly draws from it the conclusion I have just proposed. "As there is no knowledge, one might almost say that there is no jealousy, save of oneself."[8] The withheld secret Marcel anxiously pursues in others is the fantasy formula of his own desires — in short, the formula of that which sexualizes him.

Intersubjectivity in the psychoanalytic accounts I have just briefly outlined is a drama of property relations. The world dispossesses me of myself; it threatens or steals the being that is properly mine, that is my property. The Proustian, the Laplanchian, the Freudian, and the Lacanian imaginary subject must master the world in order to repossess its self. The projective, introjective, and identificatory techniques first studied by Freud are strategies designed to suppress the otherness in which my sameness is hidden from my consciousness. To paraphrase an author who made of this war between subject and object a gloriously lurid psychic drama (I refer to Melanie Klein), I must impose my good objects on the world in order to prevent the world from destroying me with my bad objects.

These are the most persuasive voices in psychoanalysis, far more persuasive than those comparatively cheerful theorists of object relations who postulate an adaptive fit between subject and object by simply dismissing the powerful speculative arguments, from Freud to Lacan, for an irreducibly intractable hostility between subject and object as well as between the individual and civilization. Significantly, when the thinkers I've been discussing imagine an alternative to the misapprehensions and the antagonisms that make of human relationality a striking case of dysfunctional evolution, they tend to do so at the expense of consciousness. In my previous work,

---

8. Marcel Proust, *The Captive*, in *Remembrance of Things Past*, trans. C. K. Scott Moncrieff, Terence Kilmartin, and Andreas Mayor, 3 vols. (New York, 1982), 3:392–93.

I have, following Laplanche, given great emphasis to that antinormative strain of thought in the *Three Essays on the Theory of Sexuality* in which Freud speaks of sexual pleasure as "a by-product . . . of a large number of processes that occur in the organism, as soon as they reach a certain degree of intensity, and most especially of any relatively powerful emotion, even though it is of a distressing nature."[9] On the basis of passages such as this one, Laplanche has formulated a theory of sexual excitement as an effect of *ébranlement* — perturbation or shattering — on the organism, an effect that momentarily undoes psychic organization. I have pushed this to the point of arguing, especially in *The Freudian Body*, that sexuality — at least in the mode in which it is constituted — could be thought of as a tautology for masochism.[10] In other words, I have been proposing that we think of the sexual — more specifically, of *jouissance* in sexuality — as a defeat of power, a giving up, on the part of an otherwise hyperbolically self-affirming and phallocentricly constituted ego, of its projects of mastery. Thus the subject enters into a Bataille-like "communication" with otherness, one in which the individuating boundaries that separate subjects, and that subjects for the most part fiercely defend, are erased.

Bypassing Laplanche, in whom it would apparently have displeased them to find any of this, the French *École lacanienne* has recently shown great interest in what it judges to be the closeness of certain aspects of American gay and lesbian studies to Lacan's reflections on *jouissance* in the 1970s. The meeting point between these improbable intellectual allies would be "la question du non-rapport sexuel," as it was recently defined in the review *L'Unebévue* — that is, the sexual as an *absence of relations, a failure to connect.* Jean Allouch evokes Foucault describing "le délire amoureux" as a "perte de soi," an experience in which the individual "no longer knows who he is," lives his pleasure as a "perpetual self-forgetting." Allouch goes on to quote, with approval, my own gloss in "Is the Rectum a Grave?" on Freud's association of sexual excitement with a loss of psychic organization and coherence — a gloss in which I say that Freud's definition "removes the sexual from the intersubjective." Allouch praises the Lacanian resonance of this comment and concludes with a definition of fucking as "a defeat of the subjective as such."[11]

9. Freud, *Three Essays on the Theory of Sexuality* (1905), *Standard Edition*, 7:233.

10. See Leo Bersani, *The Freudian Body: Psychoanalysis and Art* (New York, 1986), pp. 37–39.

11. Jean Allouch, "Pour introduire le sexe du maître," *L'Unebévue* 11 (1998): 58–59, and Bersani, "Is the Rectum a Grave?" in *AIDS: Cultural Analysis/Cultural Activism*, ed. Douglas Crimp (Cambridge, Mass., 1988), p. 197.

Much of this now seems to me a rather facile, even irresponsible celebration of "self-defeat." Masochism is not a viable alternative to mastery, either practically or theoretically. The defeat of the self belongs to the same relational system, the same relational imagination, as the self's exercise of power; it is merely the transgressive version of that exercise. Masochism consents to, indeed embraces that theft of being which mastery would remedy by obliterating otherness through a fantasmatic invasion of difference. To neglect self-defeat in sexual relations leads to that pastoralizing of sexuality that I have frequently criticized; but to privilege self-defeat in the relational field is to reduce that entire field to libidinal relationality. In psychoanalysis, the relational is tendentiously modeled on the libidinal. Perhaps the crucial move here — I'm tempted to say the crucial mistake here — is an interpretation of desire as lack. The world perceived as inherently hostile to the self (Freud), the world as withholding the "secret" of the subject's sexual being (Laplanche on the enigmatic signifier), the world as containing the subject's future completion as a coordinated form (Lacan's relationally initiating mirror stage): in all these cases the subject is either in danger of being stolen or has already suffered a loss of self. Fantasmatic — and, if possible, real — mastery places the subject in the world on the subject's own terms; no longer an agent of loss, the world is now the coerced repairer of loss. Desire is polarized between lack and possession; the *activity* of desire is what moves the subject from the one to the other. Relationality is grounded in antagonism and misapprehension, which means that to meet the world is always to see the world as a place where I am not — or, if I am there, it is as alienated and/or unrecognizable being.

Finally, misapprehension remains a fundamental relational mode even in what is probably the most interesting attempt, within psychoanalytic history, to conceptualize a productive relation of the subject to the world. I refer to Lacan's theory of desire, a theory that depends, in its most psychoanalytically original move, on a depsychologizing of desire and an emphasis on what might be called desire's ontological dignity. Desire is grounded in loss — not the loss of any particular object but rather of being itself. The sacrifice of being is the price we pay when we enter language, when we become creatures who have meaning. Wholly inexpressible, resistant to any kind of symbolization, being retroactively comes to signify lost presence and fullness. Desire is the doomed but limitlessly rich attempt to recover that fullness through objects that are ontologically incommensurable with it. There is no foundational object of desire, only what Tim Dean has called "the perpetual illusion of a secret beyond language, and it is this enigma that elicits desire."[12] In her most recent work, Kaja Silverman appeals to this Lacanian theory in order to put forth a brilliant argument about what she calls our "passion for symbolization"—the way in which we allow other creatures and things to incarnate the originary nonobject of desire.[13] The very lack of that originary object propels us toward the world and toward the future; lack and loss are the bases for our passionate interest in things, for desire's multiple relations with the world's appearances. Thus lack, in this account, is, intriguingly, the precondition for metonymic excess—for all our productively mistaken desires for real objects and real people. Logically, there is no limit to this productivity, since the objects we pursue, while they trace the design of our individual desiring histories, are meant to recover that which preexists all object-choices, to "repair," not the anecdotal, anatomical castration of oedipal anxieties but, much more impressively, the ontological castration through which we presumably entered the human community of signification. No object could ever be an adequate substitute for an objectless being that never was. The ultimate foundation of desire's productivity in this account is the pursuit of, and nostalgia for, nothingness.

Is lack necessary to desire?[14] Perhaps the founding text, in the Western tradition, of desire as lack is Plato's *Symposium*. It will therefore be all the more astonishing to see this extraordinary Platonic dialogue dismiss what appears to be its most unambiguously formulated argument. At a formal drinking party held in honor of the tragedian Agathon's first dramatic triumph, the guests agree to give speeches in praise of love. Socrates, the last to speak, is preceded by Agathon, who, complaining that those who preceded *him* had "congratulate[d] human beings on the good things that come to them from the god" of love rather than praising him "first for what he is," had eloquently enumerated Eros's qualities. Eros is beautiful, young, delicate, brave, temperate, just, and wise. Immediately after the enthusiastic applause with which the handsome tragedian's praise of love is received, Socrates, claiming—to the disbelief of the others—that he can only be tongue-tied "after a speech delivered with such beauty and variety," proceeds to demolish what Agathon has said—and, implicitly, to criticize the speeches given by all the others—for praising Eros, attributing to him "the grandest and the most

---

12. See Tim Dean, *Beyond Sexuality* (Chicago, 2000).

13. See Kaja Silverman, *World Spectators* (Stanford, Calif., 2000).

14. In *Anti-Oedipus*, Gilles Deleuze and Félix Guattari addressed this question. While sympathizing with the argument made in that book that desire does not lack anything, I will propose a way of understanding this that does not depend, as does their argument, on the denial of a desiring subject. See Gilles Deleuze and Felix Guattari, *Anti-Oedipus: Capitalism and Schizophrenia*, trans. Robert Hurley, Mark Seem, and Helen R. Lane (Minneapolis, 1983).

beautiful qualities" rather than telling the truth about him. The truth, as Socrates swiftly demonstrates in a characteristically coercive exchange with the docile Agathon, is that we desire only that which we lack: "anyone . . . who has a desire desires what is not at hand and not present, what he does not have, and what he is not, and that of which he is in need; for such are the objects of desire and love." Thus, if love is the desire of "that of which it is the love," and if, as the others have agreed, love pursues, or makes men pursue, the beautiful and the good, then love itself must be without those qualities. Love can't *be* beautiful and good if it *desires* beautiful and good things — a conclusion Agathon finds so irresistible that he readily admits not knowing what he was talking about in his speech.[15]

Desire is, then, a lack of being. The apparent importance of this position in the *Symposium* is underlined by the fact that it is the only philosophical claim made directly by Socrates; the rest of his contribution to this exercise in intellectual sociability is mediated through his memory of the lessons in love once given to him by the wise woman Diotima. Furthermore, dissatisfied with Agathon when he merely acknowledges that it "wouldn't be likely" for some-one to "actually have what he desires and loves" at the very time of desiring and loving something, Socrates insists that they agree on the necessity of the inherence of lack in desire: "I can't tell you, Agathon, how strongly it strikes me that this is necessary" (S, p. 482). Finally, in order to forestall one possible criticism of his argument, Socrates himself brings up the potential coun-terexamples of strong men who wish to be strong, tall men who wish to be tall — only to point out that what they mean is that they want to possess these things in time to come. Unable to desire things they already have, they are expressing their desire for the future health, the future tallness they now lack.

And yet even in the couple of pages in which the argument for desire as lack or need is so forcefully made, Socrates' coercive move is preceded by a logical confusion that makes us glimpse the possibility of love, or desire, as including within itself its object. Socrates begins his correction of Agathon by asking him if he agrees — and of course he will — that love must be a love of something rather than of nothing. He explains his question by saying that it's as if he were asking whether a father is the father *of* something or not — or whether a mother or a brother are mother and brother *of* something. But are these familial relations really analogous to the relation of desire to that which it lacks? If lack is intrinsic to desire, the object of desire must be absent from the activity of desiring. "Father," on the other hand, specifies a

15. Plato, *The Symposium*, trans. Alexander Nehamas and Paul Woodruff, in *Complete Works*, ed. John M. Cooper (Indianapolis, 1997), pp. 477, 481, 482, 483; hereafter abbreviated S.

relation; not only is a father the father *of* something (as desire is the desire *of* something), but the word itself includes, and therefore largely defines, the other relational term. The analogy Socrates proposes in order to elucidate his notion of desire as lack actually raises the possibility of a desire the other term of which would be an extension, another version, of that which constitutes the very activity of desiring. "Father" is not a relation of need to an object it might seek to possess; it rather evokes what we might call inaccurate replications, or a modified sameness, of itself. That which is external to it is included in that which identifies or individuates it. Thus by its very enunciation "father" moves toward "child," and this logical model of relationality not initiated by lacks or gaps of being might start us moving toward relationality acknowledged as an ontological necessity antecedent to lack. Presence is always relational; desire would be the affective recognition of something like our debt to all those forms of being that relationally define and activate our being. Desire mobilizes correspondences of being.

Much more decisively than the short passage I've been discussing, the entire text of the *Symposium* refutes the ostensibly privileged idea of love or desire as lack. On the one hand, we are tempted to give Socrates an authority none of the other figures in the dialogue enjoys. His is the last speech—as if there were a narrative movement toward a philosophical climax in which we are given the "truth" about love—and the authority of what Socrates says is reinforced by the single speech that follows it, which is Alcibiades' praise of Socrates himself. On the other hand, it is difficult to locate authority in Plato's *Symposium*. To begin with, can we even be sure that this is an authoritative account of what took place, of what was said, at that celebrated banquet? The time of the narrative is several years after the event, which has, it seems, acquired a certain notoriety among Athenians interested in hearing about Socrates. The dialogue begins with a singularly convoluted account of how Apollodorus, who will report on the events in question, learned about them himself. To an unnamed acquaintance who asks him about that dinner long ago, Apollodorus responds that another friend—Glaucon—had just a few days before come to him with the same request. Knowing that Apollodorus has made it his job "to know exactly what [Socrates] says and does each day," Glaucon, who had heard a garbled version of the banquet from a man who had himself learned about it from Phoenix, mistakenly thought that Apollodorus—who in fact has been Socrates' companion only for the past three years—had himself been at the dinner. Apollodorus rather gruffly set Glaucon straight and told him that he himself learned about it from "the very same man who told Phoenix, a fellow called Aristodemus" who went to

the party with Socrates. So Apollodorus, who had checked "part of" Aristodemus's story with Socrates ("who agreed with his account"), told it to Glaucon
and is now about to tell it again to the "rich businessman" (S, pp. 458, 459)
whose question originally led, not to Apollodorus giving straightaway the account of things he had gotten from the banquet guest Aristodemus, but rather
to that curious detour that goes from Glaucon to the man with the garbled
version to Phoenix, who may or may not have made things garbled, back to
Aristodemus. The latter, however, according to Apollodorus, "couldn't remember exactly what everyone said," and, Apollodorus adds, "I myself don't
remember everything he told me. But I'll tell you," he says to his friend,
adding two more qualifications, "I'll tell you what he remembered best, and
what I consider the most important points" (S, p. 463).

So we may have a highly selective *and* approximate account of the
speeches given during the banquet. Remember also that the *Symposium*'s
most celebrated and presumably authoritative speech is actually Socrates' report of what Diotima told him in a series of meetings, which Socrates himself
may not remember with total accuracy but which he will report on, he tells
his fellow guests, "as best I can on my own" (S, p. 484). Indirect transmission,
distance from the event, scattered sources, the perhaps doubtful credibility
of the sources: all this implicitly encourages us not to lean too heavily on
any one argument and perhaps even to reconsider what we might mean by
philosophical seriousness. This is not to put into question Plato's intellectual
commitment to the theory of Forms outlined by Diotima, the progression
from love of beautiful bodies to the love of absolute Beauty. I do mean to suggest, however, that in the *Symposium* that theory is less important than the
textual relationality in which it has its place, and, as a consequence, meaning
itself is reconceived as a certain kind of movement. Unable to be absolutely
certain that we are getting it right, that the report is entirely accurate, we are
freer to attend to what might be called the text's disseminated authority. We
note, for example, that instead of a single most authoritative voice, we have
voices — and indeed structures — that echo one another. Here are some of
them: Apollodorus repeats to the businessman the account of the banquet
he has already given to Glaucon. The speeches about love are framed by the
arrivals of two uninvited guests: Aristodemus at the beginning, Alcibiades at
the end. After the speeches on love, Alcibiades begins what is at least planned
as a second series of encomia, this time with each man present praising the
guest to his right (or perhaps choosing the topic of the speech to be given
by that guest). Socrates begins his speech about love by reporting that he
"had told [Diotima] almost the same things Agathon told [him] . . . : that

love is a great god and that he belongs to beautiful things." Diotima "used the very same arguments against [Socrates] that [he] used against Agathon; she showed how . . . love is neither beautiful nor good" (S, p. 484). None of these repetitions is exact, and the difference in the final case is especially significant. Socrates' correction of Agathon goes no further than proving that need is inherent in desire and that Eros, lacking good and beautiful things, can be neither good nor beautiful. With Diotima, Socrates, unlike Agathon with him, had drawn an apparently logical conclusion from this: "Is love ugly, then, and bad?" Shocked, Diotima admonishes him to "watch [his] tongue" and proceeds to instruct him—in a manner not unlike Socrates' instructional style with his partners in dialogue—that love is *between* wisdom and ignorance, *between* beauty and ugliness (S, p. 484). Love, like all great spirits, according to Diotima, shuttles between opposites, between ignorance and wisdom, between what is mortal and what is immortal. This between-ness is a conceptual echo of our textual betweenness, of the reader's move-ment between the inaccurately replicative voices, structures, and ideas that constitute the *Symposium*'s text.

Ideationally, the replicative structure I find most interesting is constituted by Aristophanes' and Diotima's speeches. It may seem odd to refer to these speeches as echoes of one another. Diotima explicitly (and anachronisti-cally: she instructed Socrates about love before the banquet took place) re-futes Aristophanes' contribution to the *Symposium*. Referring to "a certain story . . . according to which lovers are those people who seek their other halves," she argues that "a lover does not seek the half or the whole, unless, my friend, it turns out to be good as well. . . . What everyone loves is re-ally nothing other than the good" (S, pp. 488–89). And immediately follow-ing the Socrates-Diotima section, "Aristophanes was trying to make himself heard over [the "loud applause" and "cheers" of the other guests] in order to make a response to something Socrates had said about his own speech" (S, p. 494)—a response that has hardly begun before it is interrupted by the arrival of Alcibiades and his drunken party. The differences between the two (including the difference between the whimsical turn of Aristophanes' fable and the pedagogical and philosophical solemnity of Diotima's speech) are obvious but also somewhat misleading. Let's first of all note that Diotima sig-nificantly modifies Socrates' view that the lover of beautiful and good things desires to possess those things. The lover wants not beauty, she teaches, but rather "reproduction and birth in beauty" (S, p. 490).

Far from expressing an emptiness, Eros, according to Diotima, is the sign of a fullness, an inner plenitude that seeks to reproduce itself in the world.

She speaks of someone "pregnant" with "wisdom and the rest of virtue" (S, p. 491).[16] In philosophical discourse with the beautiful soul that acts as a catalyst, or midwife, of this self-reproduction, the lover submits his own ideas to a dialogue in which he not only "educates" the other, as Diotima says, but also "corresponds" with the dialogic modulations of his own philosophical being. An important consequence, even goal, of this exchange is to transform the loved one into a lover. This transformation is a recurrent motif in the *Symposium* (another replicative structure). In the first speech in praise of love, Phaedrus explains that the gods honored Achilles over Alcestis (who sacrificed her own life so that her husband Admetus might live) because Achilles, originally Patrocles' beloved, had made himself Patrocles' lover by his willingness to die in order to avenge Patrocles' death. With an important modification, Alcibiades, according to his own account, underwent the same transformation in his relation with Socrates. Socrates, "crazy about beautiful boys" whom, as Alcibiades puts it, he follows around "in a perpetual daze," had pursued Alcibiades. The latter, confident in his good looks, set out to seduce Socrates, inviting him to dinner, he says, "as if I were his lover and he my young prey," and brazenly offering him the sex he assumes Socrates wants (S, pp. 498, 499). Thus Alcibiades, notwithstanding the sexually "passive" role he seems willing to take for Socrates, also becomes the active lover. But now the reversal of roles is much more complexly viewed than in the case of Achilles. Alcibiades starts out by interpreting his seductive activity entirely as an acquisitive project — in terms of desire as lack. He assumed, he tells the banquet guests, that what Socrates wanted was him — to possess him — so he thought that if he "let [Socrates] have his way with" him, he, Alcibiades, would in turn make Socrates teach him "everything he knew" (S, p. 499). In this exchange of possessions, the philosopher gets the body he wants and the young man gets the philosopher's wisdom. Socrates fails to take up the offer because, as Alcibiades obscurely recognizes, he's interested in a different kind of activity in the young men he apparently pursues. If, as Alcibiades somewhat humorously

16. David Halperin has written brilliantly about the "feminine" paradigm to which Plato's erotic doctrine, as expressed by Diotima, is assimilated or, as Halperin puts it, is a paradigm Plato appropriates in order to "image the reciprocal and (pro)creative erotics of (male) philosophical intercourse" (David M. Halperin, *"One Hundred Years of Homosexuality" and Other Essays on Greek Love* [New York, 1990], p. 150). When, according to Diotima, a person pregnant with wisdom and virtue meets another soul "that is beautiful and noble and well-formed," he himself "instantly teem[s] with ideas and arguments about virtue . . . he conceives and gives birth to what he has been carrying inside him for ages" (S, p. 492). Erotic desire, as Halperin also suggests, does not lead to pregnancy but is rather caused by pregnancy; in a philosopher it climaxes in the "ejaculation" not of a baby but of "ideas . . . about virtue" (Halperin, *"One Hundred Years of Homosexuality" and Other Essays on Greek Love*, p. 140).

complains, Socrates "has deceived us all: he presents himself as your lover, and, before you know it, you're in love with him yourself" (S, p. 503), it is because, in a sense, Socrates has nothing to offer, nothing to fill the gap of a lover's desire. Just as his young lovers' beauty is what excites Socrates to give birth to the ideas teeming in his own philosophically pregnant being, so he expects those he loves to respond to his spiritual beauty by giving birth to the virtue and the wisdom in themselves. In short, the goal of a relation of love with Socrates is the loving subject's communication with himself through the other — not the suppression of the other through such psychoanalytic strategies as projection and identification, but rather the bringing to term the other's pregnancy of soul. Self-delivery fertilizes the philosophical perspective, in dialogue, of otherness.

Aristophanes' fable has of course already given us the *Symposium*'s most unambiguous version of Eros as pursuit of the same. According to that fable, there were originally three kinds of human beings: male, female, and a combination of the two. Each spherically shaped person had four heads, four legs, two faces, two sets of sexual organs. As punishment for these powerful and ambitious humans' attempt to vanquish the gods, Zeus had the luminous idea of cutting each person in two, "the way people . . . cut eggs with hairs" (S, p. 474). The result of this is that every human being is longing for his or her lost other half. "Love," Aristophanes tells his fellow guests, "is born into every human being; it calls back the halves of our original nature together; it tries to make one out of two and heal the wound of human nature" (S, p. 474). Those who were originally all male pursue other men; those who were split from a woman are, as Aristophanes specifies, "oriented more towards women, and lesbians come from this class" (S, p. 475), while the original androgynes are now heterosexuals (who, if the prelapsarian race was divided equally among the three types, would, curiously enough, make up only one-third of present humanity). Like the conversion of Achilles and Alcibiades from loved one to lover, Aristophanes' myth, as Foucault has noted, does away with the generally accepted asymmetry in ancient Greece between the lover and the loved one, the active partner and the passive partner, in a pederastic relation. But while differences of behavior remain between Patrocles and Achilles, and, more significantly, between Socrates and Alcibiades, Aristophanes establishes a perfect "symmetry and equality" between lovers. For two lovers are really a single being; each is moved toward the other by the same desire, the same pleasure.[17]

17. Foucault, *The Use of Pleasure*, trans. Hurley, vol. 2 of *The History of Sexuality* (New York, 1985), p. 232.

SOCIALITY AND SEXUALITY | 118

We are, however, left with a difficult question: is this love for our lost half motivated by lack? This would certainly seem to be the case: a lover longs for what he or she no longer has, the missing half of his or her being. Love, Aristophanes concludes, is an attempt at repossession; it "is the name for our pursuit of wholeness, for our desire to be complete" (S, p. 476). But what does it mean to lack oneself? If love in Aristophanes' fable is a desire motivated by lack or need, what the lover lacks is identical to what he is. *It is more of what he is.* This is a lack based, not on difference (as in the view of Eros desiring that which is different from it, the beautiful and the good that it is not), but rather on the *extensibility of sameness.* Aristophanes' speech makes a mythic narrative, a story, out of what I am proposing as an ontological reality: all being moves toward, corresponds with itself outside of itself. This self-desiring movement defeats specular narcissism, for it erases the individuating boundaries within which an ego might frame and contemplate itself. The self loved in what I have called elsewhere an impersonal narcissism can't be specularized because it can't be personalized; the self out there is "mine" without belonging to me. Aristophanes also makes clear that once sameness is divided from itself, desire for the same can no longer be a relation between exactly identical terms. The "ideal," he says is to "recover [our] original nature." But where is that exactly identical other half? It is of course nowhere to be found, in addition to which the splitting in two is itself a phylogenetic memory. So, as Aristophanes concedes, "the nearest approach to it is best in present circumstances. . . . Love does the best that can be done for the time being" (S, p. 476).

We love, in other words, inaccurate replications of ourselves. The philosophical lesson of the fable is that we relate to difference by recognizing and longing for sameness. All love is, in a sense, homoerotic. Even in the love between a man and a woman, each partner rejoices in finding himself, or herself, in the other. This is not the envy of narcissistic enclosure that Freud thought he detected in male heterosexual desire; it is rather an expression of the security humans can feel when they embrace difference as the supplemental benefit of a universal replication and solidarity of being. Each subject reoccurs differently everywhere.

Finally, if, as I said earlier, art is the site of being as emergence into connectedness, the *Symposium* both thematizes that emergence in speeches about love and pedagogically performs (as befits the educative mission of Socrates) its own textual emergence as inaccurately self-replicating ideas and structures. At the beginning of our philosophical and literary tradition,

Plato's dialogue makes an invaluable contribution to our own discussions of why human subjects intervene in the world, of what moves us to connect. The *Symposium* offers an account of connectedness according to which relations are initiated because they are already there. Its various registers of replication — of reoccurence of the same — disclose, bring to being what is in truth our already established at-homeness in the world.

8

Can Sex Make Us Happy?

The incompatibility of civilization and individual happiness is at once a banality and an overstatement. Everyone knows that in order to enjoy the benefits of living in civilized groups we must all sacrifice, to some degree, the satisfaction of personal interests and passions. Not only that: civilization — to utter another commonplace — actually helps to create the conditions for happiness. As Freud recognizes in *Civilization and Its Discontents*, "it is certain that all the means we use in our attempts to protect ourselves against the threat of suffering belong to this very civilization" to which he none the less assigns "much of the blame for our misery" (pp. 25, 24). In any case, it might justifiably be thought that the tensions between the claims of the individual and those of civilization constitute an argument more appropriate to sociology than to psychoanalysis. Indeed, the argument is impressively elaborated in the work of the great sociologist Georg Simmel who, in his 1910 essay "The Sociology of Sociability," formulated a thesis similar to Freud's in more measured, less melodramatic terms:

> The great problems placed before [the ethical forces of society as it is] are that the individual has to fit himself into a whole system and live for it: that, however, out of this system values and enhancement must flow back to him, that the life of the individual is but a means for the ends of the whole, the life of the whole but an instrument for the purposes of the individual.

Originally published in *Raritan* 21, no. 4 (Spring 2002): 15–30, and as the Introduction to *Civilization and Its Discontents*, Penguin Books, 2002.

For Simmel, as, it would seem, for Freud, "the great problem of association [of human groups]" is 'that of the measure of significance and accent which belongs to the individual as such in and as against the social
milieu.'[1]

In referring to the sociological banality of *Civilization and Its Discontents'*
thesis, I take my cue from Freud himself. One of the most curious aspects
of *Civilization and Its Discontents* is Freud's reiterated self-reproach to the
effect that he is not speaking psychoanalytically. The work was written in
1929, late in Freud's career, so it's not as if he hadn't had time to develop a
distinctively psychoanalytic language. You would think that by now Freud
would be 'speaking psychoanalysis' fluently. But the complaints start in Section III, where he laments that "our study . . . has so far taught us little that
is not generally known" (p. 24), little, that is, that might not have been said
without the help of psychoanalysis. Given the repetition of this complaint
three more times in the work, we should be alert to anything that breaks the
self-critical trend, to any moment when Freud might be saying: 'This is it!
Now I'm being profound, saying things that people didn't know before I said
them! Now I'm speaking the language of psychoanalysis!'

To the reader's great relief, there is just such a moment in *Civilization
and Its Discontents.* Before focusing on the crucial passage in which, apparently, Freud's investigation finally takes a distinctively psychoanalytic turn,
let's note that the argument about human misery necessarily depends on
certain assumptions about what would make us happy. While *Civilization
and Its Discontents* will singularly complicate the very distinction between
happiness and misery, twenty years earlier, in the essay "'Civilized' Sexual
Morality and Modern Nervous Illness," Freud had offered a very *uncompli-
cated* version of the presumed opposition between civilization and individual
happiness. In the 1908 piece, Freud doesn't worry about saying things that
everyone already knows, and his argument is immediately recognizable as a
psychoanalytic argument — if only in the crudest popular sense of what constitutes a psychoanalytic discourse. It's all about sex — just as the early critics
of psychoanalysis complained. "Anyone qualified to investigate the condi-
tioning factors of nervous illness will soon be convinced that the increase of
nervous disorders in our society is due to the greater restrictions placed on
sexual activity" (p. 96). Or: "the baleful influence of civilization is reduced
to the harmful suppression of sexual life in 'civilized' peoples (or classes) by
the "civilized" sexual morality prevailing in them" (p. 88).

1. Georg Simmel, "The Sociology of Sociability," in *On Individuality and Social Forms*, ed. Donald N.
Levine (Chicago: University of Chicago Press, 1971), pp. 137 and 130.

Freud anticipates the sexual liberationists of the 1960s, although he of course sounds more proper then they will even when he is making the most radical argument. Indeed, we shouldn't allow the propriety of vocabulary to obscure just how radical the argument is. Not only does civilization keep us from getting enough sex; it prevents us from having the kind of sex many of us most deeply want. "Today's 'civilized' sexual morality" permits "only legitimate reproduction . . . as a sexual aim" (p. 92); it "demands of the individual, whether man or woman . . . premarital abstinence, and life-long abstinence for all who do not enter into a lawful marriage" (p. 95). Since, as Freud had already argued in *Three Essays on the Theory of Sexuality* (1905), "the human sex drive does not originally serve the purposes of reproduction at all," but rather aims "to obtain particular kinds of pleasure," and since "whole classes of individuals" don't quite make it "from auto-eroticism to object-love, with the aim of genital union" (the presumably normative development), a monogamous heterosexual marriage is hardly a blueprint for universal happiness. The sex life of individuals whose sexual development has been arrested can in fact "take on a serviceable final form," and the sex drive of "inverts" (homosexuals) even has "a special aptitude," Freud claims, "for cultural sublimation" (p. 92). But neither inverts nor other perverts can fully display their cultural gifts, since they have to suppress their drives without, however, being able to get rid of them. The "perverse impulses," once repressed, come back in the disguise of neurotic symptoms: potentially healthy and socially viable sex drives have been transformed by "civilized morality" into culturally useless nervous illness. Not only that: the developmentally lucky ones — heterosexual men and women with a predominantly genital sex drive — are not much happier than repressed perverts. Premarital abstinence leads people to seek "a substitutive satisfaction of a neurotic kind, marked by pathological symptoms" (p. 96). Not only does it lead vast numbers of unhappy heterosexuals to expect much more, and more durable, sexual satisfaction than a monogamous union can bring; the frustrated male who has had recourse to masturbation and even homosexuality is also likely to have only "limited potency" in marriage, which in turn makes it likely that his wife — already crippled by the sexual ignorance at least theoretically mandatory for proper young women in Freud's time — will be frigid. Thus "preparation for marriage frustrates the aims of marriage itself" (p. 99); the disappointed couple "will soon abandon sexual intercourse as the source of all their embarrassments, and with it the basis of married life" (p. 102).

"'Civilized' Sexual Morality and Modern Nervous Illness" is an eloquent indictment of a repressive sexual morality. While much of it seems dated today — especially the section on the enforced sexual ignorance of unmarried young women — it would be presumptuous to congratulate ourselves on having moved significantly beyond the sexual education of young people in the Vienna of Freud's lifetime. The American Christian right has successfully seen to it that a large number of sex education courses in high school "teach" only abstinence and make no mention of contraception. Freud's essay is more a psychological curiosity than an historically obsolete document. For one thing, Freud seems astonishingly naive about the benefits of sex (lots of sex), even though, as we shall see, it is also Freud who has taught us to recognize his hymn of praise to sex as naive. Sexual abstinence (while it may be useful for "young scholars . . . "), far from producing great artists or "independent men of action or original thinkers, bold liberators and reformers," will "more often . . . produce well-behaved weaklings who later merge into the great mass of those who habitually, if reluctantly, follow the lead given by strong [that is, strongly sexed?] individuals" (p. 98). Because women are denied "the opportunity to take an intellectual interest in sexual problems . . . they are deterred from thinking at all, and knowledge loses its value for them." The "undoubted intellectual inferiority of so many women can be traced back to the inhibition of thought that is essential for sexual suppression" (p. 100). The energy with which a man pursues *all* his goals in life, Freud astonishingly and unquestioningly maintains, is a function of how "energetically [he] conquers his sex object." For "a person's sexual behavior often *sets the pattern* for all his other ways of reacting to the world" (p. 99).

Finally, Freud is extremely — and almost embarrassingly — ambiguous about all those "substitutive" activities into which premarital abstinence pushes young people. On the one hand, they are emotionally and morally dangerous. Masturbation "corrupts the character through *indulgence* in more ways than one" (masturbators will take "the easy route" in the pursuit of "significant goals"). Nongenital intercourse (the "perverse" forms of sex — presumably oral and anal) "are ethically objectionable in that they degrade a love-relationship between two human beings from something serious [that is, genital?] into a convenient game that entails no danger or spiritual involvement." Perhaps most disastrously of all, constitutionally or developmentally predestined homosexuals "are now joined by many others," who, unable to go along with "the mainstream of the libido," glide into a considerably widened "homosexual side-channel" (pp. 100–101). Worst of all — the argument is worth returning to — "all those men who as a result of masturbatory or perverse practices have oriented their libido to anything other than the normal situations and conditions of satisfaction, develop a diminished potency in marriage" (p. 101). But why? You *might* argue that when "normal" sex is finally allowed, potency would be increased: all that pent-up genitality can at last, legitimately and joyfully, explode. In "'Civilized' Sexual Morality and Modern Nervous Illness," Freud comes close to giving an anticipatory validation to homophobic fears, all too familiar to us, that heterosexuals can somehow be seduced into homosexuality and, especially, that if they do cross that line they may be permanently lost to, or spoiled for, heterosexuality. The normal, it would appear, is exceedingly vulnerable. To retaste the perverse is to lose some of our passion for the nonperverse; the danger of developmental backtracking is that we may never again have much enthusiasm for going forward.

"'Civilized' Sexual Morality and Modern Nervous Illness" is *psychoanalytically* muddled. By that I mean that its muddlement is constitutive of its limited but real interest. A rational and humane protest against the sexual abstinence imposed on sexually energetic young men and women is in fact a cry of alarm from someone who clearly — but also confusedly and perhaps unwillingly — knows something that this repressive society doesn't know (or pretends not to know). What he knows has something to do with both the power and the nature of sexuality. The apparent naiveté I referred to earlier about the benefits of lots of sex may be, more profoundly, a warning about the danger of postponing the pleasures of "normal" intercourse. More exactly, it is a warning about the danger of postponing the repressive strength of those pleasures. Society's repression defeats a more important repression (important *for* society): a repression of *the sexual as such*. For if we need frequent sex, and if having sex makes us fit for all of life's other activities, it's because sex is something like — to use an image we will find in *Civilization and Its Discontents* — an oceanic force, one that threatens to flood our lives, to drown our other interests. The immense stupidity of society is to create the ideal conditions for such a flooding — that is, to liberate sexuality through the repression of sex. If society would just allow young men and women to have (presumably) normal sex, the women will think more clearly and the men will be better artists and bolder political activists. But by interfering with the teleology, the purpose, and the direction of sexual development, society undoes one of the great conquests of human evolution: the use of reproductive sex as a sexual hygiene, a mode of sexual containment. The real substitutive activity is heterosexual genital monogamy; its milder pleasures discipline the overwhelming pleasures of perverse sex — which is to say, perhaps, the pleasures of the sexual itself. Astonishingly, then, Freud may secretly agree with the society he sternly criticizes: civilization requires sexual repression because unrepressed sexuality might destroy civilization. But *strategically* society has got it all wrong. The right way to go about the necessary damming up of the oceanic is to let people swim in the calmer waters of what might be called genital relationality: the waters of sex-cum-love, of sex promoted to, as Freud puts it, "something serious," something more than mere "indulgence," something "that entails . . . danger or spiritual involvement" (p. 101). In other words, a kind of sublimated sexuality in which what is (necessarily?) repressed would no longer produce neurosis (that is, the inevitable return of the repressed in the disguise of neurotic symptoms).

Twenty years later, *Civilization and Its Discontents* will take up the principal thesis of "'Civilized' Sexual Morality and Modern Nervous Illness," but the implicit optimism of the 1908 essay will be notably absent. Now there is hardly any suggestion that to remove the socially imposed barriers to sexual satisfaction would serve the cause of either civilization or individual happiness. For one thing, what a more liberal society might allow us to enjoy — nonmonogamous heterosexual genital sex — is explicitly presented as a pale substitute for pleasures that *no* civilized society could be imagined as authorizing. In section II, Freud tells us that the intensity of satisfactions provided by scientific or artistic work is "restrained when compared with that which results from the sating of crude, primary drives: they do not convulse our physical constitution" (p. 18). What did convulse our being, Freud suggests in the astonishing footnotes on the first and last pages of section IV, was the experience, or rather the smell of sex before we adopted an erect posture. But our sexuality fell when we stood up. Both anal eroticism and olfactory stimulation were subjected to what Freud calls "organic repression" (p. 42); the result of this "repression" is our horror of excrement and, at least according to Freud, a repugnance at sex, a shame provoked in us by our genitals and a disgust at genital odors which is so strong in many people that it "spoil[s] their enjoyment of sexual intercourse." And what a loss this was! By the end of the last footnote in section IV, Freud has transformed man's depreciation of the sense of smell in sex into the repression of "the whole of his sexuality" (p. 43). Nothing is stranger in *Civilization and Its Discontents* than the erotically confessional footnotes — that is, those moments when the distinguished (if at times both extravagant and banal) anthropological imagination of the text descends into a footnote where it enjoys the fantasy of a mythic, prehistoric convulsing of our physical being in the passionate sniffing of a male on all fours.

An unfortunate consequence of evolution is, then, what most of us, according to Freud, experience as the "unaccountable repugnance" (p. 43) that accompanies sexual love ("the model for all happiness," p. 37). At bottom, we are all insatiable and unhappily repressed perverts. We are, both ontogenetically and phylogenetically, "coded" for pleasures we can no longer legitimately enjoy. But *Civilization and Its Discontents* goes even further than this. Not only is our sexuality dysfunctional from both developmental and evolutionary perspectives; there is, it would seem, something inherently dysfunctional in sexuality itself (repressed or unrepressed). At the the end of section IV, Freud raises a disturbing possibility: "Now and then one seems to realize that this [the diminished importance of sex as a source of happiness] is not just the pressure of civilization, but that something inherent in the [sexual] function itself denies us total satisfaction and forces us on to other paths. This may be wrong — it is hard to decide" (p. 41). Wrong or not, this speculation governs the rest of *Civilization and Its Discontents*. In the footnote quoted from a moment ago and to which this sentence refers us, Freud is already trying to define that unsatisfactory something in the nature of sexuality itself. He comes up with three factors: the organic repression of our sense of smell and of anal eroticism (this is the conjecture "that goes deepest"), our inherent bisexuality (which means, he writes, that the same object is not likely to satisfy both our male and female desires) and finally that "degree of direct aggression" with which "erotic relations are so often associated . . . quite apart from the sadistic component that properly belongs to them" (p. 43).

Thus begins the reflection on aggression — the real and profound subject of *Civilization and Its Discontents*, a subject which, from section V to VIII, will be promoted to the upper body of the text. To use the image from Romain Rolland which Freud has analyzed in section I, aggression is the oceanic element that will flood the text of *Civilization and Its Discontents* — with, however, a crucial distinction. If the footnotes play the role of the psychoanalytic unconscious in this work, the material of the footnotes will be allowed into the text proper — into the quite proper text — only if its sexual components are expunged. And so, enacting compositionally his own formulation of the laws of repression and symptom-formation, Freud will devote the rest of his symptomatic upper text to the analysis of a presumably noneratic aggression. Nowhere is the troubled speculative mobility of *Civilization and Its Discontents* more evident than in Freud's ultimately failed attempt to maintain the distinction between sexuality and aggression. The text's "official" version of the aggressive drive is that it "is the descendant and principal representative of the death drive, which we have found beside Eros and which rules the world jointly with him." The reference is of course to the thesis of *Beyond the Pleasure Principle* (1920), and as in that work Freud maintains here "the ubiquity of non-erotic aggression and destruction," at the same time that he recognizes, once again, that the death drive, from which that destruction derives, "mostly eludes our perception, of course unless it is tinged with eroticism." But now Freud goes further: "Yet even where it appears without any sexual purpose, in the blindest destructive fury, there is no mistaking the fact that its satisfaction is linked with an extraordinarily high degree of narcissistic enjoyment, in that this satisfaction shows the ego how its old wish for omnipotence can be fulfilled" (p. 57).

Aggression is beginning to sound bizarrely like — of all things — the oceanic feeling, which Freud, correcting the religious emphasis given to that feeling by Romain Rolland, had defined as an ecstatic breaking down of the boundaries between the ego and the world traceable to the "unlimited narcissism" of infancy. Like the oceanic feeling, aggressiveness includes an intense erotic pleasure. Against the view that the oceanic feeling is the source of religious sentiments, Freud had argued that it is probably rather "an initial attempt at religious consolation," a delusionary cure for human suffering (p. 10). Now, however, Freud is suggesting that we suffer because civilization insists that we curb the "extraordinarily high degree of narcissistic enjoyment" that accompanies satisfied aggression (that is, the successful breaking down of the world's resistances to, or more fundamentally, differences from, the ego). The oceanic feeling is the cure that religion proposes for the suffering caused by the curbing of the oceanic feeling — which is to say that the proposed cure for the illness is an idealized repetition of its origin. The oceanic feeling is a benign reformulation of "the blindest destructive fury" (p. 57).

This mystification, however, points to a hidden truth about destructiveness: it is identical with love. Not only had Freud spoken, in the final footnote to section IV, of "a degree of direct aggression" so often associated with erotic relations; not only does he recognize, as we have just seen, the intense narcissistic pleasure of destructiveness; he had even gone so far as to assert in section V, in objecting to the communists' argument that private property created aggression, that the latter "forms the basis of all affectionate and loving relations among human beings, with perhaps the one exception of the relation between the mother and her male child" (p. 50). If we abolished the family and instituted complete sexual freedom, the indestructible destructiveness of human beings would still be with us. Only a few pages after Freud's very tentative suggestion at the end of section IV that "something inherent in the [sexual] function itself" (p. 41) *may* prevent complete sexual

CAN SEX MAKE US HAPPY? | 128

happiness, he claims, without any tentativeness at all (even while continuing to insist on the nonerotic character of this aggressiveness), that an aggressive destructiveness "forms the basis of" (p. 50) human love — which, I suggest, may be another way of saying that *destructiveness is constitutive of sexuality.* The explicit argument of *Civilization and Its Discontents* goes like this: we must sacrifice part of our sexuality and sublimate it into brotherly love in order to control our murderous impulses towards others. But the text obliquely yet insistently reformulates this argument in the following way: human love is something like an oceanic aggressiveness which threatens to shatter civilization in the wake of its own shattering narcissistic pleasure. We don't move *from* love *to* aggression in *Civilization and Its Discontents*; rather, love is redefined, re-presented, *as* aggressiveness.

Not only that: civilization itself repeats, rather than opposes, the other two terms, thereby transforming the argument of Freud's work into a triple tautology: sexuality = aggression = civilization. It is by no means certain that civilization can maintain itself as a distinct term within what might be called the oceanic textuality of *Civilization and Its Discontents*, a textuality that breaks down the boundaries separating concepts. I referred at the beginning of this discussion to Freud's dissatisfaction, expressed several times in *Civilization and Its Discontents*, with the ordinariness of his own ideas. He claims to be painfully aware of discovering nothing, in this investigation, "that is not generally known" (p. 24) It is only in the middle of section VII that Freud finally announces an idea worthy of a new science, a new way of thinking about the human mind. "And here at last an idea comes in that belongs entirely to psychoanalysis and is foreign to our ordinary way of thinking." What is that idea? It tells us, Freud continues, that while "it is at first the conscience . . . that causes us to renounce the drives, this causal relation is later reversed. Every renunciation of the drives now becomes a dynamic source of conscience; every fresh renunciation reinforces its severity and intolerance." And Freud declares himself "tempted to endorse the paradoxical statement that conscience results from [rather than is the cause of] the renunciation of the drives" (p. 65). It would seem, then, that paradox is central to psychoanalytic thinking. There is, however, something troubling in the fact that *Civilization and Its Discontents* has been dealing in paradoxes long before Freud announced the arrival of an idea worthy of psychoanalysis. We have learned, for example, that the more virtuous a man is the more severe is his superego, and that he blames himself for misfortunes for which he is clearly not responsible. Such paradoxes may be at first puzzling, but they are resolvable. To renounce satisfaction of a drive is not to renounce the desire associated with the drive; the frustration of a desire increases its intensity, and so saints, Freud remarks, are not so wrong to call themselves sinners: frustrated temptations are inescapable temptations.

Freud moves on, however, to say something quite different: renunciation itself *produces* conscience. The more familiar view, Freud reminds us, is that "the original aggression of the conscience continues the severity of the external authority and has therefore nothing to do with renunciation" (p. 65). But internalization turns out to have two very different aspects. On the one hand, the authority becomes an internal watch-dog and is thereby able to continue to exercise its prohibitive functions. Civilization thus inhibits aggression by sending it back where it came from; conscience, or the super-ego, treats the ego with the same harsh aggressiveness that the ego would like to direct towards others. On the other hand, Freud tells us, external authority — civilization and its representatives — is internalized *in order to be attacked.* The authority's imagined aggression toward the desiring subject is taken over by the subject, not only to discipline desire but also in order to attack the authority itself. The subject-ego is being punished for its guilty desires, but the punishing energy is taken from the subject's fury at the agent of punishment, who in fact also becomes its object. The child is showing the father what a good punishing father he, the child, would be, but since it is aggression towards the father which allows for this instructive demonstration, the object of it is bound to be the father, "degraded," as Freud says, to sitting in for or as the child in the punished ego. This ferociously severe conscience is already present within the renounced instinctual drives. We no longer have the paradox of virtue intensifying the reproaches of conscience, a paradox explained, and dissolved, by the role of secret desires compensating for the renounced behavior. Now we are not speaking of degrees of guilt or of moral severity but rather of an aggressiveness that accompanies renounced desire. The external authority's severe demands on the subject are fused with the subject's vengeful anger at those demands, both of which constitute the subject's renunciation: the consequence, and the content, of renunciation are a doubly reinforced conscience.

What has happened to civilization? More pertinently, *what is civilization?* What does it mean to say that civilization inhibits aggression or to assert, as Freud does in his concluding section, that "the sense of guilt [is] the most important problem in the development of civilization and the price we pay for cultural progress is a loss of happiness, arising from a heightened sense of guilt" (p. 71)? The text has by now made a quite different argument: the renunciation of aggression is inherent in its constitution. But it is a renunciation that multiplies the force of aggression. In giving up the satisfaction of a drive, we simultaneously: (1) internalize the authority presumably inhibiting the drive, (2) increase our sense of guilt by intensifying our desire for satisfaction, (3) submit the ego to the fury of an aggressiveness originally intended for the inhibiting external authority. Given the limitations of our effective power over the external world, it could be said that the curbing of aggressiveness offers the only realistic strategy for satisfying aggressiveness. And the inhibiting power of what Freud calls civilization is unintelligible — if we exclude the crudest exercise of power, in which people are physically subjected to the will of others — except in terms of those internal mechanisms that I have just outlined. In a very important sense, civilization in Freud, at least that aspect of it which he thinks of as a socialized superego, is merely a cultural metaphor for the psychic fulfilment in each of us of a narcissistically thrilling wish to destroy the world, a wish "fulfilled" in a monstrously ingenious phantasmatic scenario of self-destruction. From this perspective, civilization is not the tireless if generally defeated opponent of individual aggressiveness; rather, it is the *cause* of the very antagonism that *Civilization and Its Discontents* sets out to examine. The regulator of aggression is identical to the very problem of aggression.

We have moved very far indeed from an optimistic view of sexuality's beneficent influence on the individual as well as on civilization. A more liberal sexual ethic would, Freud suggested in "'Civilized' Sexual Morality and Modern Nervous Illness," make individuals happier, help to preserve the institution of marriage, and free the mental energy indispensable to artistic and scientific achievement. This is a psychoanalytic program closer to Wilhelm Reich than to Freud; it is psychoanalysis in the service of a gospel of sexual liberation. For the Freud of *Civilization and Its Discontents*, sexuality is certainly as important as it was in 1908, but there has been a momentous shift of perspective: now sexuality is the ineradicable, intractable source of our *un*happiness. And this view implies a distinction — absent from the earlier essay — between sex and sexuality. In the first few sections of *Civilization and Its Discontents*, Freud seems to be talking about certain kinds of *behavior* that would make the individual happy but that civilization prohibits. By the end of section IV, we are dealing with something quite different. Not only is the behavior that would make us happy a monstrous anomaly (remember that prehistoric sniffing male on all fours), but now we are being asked to look at a psychic "function," at something like a fundamental psychic posture towards the world. We may, with Freud, call that posture sexuality, but it has very little to do with sex. We may, also with Freud, wish to call it aggression, but this is an aggression of enormous erotic power, an aggression that may even be constitutive of sexuality.

It should at once be said that this blurring of distinctions is by no means what Freud the rational thinker *wants*. Indeed, the opposition advanced in *Beyond the Pleasure Principle* between Eros and Thanatos (between, on the one hand, sexuality, and on the other, aggression and a death drive) — an opposition that Freud unreservedly reasserts in *Civilization and Its Discontents* — might even be thought of as an anticipatory theoretical defense against the *collapse* of that very dualism into a nearly inconceivable sameness. Freud resolutely holds on to the notion of a nonerotic aggression at the same time that his argument moves inexorably towards a view of aggression (directed towards the world or towards the self) *as* intense erotic excitement. The latter view is the language of psychoanalysis, although it is a language at odds with what language usually does. It abolishes the differences and spaces that separate terms and concepts; it transforms oppositions into repetitions, and threatens to reduce discourse to a numbing display of redundancies. This is not to say that such redundancies cover all of reality. Psychoanalysis is not about all of reality; it treats, properly, "only" sexuality (and its detractors are right about this), but the sexuality it treats is a kind of vast tautology within the human psyche, one to which what we call the sexual act is nearly irrelevant. Psychoanalysis teaches us to recognize that tautology as an always imminent threat to our negotiations with the differences and the nonredundant spaces of the authentically nonerotic real.[2]

In terms of a particular life's history, the psychic posture just described accounts for *our never losing anything*. In psychoanalysis, nothing is ever forgotten, given up, left behind. In section I of *Civilization and Its Discontents*, Freud claims that "in mental life, nothing that has once taken shape can be lost," and, soon after this, "everything past survives" (pp. 7, 9). Everything persists; psychoanalysis classifies the modalities of persistence and return: conscious memory, slips-of-the-tongue, repression, symptomatic behavior, acting out, sublimation. *Civilization and Its Discontents* textually confirms this law. It wanders, and Freud appears to have trouble finding his subject (the function of religion, the conditions of happiness, the nature of civilization, erotic and nonerotic drives, the aetiology of conscience). And yet aggressiveness comes to include everything: it is accompanied by an intense

---

2. Ulysse Dutoit and I attempt to show what such exchanges with the world might be like (sensual exchanges that at once acknowledge and dismiss the erotic) in both *Arts of Impoverishment: Beckett, Rothko, Resnais* (Cambridge, MA: Harvard University Press, 1994) and *Caravaggio's Secrets* (Cambridge, MA: MIT Press, 1998).

erotic pleasure; like the oceanic feeling discussed in section I, it breaks down the boundaries between the self and the world; it gives expression both to instinctual needs and, in the form of conscience, to the inhibiting energy of civilization. Psychoanalysis does not deny the world's existence, but it does document the procedures by which the mind dematerializes the world, absorbs it into a history of fantasy-representations. To complain, for example, as critics have done, that Freud turned away from the real world and studied the seduction of children only as fantasy is like complaining about astronomers turning their analytic attention to the stars. Psychoanalysts are no more and no less capable than anyone else of recognizing such phenomena as real child abuse, but that recognition is irrelevant to what is "psychoanalytic" in psychoanalysis. It may not, however, be irrelevant to suggest the very limited usefulness of psychoanalysis in describing, or training us for, what I called a moment ago our negotiations with the nonerotic real. Lacan's assaults on ego psychology can be best justified as a profound fidelity to psychoanalysis itself, as a recognition that a psychology of adaptation to the world is by definition a nonpsychoanalytic psychology. Psychoanalysis gives a persuasive account not of human adjustment but of that which makes us unfit for civilized life. This should at the very least cast some doubt on the validity of *any* notion of a psychoanalytic "cure." The clinical practice of psychoanalysis is grounded in a theory that tells us why we can't be cured. The "illness" in question takes on great anecdotal variety in individual lives (and this naturally provides ample material for clinical work), but our blind destructive fury is an intractable psychic function, and positioning in the world, rather than a deviation from some (imaginary) psychic normality. We can, at best (as long as we remain within psychoanalysis), adapt to that which makes us incapable of adaptation. To go any further (again, within psychoanalysis) would be to cure ourselves of being human.

9

Fr-oucault and the End of Sex

Foucault and Freud: a large part of my work has been a dialogue (both
conciliatory and antagonistic) between the two. It is in the agitated space
between Foucault and psychoanalysis that I have been trying to think gayness and, more generally, desire and sexuality. At first, having worked with
psychoanalytic texts before I became absorbed in Foucault's work, I couldn't
help but find regrettable Foucault's unwillingness to enter into something
like a sustained dialogue with psychoanalysis. Questions that he himself
raised — principally on the nature of disciplinary networks and on the possibilities of resistance to (and from within) those networks — seemed to me
incapable of being effectively addressed without taking into account such
psychoanalytic concepts as repression and the unconscious. This was not
merely an abstract objection. I felt, for example (and I continue to feel), that
the social problem of homophobia can be only superficially understood without those concepts. In "Is the Rectum a Grave?" I suggest that the struggle
against homophobia is doomed to failure if we ignore the psychic yearn-
ings and anxieties that sustain homophobia. For many heterosexual men
(the major source of homophobic persecution), homophobia has been a displaced, more "acceptable" form of misogyny. It is the symptom of a fascination with and terror of the ego-disintegrating *jouissance* of a fantasized female
sexuality — a *jouissance* available to the male body, according to this fantasy,
in "passive" anal sex. Thus Foucault's claim, in interviews for *Salmagundi*

Lecture given at the University of California — Berkeley at the symposium "Foucault at Berke-
ley/Twenty Years Later," October 2004.

and *Mec*, that what people find intolerable in gayness is not the sex act but the spectacle of postcoitum happy gays could strike me only as bizarrely simplistic. After all, the scene Foucault describes (one he probably saw many times on the streets of the Castro in the gloriously sex-wild pre-AIDS days of the late 1970s in San Francisco) is hardly a gay prerogative. Millions of straight couples look just as happy after a good fuck, and now that gays are anxiously rushing to take matrimonial vows, it is likely that they will look just as *un*happy, or bored, as countless straight couples after five or ten years of monogamous intimacy.

And yet it was this simplistic, easily derided view of homophobia that helped to dampen my enthusiasm for psychoanalytic interpretations. First of all, Foucault's reductive comment is of course deliberately, strategically polemical. More important, it is the result of his conviction, which may have been more of a hope, that gays might invent less oppressive lifestyles (intimacies as well as more general social relations no longer structured by fixed positions of dominance and submission, of superiority and inferiority) — in short that we might become models for what he called "new relational modes." My book *Homos* is a difficult balancing act between a lingering allegiance to psychoanalysis and my growing conviction that psychoanalysis will not be very useful in helping us to reconfigure relationality. And this is not only because (as Didier Eribon has argued with great force) psychoanalysis may be irrevocably committed to a normativizing sexual ethic. Perhaps even more significantly, what I have come to think of as the most invaluable aspect of psychoanalytic thought is inherently inhospitable to the admittedly utopic but no less indispensable goal of "new relational modes." I'm thinking of the drive to destroy — to destroy both the world and the self — which Freud, especially in *Civilization and Its Discontents*, defines as intractable because it is also the source of the most intense pleasure we can know. As such, destructive *jouissance* would be resistant, as Freud claims, to any social transformations whatsoever. A question that interests me very much is: is it possible to invent "new relational modes" while taking into account the intractability of the death drive?

It's true that Foucault himself didn't go very far in defining what those "new relational modes" might be like. I actually find this to be a beneficial limitation, since more specific suggestions about, as he put it, how we might "become gay" could operate as a constraint on our very effort to do so, while his underconceptualizing of that notion can serve as a generous inspiration, leaving the field open for all sorts of experiences and experiments. My recent collaborative work with Ulysse Dutoit on the visual arts could be thought of as speculative experiments inspired by Foucault's interest in relational innovation. *Caravaggio's Secrets*, in particular, moves from a psychoanalytic reading of what we call the erotic invitation in Caravaggio's early portraits of provocatively seductive boys to an analysis of a relational field that proposes a kind of pleasure different from the *jouissance* associated with sexual desire (and sexualized aggression). *Caravaggio's Secrets* is an antipsychoanalytic study in the sense that it proposes the relational foundation for a sensual pleasure that has renounced, or gone beyond, the exciting mysteries of desire. Thus, in our analyses of paintings we repeat, in our own terms, Foucault's distinction between desire and pleasure. We find in Caravaggio's work, in opposition to the psychoanalytic insistence on the lack inherent in desire, visual representations of the pleasures of perceiving partial self-replications, everywhere. In sum, an erotics of presence and plenitude rather than one based on efforts to appropriate and to find our pleasure in that which we lack. The connection to Foucault is even more pronounced in that the pleasure we speak of is at once an aesthetic phenomenon (produced by the perception of formal correspondences between the subject and the world) and an effect of a certain ascesis (of a work on and, to a certain extent, against the self). Ascesis and aesthetics: two terms central to Foucault's elaboration, in *History of Sexuality* of a *souci de soi*, en ethic of the self, in Greco-Roman antiquity.

And yet: another reading of Foucault for a seminar I gave at Northwestern University a few years ago unexpectedly reilluminated psychoanalysis for me and even brought Freud and Foucault in an at least temporarily harmonious reencounter. With an obvious antipsychoanalytic intention, Foucault announces, in the first sentence of chapter 3, part 4, of volume 1 of *History of Sexuality* that "sexuality must not be described as a stubborn drive. . . . " Instead, "it is the name that can be given to a historical construct . . . a great surface network in which the stimulation of bodies, the intensification of pleasures, the incitement to discourse, the formation of special kinds of knowledge, the strengthening of controls and resistances are linked to one another, in accordance with a few major strategies of knowledge and power." Even more original, and this time somewhat bizarre, is Foucault's insistence, in the final section of the same volume, on the nonexistence of sex. There is an important distinction here: sexuality exists as strategic deployments, but those deployments depend on the invention of "sex in itself" as "the center around which sexuality distributes its effects." Sex is nothing more than "the most speculative, most ideal, and most internal element in a deployment of sexuality organized by power in its grip on bodies and their materiality, their forces, energies, sensations, and pleasures." Nothing, it would appear, erases more effectively the entire field of psychoanalysis than this affirmation of sex as the myth required to support a historical construct named sexuality.

We read some Freud in the same seminar, and it was perhaps his textual proximity to Foucault that led us to the startling conclusion that, proceeding from wholly different analyses, Freud comes to nearly the same conclusion as Foucault. That is, the founder of psychoanalysis also erased sex from the human body. The entire text of *Three Essays on the Theory of Sexuality* deploys sexuality as a construction: it defines the stages — oral, anal, and phallic — through which the human subject must pass in order to reach the goal of normative genitality. But after so carefully tracing the presumably necessary development of sexuality in the child, Freud comes to the astonishing "unsatisfactory conclusion" in the final sentence of his book that we know so little about "the essence of sexuality" that in fact we cannot construct a theory "adequate to the understanding alike of normal and pathological conditions." But this is exactly what, until that final sentence, *Three Essays* has more or less confidently been doing: constructing a theory of the normal and pathological conditions of sexuality. Reread in a Foucaldian perspective, Freud's work has been doing something quite different. *Three Essays* has deployed the guidelines for a therapeutic discipline. It has both provided a content for sexual development and structured that content as a teleological narrative. But Freud exposes that narrative as pure construction by acknowledging the absence, or at the very least the unknowability, of, to paraphrase Foucault, the ideal point made necessary by his own deployment of sexual development. (Add to this the fact that within the text itself sex becomes a property of the entire body — of the skin and of internal organs — and sexual pleasure can be triggered by such things as reading and riding in trains.) The validity of that deployment, of that narrative, depends on there being a knowable "sexual essence" — a biological referent that Foucault calls "sex." It is as if in the main narrative thrust of the essay Freud was confirming his role in the history of those strategies of knowledge and power that Foucault called sexuality; but then he moves from being one of the cultural "objects" demystified by Foucault's analysis to becoming himself one of its demystifiers. Thus psychoanalysis anticipates and performs Foucault's deconstruction of it. Has Freud anticipatorily mutated into Foucault? In any case, when we add to this astonishing self-defeating move the collapse of sex into the *jouissance* of aggression twenty-five years later in *Civilization and Its Discontents*, we may feel justified in arguing that Freud initiated Foucault's major enterprise of what might be called *corporeal clearance* — that is, stripping the body of its imposed and unnecessary sexual identity and presenting it as a marvelously variegated surface of flesh available to as yet unarticulated pleasures suppressed and crippled by the at once authorized and prohibited excitement of something called sex.

But why return to Freud by way of Foucault if it is only to read Foucault as Freud? First of all, Foucault can help us to see — in spite of himself — that psychoanalysis, which he certainly considered, as most queer theorists do today, as operating a massive reinforcement of old relational modes, in fact may have cleared the field — in spite of itself — for "new relational modes." At the same time, however, psychoanalysis powerfully argues against the illusion that new ways of structuring relations can simply be "performed," that they depend on our consciously choosing them — an illusion nourished, involuntarily or deliberately, by some early queer texts. The possibility of inventing new forms of intimacy and perhaps even new modes of pleasure must, I believe, take into account that intractable resistance to life that Freud called the death drive — and that Jean Laplanche has identified with sexuality itself in Freud. In political life, the promotion of murderous projects can perhaps be explained in terms of ego-motives, but the more or less passive support of, and therefore collaboration with, those projects on the part of millions of people who have no self-interest in their fulfillment can be understood only in terms of a perhaps universal, and incurable, drive to destroy. In other words, while there can be no excuse for not struggling against the multiple forms of oppression, psychoanalysis teaches us (against a certain naive complacency about the effectiveness of political reform) that there is never *only* an opposition between the oppressor and the oppressed, and that we are all, so to speak, oppressed by the appeal of murderous *jouissance*.

The complacency I refer to has often justified itself by a serious misreading of Foucault. In fact, the psychoanalytic death drive can bring us back — in a penultimate turn of the screw — to those aspects of Foucault that provide a nonpsychoanalytic and yet persuasive account of how new relational modes can be blocked. They will always be blocked, more or less successfully, by the drive to power inherent in movement itself. Remember that for Foucault power is not simply something exercised by those "in power," those who exercise power; rather, power is "omnipresent," "immanent" in all "types of relationships," it is "produced from one moment to the next, at every point, or rather in every relation from one point to another." In a sense, power, as well as the inevitable resistances to power internal to its movement (resistances are the "irreducible opposite" of power, the "odd" terms that can deflect and reorient the always mobile trajectories of power) — all this, power and resistances to power, is the mobile energetics of life itself. In more concrete terms, Foucault thus implies that the frictions, the inherent antagonisms and oppositions of power, can never be eliminated from social groupings, and that they must therefore be allowed their place in any project of social reorganization. Power operates relationally; there is no relationality without power. This kinetic ontology of power is the Foucaldian version of intractability, an intractability defined more fully, and more satisfactorily for me, by the psychoanalytic appeal to unconscious drives. So to schematize in oversimplified fashion this dizzying back and forth movement between Foucault and psychoanalysis, let's say that psychoanalysis "needs" Foucault's utopic call for "new relational modes," while Foucault "needs" the psychic density within which, in terms psychoanalysis has made available to us, *jouissance* always risks corrupting pleasure.

For my final move — or at least my most recent one — I want to suggest that a psychoanalytically conceived unconscious can be not only the source of the risks I just mentioned, but also a collaborator in the extensions of pleasure and the rethinking of relationality. This would mean enlisting the unconscious in the service of "new relational modes." The body, once it is relieved of the burden of sex and especially of the prejudicial view of lack as constitutive of desire (and of our relation to the world), can, in its openness to the world, be the site of an inscription of the unconscious. Is a Foucaldian rethinking of the unconscious possible? It could be maintained that Lacan has prepared the way for this project, especially in connection with his attempt to dissociate psychoanalysis from a depth psychology. The unconscious, Lacan argues, is between perception and consciousness. To speculate on this proposal (which I would locate somewhere between Freud and Foucault) might be the start of a reconstruction of subjectivity (a task more general, and more radical, than the delineation of a so-called gay subjectivity) on which all effective political reconstructions ultimately depend.

10

Psychoanalysis and the
Aesthetic Subject

We are neither present in the world nor absent from it. The intelligibility
of this assertion will depend on our success in redefining the usual referent of "we," a success made problematic by the fact that the redefining
agency is a function of the very object—or, more properly, subject—to
be redefined. We may, however, be encouraged by the thought that both
art and psychoanalysis offer ample evidence of the human subject's aptitude for exceeding its own subjectivity. By that I mean an aptitude for
modes of subjecthood in excess of or to the side of the psychic particularities that constitute individualizing subjectivities. Only those modes of
subject-being can both recognize and initiate correspondences between
the subject and the world that are free of both an antagonistic dualism
between human consciousness and the world it inhabits and the anthropo-
morphic appropriation of that world. While it seems to me that the most
profound originality of psychoanalysis has been that it demands of itself a
conceptual account of such correspondences, I also feel that it has largely
evaded that demand by misinterpreting itself as a depth psychology. The
depsychologizing of psychoanalysis—implicit in Freud and reinitiated,
most notably, by Lacan—is imperative if psychoanalysis is to be more than
the therapeutically oriented classification of the human subject's failed
communications with the world.

If psychoanalysis invites us to think a register of being radically different
from a subjectivity grounded in psychology (it calls that other mode of being

Originally published in *Critical Inquiry* 32 (Winter 2006): 161–74.

the unconscious), it has also, for the most part, failed to see how that discovery reconfigures the subject in ways that open us to the solidarity of being both among human subjects and between the human and the nonhuman. It is this failure that accounts most profoundly for the limitations of psychoanalytically inspired approaches to art. Psychoanalysis describes our aptitude for transforming the world into a reflection of subjectivity. It has treated the work of art as a double model of subjectification: a privileged representation, in its contents, of subjectifying strategies as well as an exemplification, in its structural and stylistic enunciations, of the artist's subjectifying resources. Psychoanalysis has been the most authoritative modern reformulation of the Cartesian and the Hegelian opposition (qualified by Hegel as "necessary absolutely") between Nature and Spirit or between the *res extensa* and thought. The clinical subject of psychoanalysis successfully strips (I quote from Hegel) "the external world of its inflexible foreignness [in order to] enjoy in the shape of things only an external realization of himself," in order to find again "his own characteristics," which Hegel attributes to the "free subject." Thanks to the ruses of desire, the psychoanalytic subject lives what Hegel defined as "the really beautiful subject-matter of romantic art": the emergence of subjectivity from itself "into a relation with something else which, however, is its own, and in which it finds itself again and remains communing and in unity with itself."[1]

The projective, introjective, and identificatory techniques first studied by Freud are strategies designed to suppress the otherness in which my sameness is hidden from my consciousness. To paraphrase an author who made of this war between subject and object a gloriously lurid psychic drama (I refer to Melanie Klein), I must impose my good objects on the world in order to prevent the world from destroying me with my bad objects. For Klein, it is the bad object that gives birth to the object as object; the latter is originally constituted in the human subject. From the very beginning, the object as conceived by psychoanalysis is inherently a bad object, or a fundamentally foreign object that I must struggle to appropriate, or, finally, an object in whose depths the subject risks discovering his own psychic wastes. "At the very beginning, it seems," Freud writes in the 1915 essay "Instincts and Their Vicissitudes," "the external world, objects, and what is hated are identical." Not only at the very beginning: "As an expression of the reaction of unpleasure evoked by objects," he goes on, hate "always remains in an

1. G. W. F. Hegel, *Aesthetics: Lectures on Fine Art*, trans. T. M. Knox, 2 vols. (Oxford, 1975), 1:465, 31, 533.

intimate relation with the self-preservative instincts."[2] Given the (perceived) fundamental hostility of the world to the self, the very possibility of object relations depends on a profound mistrust of the object and, consequently, on different modes of appropriating objects.

"It is obvious," Lacan writes in the 1959–60 seminar on *The Ethics of Psychoanalysis,*

> that the libido, with its paradoxical, archaic, so-called pre-genital character-
> istics, with its eternal polymorphism, with its world of images that are linked
> to the different sets of drives associated with the different stages from the oral
> to the anal to the genital—all of which no doubt constitutes the originality
> of Freud's contribution—that whole microcosm has absolutely nothing to do
> with the macrocosm; only in fantasy does it engender world.

Lacan goes on to say: "This is a point whose importance does not seem to have been noticed, namely, that the Freudian project has caused the whole world to reenter us, has definitely put it back in its place, that is to say, in our body, and nowhere else."[3] Having removed the desiring subject from the world, and having relocated the world within the subject, Lacanian theory would seem to have nothing to say about the world as such or about the subject's presence in that world. But this is not exactly the case. Lacan relocates the subject—or at least parts of the subject—in the world, not as projections, but rather as that which has been detached, cut off from the subject, as a result of our entrance into language as signification; we are in the world as the psychic dropping that will be identified with the *objet petit a.* In Lacanian aesthetics, especially as outlined in the ethics seminar, beauty, or form, is what protects us from the *objet petit a,* that is, from the unacceptable, hidden, lost cause of our desires. "The function of beauty," Lacan announces in the essay "Kant avec Sade," is to be "an extreme barrier that forbids access to a fundamental horror."[4] It is this invisible, literally unspeakable presence that gives to beauty its blinding brilliance, the seductive and protective shining of form.

Thus, psychoanalytically conceived, the world interests us, seduces us, even dazzles us to the degree that it contains us—whether it be as a

2. Sigmund Freud, "Instincts and Their Vicissitudes" (1915), *The Standard Edition of the Complete Works of Sigmund Freud,* trans. and ed. James Strachey, 24 vols. (London, 1953–74), 14:136, 139.

3. Jacques Lacan, *The Ethics of Psychoanalysis, 1959–1960,* vol. 7 of *The Seminar of Jacques Lacan,* trans. Denis Porter, ed. Jacques-Alain Miller (New York, 1992), p. 92.

4. Lacan, "Kant avec Sade," *Écrits* (Paris, 1966), p. 776; my trans.

projection, an identification, or an original loss. We might note in passing that the relational mechanisms studied most thoroughly by psychoanalysis — identification, projection, introjection — could perhaps only have been theorized in a civilization that has privileged an appropriative relation of the self to the world, one that assumes a secure and fundamentally antagonistic distinction between subject and object. I want to ask the following question: can the work of art, contrary to psychoanalytic assumptions, deploy signs of the subject in the world that are not signs of interpretation or of an object-destroying *jouissance*, signs of what I will call correspondences of forms within a universal solidarity of being? What I have tried to show in my work on psychoanalysis and art and especially in work done in collaboration with Ulysse Dutoit — in studies of art as diverse as ancient Assyrian sculpture, Plato's *Symposium*, Caravaggio's painting, Proust's literary monument, Mark Rothko's and Ellsworth Kelly's art, and the films of Resnais and Godard — has been how art can in effect position us as aesthetic rather than psychoanalytically defined subjects within the world.

Our notion of correspondences has been elaborated almost entirely through studies of the visual arts. That is to say, certain perceptual recognitions — ours, and, it has seemed to us, those of the artists we have discussed — have provided the evidence for our argument for the human subject's nonprojective presence in the world. Our fundamental claim has been that the aesthetic subject, while it both produces and is produced by works of art, is a mode of relational being that exceeds the cultural province of art and embodies truths of being. Art diagrams universal relationality. How might that relationality be diagrammed in literary works? Pierre Michon's 1996 novel *La Grande Beune* begins by locating itself in a comfortably familiar Balzacian fashion: "Between les Martres and Saint-Amand-le-Petit lies the town of Castelnau, along the Beune [river]. I was posted to Castelnau in 1961."[5] As we learn in the first pages, the narrator was twenty years old in 1961, and it was at a small public school in Castelnau that that he had his first teaching position. He lodges at the town's only hotel, Chez Hélène; its proprietress, Hélène, is a widow whose son, called Jean-le-Pêcheur, is, as his name suggests, the region's most renowned fisherman. The place is unremarkable except in two respects: it is an area famous for its prehistoric caves (among them, Lascaux), and the woman who runs the local shop where the young teacher buys cigarettes and postcards is a beauty he describes as "a nice piece" (*un beau morceau*), an animal and a queen, a beauty who instantly makes "abominable

5. Pierre Michon, *The Origin of the World*, trans. Wyatt Alexander Mason (San Francisco, 2002), p. 3; hereafter abbreviated OW.

thoughts" run through his blood (OW, p. 12). He immediately desires this radiant specimen in terms remarkably free of the romantic idealization one might expect from an ordinary twenty-year-old: "I gutted her" (*Je l'étripais*) is his concise formulation of his erotic fantasies about her (OW, p. 25). His interest in Yvonne remains silent, perhaps especially because he discovers — or infers — that she is having an affair with another, older, man. Not only that: surprising her returning home, or so he assumes, from an assignation with her lover, he notices bruises on her neck and concludes that she enjoys and suffers from her lover's violence, that her entire, splendidly white body is inscribed with the dark welts inflicted by the lashes of her beloved's whip. This discovery, or sadomasochistic fable, far from repelling him, inflames the young man's passion even more. One day the narrator and Mado — a young woman with whom he is having a considerably more banal sexual relation — are taken on a tour of one of the less known prehistoric caves. Their guide is Jeanjean, whom the narrator recognizes as the man he had judged, by the way he and Yvonne had once exchanged a few words in her tobacco shop, to be her cruel, happy lover. The main attraction of the cave they visit, much to Mado's slightly exasperated amusement, is a room with completely blank walls. The short novel ends with an account of how the narrator, in his frustration at not being able amorously to torture Yvonne, mistreats her seven-year-old son, one of his students, and, on the final pages, with a description of the rare carp — not the usual scaly kind of fish, but rather the unusual leather-carp without scales, smooth as water, shimmering, and with completely bare skin — that Jean-le-Pêcheur proudly brings to his mother's inn one evening. The narrator compares the capture of this precious fish to the mythic capture of "queens that are carp from their bellies down" and who "are surprised in their baths by an ardent man," one who might threaten to lift them from their pool as the narrator imagines Jeanjean, at the same moment, raising and lowering an ecstatically submissive Yvonne from and back into the water of her bath, Yvonne accepting and announcing to her lover over and over again her imminent and indefinite death (OW, pp. 83–84).

It would be tempting to read this rather sordid tale as an anatomy of sexual fantasy. Since everything we know about Yvonne is filtered through the young man's point of view, she — and the sadomasochistic adventure he attributes to her — exists for us only in his imagination of them. In this reading of the novel, everything proceeds from a psychic inwardness; the fantasy is so powerful that it affects the narrator's entire world. The dead fox hanging on poles carried by a group of boys, the remnants of prehistoric weapons used to slaughter animals on display at the back of the classroom, the fish unlucky enough to be caught on Jean-le-Pêcheur's hook, the images of wounded animals on the walls of the region's caves: everything is contaminated by the narrator's brutal sexual obsession. Michon's work would be a rigorous demonstration of the way in which what Lacan calls a fundamental fantasy structures the subject's perception of the world. More exactly, it demonstrates the nonexistence of the world from the perspective of a psychoanalytically defined fantasy. The world is the narrator's sadomasochistic fantasy; it has become an immobilized structure that, however frightening it may be, is also somewhat protective or defensive. The young man's lurid projections and displacements shape the world. It is as if reality were, before this psychic intervention, as blank as the cave wall Jeanjean takes him to. In a sense, the narrator is as much an artist as the prehistoric men who covered the walls of other caves in the same region. But, unlike those ancient artists who resurrected in their art the recently slaughtered animals whose migration from the Atlantic coast every spring to the green fields of Auvergne provided food for their hunters and their families, the narrator writes, or paints, the world with his desire. Everything becomes an image of Yvonne's tortured body — the painted cattle caught leaping in pain, the naively designed martyred St. Gabriel on the postcard the young man buys in Yvonne's shop — just as those images are superimposed on Yvonne herself, whose joyously suffering body takes on layers of tortured identities. The world thus acquires the stable thematic unity, and monotony, of a work of art signed by the narrator's distinct desiring fantasy. If there is a beauty in this picture, it is a beauty that emanates from a certain kind of power, the human power not exactly to satisfy desire but to see a desire everywhere, to be thrilled by the universal representation of that which it lacks.

But this aesthetic grounded in control is at once illuminated and threatened by something more terrifying — and perhaps more thrilling — than the visions of lack that sustain it. Walking through the dark, narrow passages that lead to the room with unpainted walls, the narrator feels that he is being breathed on by some invisible beast crawling along the crumbling stones above them, some "great ambulatory abstraction, chaotic and ready to manifest in the low lamplight . . . the universal miasma with the head of a dead sheep and the teeth of a wolf, straight ahead and upon you in the shadows and watching you" (OW, p. 64). This hybrid monstrosity lacks the features of a desiring fantasy. It is at once an amalgam of animal being and an "idea," an abstraction, without any substance whatsoever. It is the horror of undifferentiated being that we can never see but that, always hovering, always moving with us, never stops looking at us. Deep within our brain there is the unimaginable imagination of an identityless miasma, of something before articulated being, which the human can only "think" as before the realization of any being whatsoever, as something from which the peace of inorganic stasis, of the death drive fully satisfied, might rescue us. Failing that salvation, there is the pleasure of negating the world that emerged from the originary miasma, the pleasure of repainting, of re-creating the world as the deceptively variegated sameness of our desire.

With each step of our reading so far, we have descended further into the psyche — moving from the young man's conscious desire for Yvonne, to a fantasy about her that he inscribes on the external world, and finally to a psychic terror of the individual psyche itself being engulfed in a slough of undifferentiated being. In this cave of interiority, the world as world is left behind just as surely as it no longer exists in the prehistoric caves where, as the narrator says, the curious visitors wander in a darkness deeper than the layers of earth where the dead are buried. And yet I want to propose, against the reading I've just offered, that interiority in *La Grande Beune*, far from refashioning the world into the structure of a psychic obsession, is actually produced by the world. The narrator's subjectivity is an effect of external reality. Let's note first of all that this narrator, of whom we presumably have the most intimate knowledge, is never named. He is perhaps waiting to be named, or, to put this in other terms, he may be an empty subject; he is not exactly, in psychoanalytic terms, a subject without an unconscious, but one whose unconscious can only come to him from the outside. The narrator receives from the world the material that will be fashioned into his particular fantasy of violence. There are the images evoked by the objects in the display case; there is the postcard representation of a tortured Saint Gabriel; there is the dead fox carried on poles by boys who, imitating an ancient ritual, display the fox outside village homes where, repeating an old gesture of gratitude to the hunters who rid them of this dangerous animal, the residents will give something — eggs, a little money — to the young transporters of the dead fox. And there are above all the scenes reminiscent of the hunt painted on the walls of the caves the narrator visits with Mado.

Let's look more closely at the scene with the dead fox. Late one afternoon the narrator finds only Yvonne's seven-year-old son taking care of the store. He rushes out of the village toward the fields and the edge of the woods where he had often seen Yvonne returning, so he had imagined, from a tryst with her lover. His frantic searching eyes evoke the phantom Yvonne he had imagined seeing a thousand times emerging from the forest, in her stockings, her hips naked in the cold, and reminding him of some "big game" (*un gros gibier*). It is just at that moment that the boys appear carrying the dead animal. In the place of the fox, the young man hallucinates Yvonne tied to the poles and, instead of the fox's red hair, wet black pubic hair foaming, he writes, "on the bitch's thick thighs" (*aux cuisses épaisses de cette garce*) (*OW*, pp. 36, 38). Just then, Yvonne really does come into view, and he sees the black marks on her cheek and neck that he attributes to her lover's expertly handled whip. The scene is the novel's most extreme example of a delirious projection that appropriates the world as a setting for a private fantasy, while at the same time a certain reality distinct from this fantasy persists, independently but analogously. The substitution of Yvonne for the dead fox is an erasure of the world as world. When Yvonne appears, it is as if the private fantasy had to accommodate her real presence (she is part of the world as world). But the fantasy is of course no longer entirely private. The word "gibier," thought before the boys appear, "meets," by chance, its objective correlative in the dead fox, to which "gibier" "responds" by inventing a specifically human version of violence: the violence of a sadomasochistic exchange between lovers. The real marks on Yvonne's cheek and neck correspond both to and with the fox through the fantasmatic activity that interprets the marks as inflicted by a whip and extends them down Yvonne's hidden body, blackening the dazzlingly white skin of her legs under her stockings with an extension of the "absolute writing" (*l'écriture absolue*) just seen on her face.[6]

In our work on the visual arts, Ulysse Dutoit and I have been studying film and painting as documents of a universe of inaccurate replications, of the perpetual and imperfect recurrences of forms, volumes, colors, and gestures. We have spoken of these recurrences as evidence of the subject's presence everywhere, not as an invasive projection or incorporation designed to eliminate otherness, but rather as an ontological truth about both the absolute distinctness and the innumerable similitudes that at once guarantee the objective reality of the world and the connectedness between the world and the subject. We are born into various families of singularity that connect us to all the forms that have, as it were, always anticipated our coming, our presence. I'm now attempting to describe a more specifically psychic version of these correspondences, one in which desiring fantasies both determine and are determined by their replications in the world. Successfully realized, this project might be the basis for a reconciliation of psychoanalysis both with the world as such and with the aesthetic subjectivity that eschews psychologically

6. Translated by Mason as "absolute authorship." See Pierre Michon, *La Grande Beune* (Lagrasse, 1996), p. 50.

motivated communication and replaces such communication with families of form.

In the passage I've just been discussing, except for the momentary substitution of Yvonne for the fox just before Yvonne appears, the world is not overwhelmed by fantasy. There is a distinction between what the narrator imagines and the procession of the schoolboys with the dead fox, and yet it is difficult to mark a precise boundary between internal and external worlds. In the regime of correspondences that we have been studying, differences are inviolable, although they are not governed by or grounded in a fundamental difference of being between inner and outer. The object never becomes the subject, and the subject, or the subject's ego is never, as Freud would have it, simply the sum of its history of object choices. There is neither a subject-object dualism nor a fusion of subject and object; there is rather a kind of looping movement between the two. The world finds itself in the subject and the subject finds itself in the world. What the world finds in the subject (in addition to physical correspondences) is a certain activity of consciousness, which partially reinvents the world as it repeats it.

The image of a whiplashed Yvonne is the narrator's contribution to the universal singularity of violence inflicted upon living bodies. The ancient hunt, fishing, the medieval martyr, the slaughtered foxes, war, torture, sadomasochistic eroticism: all these scenes, which inaccurately replicate one another, belong to an enormous transversal cut of being. Taken separately, it's true, each one raises specific historical, affective, and ethical questions; ontologically considered, however, they delineate the variegated character of one vast potentiality. Seen in this way, present and past variations on any mode of being permanently persist because they *are not fully*; to remember events is to recognize ourselves in their imaginary presence. From this perspective, the past is what has passed from the phenomenological to the virtuality of the imaginary. The past's disappearance as events is the condition of a new permanence, the permanent persistence of possibility. The narrator's cruel fable about Yvonne is his manner of corresponding with the persistent cut of violent being that surrounds him; he is the site where different images of violence intersect. This is the power of the aesthetic subject, fashioning from the "miasma" of a psyche that, like all human psyches, can be at once everything and nothing, its individuating responsiveness to the world.

Does this fable give expression to unconscious impulses? In the reading I'm now proposing, there is no specified unconscious prior to the material from the external world in which it at once recognizes and constitutes itself. The unconscious never is; it is perhaps an essentially unthinkable, intrinsically unrealizable reserve of human being—a dimension of virtuality rather than of psychic depth—from which we connect to the world, not as subject to object, but as a continuation of a specific syntax of being. A continuation that is also an accretion: the psychic designates its place in the vast family of stored past and present being by contributing new inscriptions—in *La Grande Beune,* the inscription of the young protagonist's fable of erotic violence. It is as if the world stimulated the activity of desiring fantasy, not by lacking objects of desire, but by their very proliferation. The narrator is excited by the abundance of images of violence, and he implicitly recognizes their imaginary status by responding to their call, not with an act, but with other images, the images of fantasy. From this perspective, fantasy is not the symptom of an adaptive failure. On the contrary, it is the sign of an extremely attentive, highly individuated response to external reality. It is not the result of pressure from preexistent, dominant unconscious impulses; the only sense in which it is revealing about psychic depths is that an intrinsically undifferentiated unconscious provides the material for a psychic composition. Fantasy is thus on the threshold between an invisible (and necessarily hypothetical) inner world and the world present to our senses. It is not a symptom to be cured; rather, it is the principal ontic evidence for an ontological regime of correspondences in which the discreteness of all things (including human subjects) is superseded, not by universal fusions, but by the continuation of all things elsewhere. In this regime, the distinction between inner and outer is wholly inadequate to describe universal reoccurrence. The human subject does of course exist and act discretely, separately; but its being exceeds its bounded subjectivity. There is a perspective on fantasy that would imprison it within subjectivity. This perspective is consistent with the limited individuality traced by a psychologically defined subject. I'm suggesting something different: fantasy as a function more of contingent positioning in the world than of psychic depth.

Furthermore, if fantasy is a major site of our connectedness to the world, it is not an act that touches or changes the world. It represents the terms in which the world inheres in the fantasizing subject, terms that can change as our position in the world changes. An undifferentiated unconscious lends itself to diverse representations of the interface between the moving subject and a world whose relational map is itself continuously modified by the moves of all the units—including the human units—that constitute it. All these figures do not have the finality of acts that materially modify the world—such as the actual slaying of a reindeer, the torture of a monk, the whipping inflicted on Yvonne's real body. On the contrary, they are the possibility of the act that may of course precede the act, but that can also follow the act, when the latter moves back from the real, so to speak, in order to become always present, permanently imaginary. Psychic fantasy is a type of unrealized or derealized human and world being, the figure, not for a taking place, but rather for all taking place — for all relationality — in its pure inherence. Painting can illuminate this inherence, and it is significant that, as I have argued elsewhere, for thinkers and artists as different as Caravaggio, Proust, Heidegger, and Lacan the sign of beauty is a certain brilliance or shining — as if the disappearance of the material world as object and event were best figured by an unnatural lighting (one that in Caravaggio is not projected on objects but seems to come from within objects), a lighting that signifies a withdrawal from the visible world into the superior visibility of what has been derealized. Art leads us back from objects, or the actual hunt, to the vast repertory of virtual being that constitutes what Michon's narrator calls the "marvels" that art seeks beyond its own visibility.

Psychoanalysis, with its notion of a subject divided between conscious thoughts and affects and an atemporal unconscious is, or should be, hospitable to the notion I have been tracing of an aesthetic subject. In mental life, Freud writes in chapter one of *Civilization and Its Discontents*, "everything past is preserved."[7] We might reformulate this in the following way: memory is an illusion of consciousness, as there is no past to remember; instead, there are innumerable inscriptions of the world that define us by mapping particular positionings in the world and that simply persist, immanently. These inscriptions are the world, and they are the subject. While consciousness continuously forms affectively motivated projects that essentially oppose us to the world, projects whose satisfaction requires mastery of otherness, we never cease corresponding unconsciously with that otherness. Mind moves not only to master the world but also to acknowledge its own reappearances in the world — that is, the reappearances of itself as self-world. The world configurations that constitute and individuate a subject wait to be received by the subject; to put this differently, the subject is in the world before being born into it. The unconscious is not the region of the mind most hidden from the world; it resists being known because it so vastly exceeds what might know it, because it is not of the same order as what might know it. For the most part, however, psychoanalysis has added depth to classical psychology rather than elaborating the truly radical notion of a nonsubjective interiority. It is, I have been arguing, only the latter notion that might speak persuasively of

7. Freud, *Civilization and Its Discontents* (1930), *The Standard Edition of the Complete Works of Sigmund Freud*, 21:71.

a subject inherently reconciled with the world. The antagonism between the subject and the world might then be seen as contingent (if, at times, no less catastrophic) violations of a fundamental correspondence between the world and subjects, a view significantly different from the more prevalent one that posits antagonism as the natural consequence of an irreducible opposition between subject and object. These are not "merely" theoretical considerations; human subjects are educated into how they see themselves as being-in-the-world. Negotiating difference has been the dominant relational mode in our culture. Such negotiations have primarily consisted in attempts to overcome or destroy difference or, at best, to tolerate it. Our most liberal injunction has been: learn to communicate (or pretend to communicate) with a world where differences practically guarantee failed communications. We have yet to elaborate the concrete steps (in education, in politics, in the practice of sociability, in the organization of living spaces) that might help to erase the hegemony of this relational regime and institute a relationality grounded in correspondences, in our at-homeness in the world's being.

Michon's *La Grande Beune* is a document of correspondences, a particularly courageous one in that what I have called the cut of being it traces is perhaps the one most likely to be co-opted by the prejudice of psychic lack, a prejudice that conveniently justifies invasive appropriations of the world's seductive and threatening otherness. The inevitable resistances within the family of being — resistances inherent in the inaccurately replicative nature of correspondences — facilitate a certain backtracking into an oppositional, subject-object relationality. Correspondences do not eliminate frictions, and frictions can exacerbate the appetite for fusions perhaps endemic to sexual desire. Psychoanalysis — especially Freud, Laplanche, and Lacan — has profoundly conceptualized the inseparability of *jouissance* from aggression. Psychoanalytically defined sexuality is not a relation; it is the fantasized ecstasy of a oneness gained by the simultaneous destruction of the self and the world. This ecstatic destruction of the subject is the most extreme consequence of a psychological subjectivity, a subjectivity for which the world as lack is an object of suspicion and of desire. To enter the region of being characterized by the violence of countless versions of subject-object collision is perhaps also to be tempted by the psychological derivative of inhabiting that region, which is sadomasochistic desire. This temptation, inscribed in the language of *La Grande Beune*, accounts for the novel's rich relational indeterminacy. It would be difficult to eliminate psychological expressiveness from a critical reading of Michon's novel. The intense affectivity accompanying the young

man's fantasies compels us to think of them as expressing and partially satisfying an otherwise suffocating sadism, at the same time that his anonymity, the
absence of any perspective that might confirm or invalidate his erotic fable
about Yvonne, and above all the placing of the narrative within a region of
France whose past is present as a pervasive immanent violence — all this
encourages a view of fantasy as a subject's desubjectifying insertion within a
particular region of being.

And, yet, contrary to Michon's presentation of a world that corresponds to
but is independent of the protagonist's fantasies of violence, the novel does
seem to cultivate a dream of the world's disappearance. It is even as if we were
being given a key to *La Grande Beune* as a demonstration of fantasy's power
to remake the world in its own image when the narrator says, just before the
end of his story, that the rain that never seems to stop allows us to substitute
our dreams for the world, to live "the satiety of our dreams behind this grey
curtain where everything is permitted" (OW, p. 81). Behind the curtain of
rain the founding desire of all particular desires might be realized: to make of
the entire world the mirror of our dreams, the place where nothing is different, where nothing resists, where an omnipotent subject can write anything.
Michon often seems to be writing about writing, to be using his own text
in order to satisfy a dream of total reinscription by making of his novel an
emblematic deployment of that dream. (Even fishing is at one point called
writing on the water.) Thus the fantasized whip marks on Yvonne's body can
be described as "an absolute writing": "absolute" because the nonresistant
exceptional whiteness of her flesh is marked only by the material signs of another subject's power and desire. Indeed, receptive whiteness haunts the entire text. There are the blind "albino fish" Yvonne's lover has found floating
in an underground pool, killed by the electricity brought into the caves; the
white leathery skin of Jean-le-Pêcheur's rare "mirror carp"; and perhaps most
notably the "inexhaustible whiteness" of the room to which Jeanjean brings
Mado and the narrator, a room with, as he says, in a strangely triumphant
manner, "absolutely nothing" on its walls (OW, p. 66). This, the narrator
conjectures, was Lascaux before the paintings, but with the hunter-painters
already there, preparing their materials, "conceiving" the scenes with which
they would cover the walls. The whiteness of the walls reminds us of a certain
precariousness in the transfer from the phenomenological to the ontological. That which has taken place — settled being — may not recede into the
permanently potential. It may, as it were, stop at a "point" where potentiality
itself is merely potential. Jeanjean's prized room puts Lascaux into question.

Its whiteness could be taken as an emblem of the susceptibility of all potential being to nothingness — as if potentiality could itself fail to "take place" (in fantasy, and in art), could tilt the universe backward into the void, thus failing to reinscribe the history of the universe in a vast present in which nothing is lost, a present identical to the persistent intransitivity of being. Whiteness — or an indefinitely prolonged possibility of possibility — is the gravest threat to ontological intransitivity.

In his seminar on identification, Lacan asks: What is the difference between my dog and the human subject? He answers that his dog never mistakes him for someone else, while misidentification of the other is constitutive of the human. In a sense, then, Lacan's dog is a better observer of the world as world than his master. In the light of what I have been arguing here, we might say that misidentification is inherent in our inability, or refusal, to acknowledge the world's independence. That refusal may itself be the consequence of the human infant's prolonged helplessness — unique among animals — and dependence on others. If, as Freud says, "at the very beginning . . . the external world, objects, and what is hated are identical," and if, as he also claims, "as an expression of the reaction of unpleasure evoked by objects, [hate] always remains in an intimate relation with the self-preservative instincts," this is because the external world is a potential threat, one against which, for an exceptionally long period at the beginning of our lives, we have neither the physical nor the psychic resources to defend ourselves. A human subjectivity is thus developed on the ground of a profound insecurity, one that might be lifted only if the world didn't exist — or, put differently, only if we could substitute ourselves for the world. Psychoanalysis has, on the whole, been so committed to studying and "treating" the mechanisms of this attempted substitution that it has failed to elaborate a concept of the world as much more than a vaguely specified (or, at best, normative) reality to which we must learn to "adapt." To do so would mean recognizing that the subject's need to project himself on the world is not entirely necessary. While a certain degree of anxiety about an unmastered world is inevitable, it is also true, as I have been demonstrating through Michon's novel, that we correspond to the world in ways that don't necessitate or imply the world's suppression. The world will always resist embodying our anxieties, or our desires, but we are also in it independently of our need to master it. External reality may at first present itself as an affective menace, but psychoanalysis — like art, although in a more discursive mode — might train us to see our prior presence in the world, to see, as bizarre as this may sound, that, ontologically, the world cares for us. Finally, however, as Michon's exceptional novel suggests, it is part of the complexity of a human destiny that we may fail to find that care sufficiently satisfying, and so we will undoubtedly never stop insisting — if only intermittently — that the *jouissance* of an illusion of suppressing otherness can surpass the pleasure of finding ourselves harbored within it.

11

The Will to Know

In the three published volumes of *The History of Sexuality* (which could more accurately be called *The History of Subjectivity*), as well as in the lectures at the Collège de France that were both the raw material and, for Foucault's readers, the indispensable amplification of that history, Foucault studied the changing positions of knowledge of the self and what he called "care of the self" in the history of the Western subject's conceived relation to truth. From the shifting emphases given in Greek and Roman antiquity to, on the one hand, the philosophical theme of how to gain access to knowledge and, on the other, the more specifically ethical *souci de soi* (how the subject must be transformed, "cared for," by a teacher and/or by the subject himself) in order to reach truth, to the relation in Christian thought between self-renunciation and self-confession, and to the secularizing of the methods and goals of self-confession in modern medicine, pedagogy, and psychiatry and psychoanalysis, Foucault's ambition was to trace, in the Western configurations of subjectivity, the opposition as well as the interpenetrations between philosophy of knowledge and the care of the self that he also called spirituality. While aware of the complexities, and perhaps above all of the non-, even antilinear nature of this history, Foucault nonetheless identified the beginning of the modern age in this history with what he called "the Cartesian moment," the moment when knowledge and knowledge alone — to the detriment of spirituality — became the subject's path to truth. Even more: the Cartesian type of knowledge, Foucault claims, substitutes a knowledge of objects — and, ultimately, the acquisition, through science, of power over the world — for the notion of an access to truth.

We may of course, for all Foucault's nuances and qualifications, be reluctant to accept Foucault's own grand oppositions as corresponding to "historical truth." However, given both the slipperiness and the tendentious use of that concept, Foucault's fundamental distinction seems to me to have, at the very least, a heuristic value. It lends itself to being reformulated as a distinction between two modes of positioning ourselves in the world: either as subjects for whom knowledge is the principal aim in a struggle to appropriate the irreducible and always potentially menacing otherness of the world, or as subjects who connect, who correspond to, and with, the world's essentially hospitable being.

I say reformulated because in the Foucaldian scheme, the *souci de soi* does not necessarily imply a shift in epistemological assumptions. Both self-knowledge and care of the self are exercises of the self on the self; they are not, inherently, different views of the relation between the self and the world. The function of the Epicurean emphasis on the study of objects and of other men, for example, is, as Foucault puts it, "to modify the subject's being." We might say that both self-knowledge and care of the self are different techniques grounded in a shared assumption of the fundamental difference between the subject and the world. Care of the self is another strategy within that relational assumption rather than a modification of what is taken for granted about relationality itself. Foucault was far from naively believing in the possibility of adopting the ancient version of the *souci de soi* for ourselves. Nonetheless, he insisted, in his 1981–82 course at the Collège de France on "The Hermeneutics of the Subject," on what he called the "urgent, fundamental, politically indispensable task" of constituting an "ethic of the self" today since, as he believed, "there is no other point, first and last, of resistance to political power than the relation of the self to the self." I don't, however, see any possibility of this taking place without a concomitant change in the modes we adopt of positioning ourselves in the world. To speak of the Cartesian absolutizing of knowledge as a liquidation of spirituality or a renunciation of the goal of accessing truth seems to me an inadequate specifying of that presumed moment. The exclusiveness of knowledge is, after all, both grounded in and authorized by a rigorous distinction between mind and nonmind, between the *cogito* and the *res extensa*. Descartes' occasional military metaphors are justified by the ontological war inherent in that distinction: knowledge, and especially scientific knowledge, is necessary in order to conquer alien territory. The political viability of the care of the self depends, if it is to be more than a superficial self-aestheticizing, on the discovery, or the rediscovery, of the continuity of being between the subject and the world, a continuity that alone explains why the aim of knowledge of others and objects for the sake of appropriation of others and objects is an ontological illusion. From this perspective, a new "ethic of the self" could be conceived of as a discipline of self-attunement, of the self attuning itself to something like its own inexistent autonomy, or at the very least to the permeability of the boundaries between itself and what Ulysse Dutoit and I have called its innumerable inaccurate replications in the world.

I want to focus on what could be thought of as a radical, perhaps inherently implosive stage of the historical *episteme* baptized by Foucault as the Cartesian moment. I'm thinking of a field of knowability most fully, if ambiguously, exemplified by psychoanalysis and, in literature, by Proust. Psychoanalysis has reformulated the epistemological imperative of self-knowledge as a theory and practice of psychic truth. For classical psychoanalytic theory, analysis is an investigation of a personal past. From this perspective, analysis could be thought of — indeed has been thought of — as the epistemological conquest inherent in a depth psychology: the unconscious would add to our knowledge of the mind psychic contents never imagined by pre-Freudian psychology. Viewed in Foucaldian terms, Freudian talk therapy is a massive psychic confession on the part of the analysand. It reinstates the Cartesian subject-object dualism in a relation between two human subjects. If the analysand ultimately becomes "the one who knows" (about him or herself), and if analysts never entirely lose their ignorance of the psyche they help to bring to self-knowledge, the analyst's prestige as "the one who knows" is nonetheless what initiates and sustains (and, by no means incidentally, justifies the cost of) what is perhaps not quite accurately referred to as the psychoanalytic dialogue. An emphasis in post-Freudian therapy on the phenomenon of countertransference has, it's true, brought us a long way from Freud's dictum, in the 1912 essay "Advice to Doctors on Psychoanalytic Treatment," that "for the patient the doctor should remain opaque, and, like a mirror surface, should show nothing but what is shown to him." Yet even this awareness of projective identifications from analyst to analysand (and not merely in the opposite, strictly Freudian direction) has not, it could be argued, changed the essential inequality of the analytic exchange. In the analytic exchange, one interlocutor is vastly more voluble, exposed, and uninformed (about both himself and his dialogic partner) than the other. Even if we allow for what have become fashionable disclaimers of the analyst's position as "the one who knows," the analytic contact is motivated, and in effect determined, by the analysand's ignorance and his reliance on a certain type of knowledge presumed to be possessed by the analyst, a knowledge intended to make the patient more knowledgeable (intellectually, affectively) about himself.

Foucault saw the psychoanalytic version of the Western philosophy of self-knowledge as a moment — an essentially sinister moment — in the exercise of power in Western history, as having served a massive power strategy of normativizing subjectivity. In the first volume of *The History of Sexuality*, Foucault insists on the importance of desire as constitutive of a modern subjectivity, but he finds the desire produced by specifically modern exercises of power (psychoanalysis would be exemplary here) as the subject's desire *to know his desire*. The peculiarity of this extended moment in the history of power (our moment) has, in Foucault's argument, less to do with the particular contents of the modern subject's desires than with the subject's acquiescing in the view (promoted by power) that his desires (and especially his sexual desires) are the key to his being. The defining desires themselves are secondary to this epistemological hunger, almost irrelevant to the classifications and consequent management made possible by our knowledge of them. Authoritarian systems of government naturally profit from the confessional habits produced by the diffuse exercises of power analyzed by Foucault. Confession makes subjects visible, and their visibility (ideally, the visibility of desires which, they have been made to believe, constitute their essence) is a precondition of their political subjection.

I might, at several points of what I have been saying, been speaking not only of psychoanalysis but also of Proust, who has given us the most incisive and thorough representation of what we might call the psychoanalytic subject. For example, and most notably, the sequestering and relentless questioning of Albertine by Marcel in *La Prisonnière* is an attempt, on Marcel's part, to lead Albertine to a confession of her desires that will, he believes, make her innermost being visible. The imprisoning of Albertine is a power strategy designed to penetrate the secrets of her subjectivity. Proustian love exemplifies the Cartesian absolutizing of knowledge — with, however, an important difference. Once intersubjectivity is conceived of not as an exchange of being (more on this later) but in terms of a subject-object dualism, the object of knowledge can will its own opacity, can hide behind its fundamentally differential otherness. Proustian love is the pursuit of that difference and the desire to possess and annihilate it. First of all, we should note that the amorous pursuit in Proust is much more an epistemological than an erotic adventure. At the very moment the narrator speaks of his intense suffering when he learns, at the end of *Sodome et Gomorrhe*, that Albertine is a friend of Mlle. Vinteuil (and therefore perhaps also a Gommorhean), he notes that the discovery of "the most terrible reality" also brings with it "the joy of a beautiful discovery," one that leads, however, to another epistemological impasse: how to penetrate the inconceivable "truth" of Albertine's desires? Behind Albertine's physical presence, Marcel no longer sees "the blue mountains" of the sea at Balbec, but rather the bedroom at Montjouvain where she has perhaps fallen many times into Mlle. Vinteuil's arms with a laugh containing her mysterious pleasure, *"le son inconnu de sa jouissance."*

And yet, for all this emphasis on the mystery of Albertine's desire, it's not at all clear that she is the object of Marcel's need to know. The women he has loved the most, the narrator confides, "have never coincided with my love for them." If they were able to awaken a very real love, indeed to bring that love to its most extreme intensity, they were nonetheless not the "image" contained within that love.

> When I saw them [the mistresses whom I have loved most passionately], when I heard their voices, I could find nothing in them which resembled my love and could account for it. And yet my sole joy lay in seeing them, my sole anxiety in waiting for them to come. It was as though a virtue that had no connexion with them had been artificially attached to them by nature, and that this virtue, this quasi-electric power, had the effect on me of exciting my love, that is to say of controlling all my actions and causing all my sufferings. But from this, the beauty, or the intelligence, or the kindness of these women was entirely distinct. As by an electric current that gives us a shock, I have been shaken by my loves, I have lived them, I have felt them: never have I succeeded in seeing or thinking them.

In this extraordinary passage, we can see traces of a momentous redirection in the trajectory of the Foucaldian history of self-knowledge, knowledge of the object, and spirituality (or "care of the self"). It is as if, brought to its paroxysm, knowledge of the object turns in on itself and becomes self-knowledge — not, however, of a self identical to itself, but of a self alien to the subject in whom it is hidden. The subject-object dualism remains; but now it is re-created within the subject. This, I think, is the only way we can understand the narrator's strange and significant remark, in the passage I have been discussing, that as Albertine moved away from him to get off the train at Parville, the visible "spatial separation" between them was only an "appearance," and that, "for someone who might have tried, according to what was truly real, to re-design things, it would have been necessary to place Albertine now, not at some distance from me, but within me." Marcel's anguished determination not to let Albertine leave him, even for the briefest time, is exactly identical to her irrelevance to that determination. The uncrossable distance separating them is now an internal distance. Since Marcel seems to understand this clearly enough, why, we might ask, is he so insistent on keeping her close to him — even more strangely, on relentlessly quizzing her about her desires? It is as if the other could become, or could embody, an alien self, a self that at once "belongs" to the subject and is perhaps inconceivably external to him. We might apply to this relation Jacques-Alain Miller's term "extimacy": the subject's most intimate "I" is also outside the subject. The human subject is divided: the unconscious, and its "distance" from a knowing consciousness, makes obsolete any notion of a unified self. The "inconceivable truth" of Albertine's desire is a projection of the inconceivability of Marcel's desire. "All jealousy," the narrator profoundly notes elsewhere, "is self-jealousy," which we might take to be the Proustian formulation of Freud's argument in his 1914 essay on narcissism that the loving subject projects onto the loved one his own idealized and now lost infantile ego.

Proustian love anticipates a well-known Lacanian dictum: the object of my desire is not the cause of my desire. This could in turn be thought of as an extrapolation of Freud's argument in *Three Essays on the Theory of Sexuality* concerning the relation between sexual desire and its objects. Unlike others before him who had merely noted that desire can swerve from the object to which, presumably, it is "naturally" attached, Freud insisted on the intrinsically free-floating nature of desire: it is available to any object and must be trained to focus on the "proper" object. The sexual is defined not in terms of predetermined object relations, but rather as the effect nearly any object can have on the structure of the ego. Sexuality, according to passages in the *Three Essays* which, following Jean Laplanche's analysis in *Life and Death in Psychoanalysis*, I have commented on in *The Freudian Body*, would consist in a shattering of ego boundaries produced by any number of unaccountable, unclassifiable objects. There are degrees of self-shattering, ranging from such examples of sexual stimulation (given by Freud in the *Three Essays*) as intellectual strain, verbal disputes, and railway travel, to the ultimate devastation of the ego and of the subject in death. Thus Laplanche, reversing Freud's domestication of his own early definition of the sexual by opposing it to the death drive in *Beyond the Pleasure Principle*, identifies the death drive with sexuality. What all the different stimuli mentioned by Freud have in common is their ability to set affect free from psychic organization; unbound affect produces the excitement of *jouissance*. *Jouissance* has little to do with what we ordinarily think of as sexual pleasure. Indeed, it may more properly be thought of, as Lacan suggests, as the enemy of pleasure. Following this line of thought, we can say that, far from promoting the pansexualism it was for a long time accused of, psychoanalysis proposes a definition of sexuality that has very little to do with what we think of as sex (which may be little more than a contingent manifestation of it). Interestingly, this radical current in psychoanalytic thought (which seems to me central to the originality of psychoanalysis) is echoed by Proust. Proustian passion is curiously — and, from a psychoanalytic perspective, appropriately — detached from sexual desire. Remember that Odette is not Swann's sexual type; what changes his mildly sensual interest in her into a frenzy of jealous passion is simply his not being able to find her one evening. Her unlocatability (which, as I have been suggesting, may be Swann's own unlocatability) shatters him into love for an object whose inaccessibility will be her principal seductiveness. Similarly, immediately after the passage from *Sodome et Gommorhe* I quoted a few moments ago, the role of sex in love is literally reduced to a parenthetical remark. Physical pleasure, the narrator notes, accompanies love but is insufficient to create it, and this is because our desire is in reality directed toward those "invisible forces" by which it is accompanied, forces that don't belong to the loved one but which, as it were, have momentarily lodged themselves within her.

Within the Western literary tradition, Proust is perhaps the principal avatar of — to return to Foucault's historical scheme — a reappearance of a project of self-knowledge within the subject-object dualism of the Cartesian opposition between mind and non-mind. But now the dualism is between subject-mind and object-mind. The psychoanalytic turn given to this impossible project of appropriating another consciousness is to make of the other's consciousness a screen for the otherness hidden within the subject's own consciousness. Love for the other is from this perspective a displaced self-love, or a blind narcissism.

I want, however, to suggest that at this extreme point in its history, the pursuit of self-knowledge gives rise to what may be a new *episteme* and, correlatively, to the discovery of a new relation to the world. The object returns, so to speak, to the world, but not as an unknowable object. Rather, the world is seen as a field of extensibility for the self, the site of innumerable correspondences of being. In Proust, this radical shift takes place in his reflections on art, more specifically on the type of individuality expressed in art. Art elaborates an individuality more general than individuals: in French, the *individuel* (a type of individuated being more general than a personal psychology or individuality) rather than the *individu* (a particular person). The world expressed in art, as Deleuze has put it in his book on Proust, "does not exist outside of the subject which expresses it, but is expressed as the essence, not of the subject itself, but of Being, or of the region of Being which is revealed to the subject."

The Proustian notion of art is perhaps, most profoundly, a prioritizing of shared being over appropriated knowledge. Art would be a model for the relation of the self to the self and to the world that would be neither one of self-knowledge nor one of an attempted knowledge of the world. It would thus return us to something like the "spirituality" that Foucault opposes to knowledge in his history of Western subjectivity. What I have in mind is not, however, identical to what Foucault calls care of the self, which, as he emphasizes, was a discipline of the self exercised on the self rather than a transformation of the subject's fundamental relation to the world. And it seems to me that it is a transformation of this sort—of our relation to the world—that Foucault had in mind when he summoned us to invent "new relational modes." If there is no solution easily recognizable as "political" to the violence in which, directly or indirectly, we are all implicated, it is, Foucault believed, because no recognizably political solution can be durable without something approaching a mutation in our most intimate relational system, a mutation involving a shift in the conditions and the very field of knowability. Foucault's call for "new relational modes" struck some of his readers as politically evasive; it seems to me, on the contrary, that his summoning us to rethink relationality is at once an instance of political realism and a moral imperative.

It is likely that Foucault would have been astonished, and perhaps even displeased, to learn that in our recent book, *Intimacies*, Adam Phillips and I enlist psychoanalysis in our attempt to trace the contours of an as yet unfamiliar antiepistemological *episteme*. Ideally conducted, analysis can lead to the dissolution of the self—that is, to the loss of the very grounds of self-knowledge. Psychoanalysis could undo the subjectivity necessary to a psychological philosophy of knowledge. Seen in this way, psychoanalytic treatment would not be primarily a subject-object relation in which the analyst helps the analysand to excavate and to know the secrets or drives that have brought him or her to treatment. Rather, it would be an exercise in the depersonalizing of both analyst and analysand, in the creation of a new, third subjectivity to which no individual name can be attached, a subjectivity in which the two find themselves corresponding—co-responding—in the transindividual being which, they have discovered, "belongs" to neither of them, but which they share. Our claim, then, is that even the analytic dialogue can be conducted as an "experience of exchange . . . , of desire indifferent to personal identity," no longer ruled by "a collusion of ego-identities." We call such an exchange an experience of impersonal intimacy. If, however, such intimacies are focused on the future since they are not dependent on personal pasts, our emphasis on the future would be glibly utopic if it were not grounded in a reimagining of the analytic past. If, as Phillips writes, "impersonal intimacy asks of us what is literally the most inconceivable thing: to believe in the future without needing to personalize it," that belief becomes at least somewhat conceivable if we can believe, to begin with, in an impersonal past. Christopher Bollas's fascinating discussion of "the transformational object" helps us to spell out developmental alternatives, within a person's past, to the personal. A psychoanalyst's interest in the past can, it turns out, be entirely compatible with an impersonal relationality. The mother of early infancy may be one, to quote from Phillips's reading of Bollas, "whose selfhood we need not recognize. Indeed, it is our very powerlessness to do so at that stage that makes [the] cumulative transformations [evoked by Bollas] possible." In *The Shadow of the Object*, Bollas describes a "being-with, as a form of dialogue," that enables "the baby's adequate processing of his existence prior to his ability to process it through thought." Phillips, elaborating on this wordless "dialogue," speaks of mother and infant being "attuned . . . to what each is becoming in the presence of the other." (Bollas speaks of the baby being transformed by the mother's "aesthetic of handling.") Love is perhaps always — as both Plato and Freud suggest — a phenomenon of memory, but what is remembered in the expansive narcissism of an impersonal intimacy is not some truth we know about the self, but rather, as Phillips says in *Intimacies*, "a process of becoming," or, in other terms, evolving affinities of being. The subject's need to know the other, rather than being valued as our highest relational aspiration, should be seen, as Phillips writes of the relation between mother and child, as "a defence against what is unknowingly evolving, as potential, between them." This potentiality is originally initiated by the mother's "aesthetic of handling" and repeated but also modified and recategorized in the splintered, nonassignable subjectivity between analyst and analysand.

The key words for the new relational field toward which I have been moving in the second half of this discussion (a field no longer dominated by a Cartesian dualism between a knowing subject and a vast domain of objects principally conceived of in terms of their knowability or nonknowability) are:

potentiality, the transindividual, impersonal correspondences, and a general typology of being beyond, or perhaps before, psychological individuality. I will conclude with a brief discussion of a major figure in this reimagining of the relational. Jean-Luc Godard's 1982 masterpiece, *Passion*, is a finished film about, apparently, an unfinished film. I say "apparently" because the word "about" immediately commits us to the kind of narrative statement that Godard's film (principally through Jerzy, the director of the internal film) relentlessly mocks. As far as we can tell, Jerzy's film (also called *Passion*) is "about" nothing but a series of at times mobile, at times immobile *tableaux vivants* of famous paintings by Rembrandt, Goya, Ingres, Delacroix, and El Greco; the reconstruction of these paintings is accompanied, as are many other scenes in Godard's film, by excerpts from music by Ravel, Mozart, Fauré, Beethoven, and Dvořák. The film that contains this enigmatic, fragmented visual and aural feast has, it's true, considerably more narrative substance. Jerzy is torn between Hana (the owner of the hotel where the crew is staying) and Isabelle (who is trying to organize a protest with her co-workers against the working conditions at the factory owned by Hana's husband, Michel). Godard has spoken in an interview of an analogy between these workers' discontent and what seems to be a fitful rebellion on the part of the extras in Jerzy's film. Within the film, the connection between work and love is made by several characters. "Work has the same gestures as love," Isabelle says, a likeness affirmed by Godard himself in his short film *Scenario for Passion*, where he speaks of having noticed that resemblance in a Tintoretto painting (one not, I should add, present in the film *Passion*).

There is, then, some potentially heavy thematic and narrative material in *Passion*. What I find most striking about the film is, however, the multiple ways in which it seems to be pulling away, or withdrawing from, not only a development of such material, but also from any sort of finished statement whatsoever. It is as if Godard were trying to decompose his film, to withdraw it into the not-yet-having-taken-place condition of Jerzy's film. Much of *Passion* consists of the filming of scenes from Jerzy's *Passion*, not, however, in the form of fully reconstituted paintings, but rather in the partially realized form of paintings that appear to have been unmade in order to be cinematically put together again tentatively, and at times somewhat differently, from the originals. Jerzy even seems peculiarly detached from his film: he never discusses it except to complain about the lighting which, to judge from a talk he has with his friend and assistant Laszlo, he conceives of mainly as between rather than directly on parts of the paintings, much as Jerzy himself, as he says, is affectively suspended between Hana and Isabelle. Furthermore — and this is a Godardian trademark — the sense of statements is undercut by the frequent desynchronizing of the aural and the visual (we see characters moving their lips as we hear other characters' voices), as well as by the many, at times unattributable, voice-off remarks and by the superimposing of different, unconnected sounds and voices (Léo Ferré reciting Villon's "Ballade des pendus" as Jerzy, Patrick and Sophie talk about paying the actors and what scenes they are now going to film, or the sound of a car horn blaring into a passage of music).

Godard has other tricks for impeding, or blocking, the sense of otherwise conventionally synchronized voices and presences. Isabelle stutters, Michel's sentences are cut up by his persistent cough, the producer speaks only Italian, Jerzy and Hana have foreign accents and at times slip into their native Polish and German. The characters have been given the first names of the actors who play them; for the most part, the actors' last names have disappeared or, in the case of Michel Piccoli, been changed. Isabelle's grandfather stubbornly refuses to "say his sentence," apparently a pre-bedtime ritual: "*Dis ta phrase,*" she implores, a sentence repeated several times a few minutes later by François as he appears to be sexually penetrating Magali from behind in a doorway. Toward the end of the film we hear Michel's voice plaintively complaining: "I'm looking for a definitive sentence, but I can't find one," a failure Jerzy's film seems complacently to prolong and toward which Godard's film perversely, and more or less successfully, strives. At the end, Lazlo goes to Hollywood to work on the film for Metro, where it has been accepted, but Jerzy drops the whole project and starts driving home, to Poland. In another car, Hana and Isabelle, whom Hana picks up walking on the road, also set out for Poland, which, however, can hardly be said to be a place any of them realistically set out for. If it has somehow become "home" for several of the characters (Polish or not), and while we should of course remember that the film takes place during the struggle between Solidarity and the Polish Communist government (an event the film refers to), Godard doesn't bother to give any psychological or political plausibility to this sudden exodus to Poland. Poland is perhaps nothing more than the arbitrary metaphor for the whiteness into which we see the cars disappear, the misty whiteness of a snow-covered landscape. That whiteness recalls or, more exactly, anticipates the blank page Godard refers to in the *Scenario* as the Mallarmean *page blanche* that precedes and, more profoundly, defies all realized art. *Passion* is an aesthetic adventure in moving backward: from the film Godard actually made, to the other cinematic *Passion* Jerzy is always stopping work on, to the renunciation of that film and the dispersal of its players (as well as of Godard's other characters), and, finally to the *Scenario* that came out after *Passion*, as if Godard's time had become a reel he could rewind — that is, not a time from a scenario to a finished film, but rather from the film that has been made to its tentative form that must have preceded but now follows it, and, finally, to that blankness pre- and postfigured in the film's final shot, the strangely displaced point of arrival of the film's actual point of departure, which was its pure virtuality in Godard's mind.

The Godardian movement backwards, far from negativizing or simply erasing the finished being it leaves, actually expands it by potentializing it. Partially derealized being is virtual being. A difficult but fundamental question remains: What is the activity of virtuality? Or, put in other terms, Godard must discover, or invent, a type of relationality that is at once the phenomenological operator and the sign of the real becoming the potential. Or, in still another formulation, what is potentiality's syntax? For Jerzy and for Godard, the syntax of stories is a form of accounting. The story-hungry Italian producer is also obsessed with the cost of things; Laszlo takes him through the studio ("the most modern in Europe," Sophie says), mentioning the prices of the equipment and the costumes. In story telling, elements are added to one another in order to make a sum of completed meaning; the sense we get from narratively coherent stories is, Godard suggests, determined by their epistemologically additive bias. This does not mean, however, that Godard's film — perhaps unlike Jerzy's film — is structurally incoherent. There are, most notably, couplings that give to Godard's work a certain structural connectedness: the relation of Godard's *Passion* to Jerzy's *Passion*; the aesthetic couples of film and painting, as well as of music and the visual arts; the two types of love — open and closed, Jerzy says — embodied in Isabelle and Hana; the mingling as well as the opposition of home and foreignness (and of the irreconcilable destinations of Hollywood and Poland); and of course the thematic coupling of work and love.

Instead of being encouraged to answer the question of how, most notably, love and work are alike, we are compelled to ask the more fundamental question of what "alikeness" means for Godard. Take, for example, the incongruous symmetry of the "traces" that are at the beginning and near the end of *Passion*. The film opens with shots of the long white trace left by a plane in the sky; much later, when Jerzy and Isabelle are making love and he says that now he will take her from behind, she assents, saying, "Yes, there mustn't be any traces." This last scene is immediately followed by a shot of El Greco's *Assumption of the Virgin*, a tribute to the human vessel of the momentously untraceable event of Christ's conception. So one kind of trace starts the film, while negations of a very different sort of trace conclude it, negations that are also incongruously "like" Godard's derealizing movements I discussed a moment ago. In what way is Isabelle at once losing and keeping her possible virginity (she answers "perhaps" when Jerzy asks her if she is a virgin) "like" Mary's at once conceiving Jesus and negating the conception presupposed by a human birth? One of the first things we hear (barely hear) Isabelle say as she works is "Why have you abandoned me?"—a question she repeats to Jerzy a few minutes later as she runs alongside his slowly moving car, but which also recalls the vastly more momentous question, at least as reported by Mark, of Christ on the cross.

Godard's similitudes are radically different from Proustian metaphors. For Proust—at least ideally, or theoretically—to juxtapose the two terms of a metaphor would disengage the essence they have in common. Diffrerences would be subordinated (if not erased) to a shared identity; phenomenological diversity would be superseded by ontological oneness. Godard's similitudes make no such claim. Isabelle and the Virgin, Jerzy abandoning Isabelle and God the Father abandoning His Son, the gestures of work and the gestures of love: alikeness here has none of the substantive identity of Proustian metaphor, but seems more like a possibility that might reduce the incongruity of the comparison. It's as if Isabelle's sense of being abandoned, and the gestures of her work, were reaching toward the terms to which they are compared, were not the discovery but rather the experimental initiation of a connection, or a correspondence. The alikeness of the terms is an essentially unrepresentable virtuality, the beginning of a rearrangement of the field of knowability. The unfinished and the incongruous are the principal features of Godard's extraordinary proposal about how we might both see and think the universe. Desynchronization accounts for much of what is hectic and ungraspable in a Godard film; more profoundly, it is the condition of possibility (if not, to use a distinction emphasized by Jerzy, probability) of recomposed relationality.

A certain gravity, even melancholy, in the episode that alternates the filming of the El Greco painting with the scene of Jerzy and Isabelle in Isabelle's bedroom (an episode accompanied by Fauré's *Requiem*) is perhaps the affective sign of Godard's consciousness of the "expense" of desynchronization, the provisional lessness consequent upon a loss of coherent being. The passion of unfinishing, even crucifying, his own work and the identity that might be traced by that work ("I began to mourn myself at an early age," Godard says in *JLG by JLG*) is at once exhilarating and tragic. Tragic in that possibility itself might disappear into the undifferentiated whiteness of the road to

Poland; exhilarating in that a floating, tentative, improbable relational field multiplies connections, creates a space for new, unpredictable, unclassifiable relations. The unfinished and the incongruous have what we might call a flotational effect on the real, an effect figured by the curiously unsettled figures in the El Greco painting, figures suspended between two subjects (certain critics have spoken of the painting as an Immaculate Conception) and who are filmed in a way that makes them appear to be floating, even mutating, in space. Godard has been a major agent in a contemporary reformulation of the aesthetic, the aesthetic as no longer confined to objects culturally tagged as art (a tagging accompanied by a reactive, reactionary anxiety about what art "is"), but as carrying the privilege and the responsibility of an otherwise inconceivable concretizing of the metaphysical. In Godard's film, the aesthetic passion of desynchronizing the elements of an artwork is doubled by the ontological passion of derealized being. What "knowledge" might mean or be under these conditions remains to be defined — if, that is, the question itself is not dismissed. Perhaps we should simply try to engage in other exercises in incongruity, as I have tried to do by juxtaposing Foucault, Proust, the psychoanalytic dialogue, and a film by Godard as remotely similar demonstrations of the proliferative nature of unripe, virtual being.

The discussion of Godard beginning on p. 163 was written in collaboration with Ulysse Dutoit.

PART 3
3
Two Interviews

12

A Conversation with Leo Bersani

with Tim Dean, Hal Foster, and Kaja Silverman

Hal Foster: I thought we could begin with the topos of failure. It is a primary subject of your recent work: a critique of redemptive practices in *The Culture of Redemption* [1990]; an argument for impotent aesthetics in the recent book coauthored with Ulysse Dutoit, *Arts of Impoverishment* [1993]; an analysis of failed subjectivity in *Homos* [1995]. But it is a principal method as well: for example, in *The Freudian Body* [1986] you focus on the points in Freud where his thought breaks down, and these you regard as the most provocative, even the most productive (if that is not too un-Bersanian a value). In what ways is failure a method for you, and how does it differ, say, from a dialectical concern with contradiction or a deconstructive concern with aporia?

Leo Bersani: That's an interesting way to begin, even though it sounds inauspicious. My interest in failure has, I guess, been fairly constant. It's there in the early books, too, when I talked (optimistically) about mobility and immobility of desire in Baudelaire [*Baudelaire and Freud* (1977)], as well as in several French novelists in *Balzac to Beckett/Center and Circumference in French Fiction* [1970]. The latter explored the notion of a circumferential expansiveness of the self against a fixed anchoring of the self. *A Future for Astyanax* [1976] strikes me as the most coherent statement of this early position, of this version of the argument against the immobile, centered, self-contained subject.

Failure first played an explicit role in *The Freudian Body*, where it

Originally appeared in *October* 82 (Fall 1997): 3–16.

really concerns a collapse of the text. This was not like deconstructive readings that tend to reconstruct texts according to rhetorically determined thematics that run counter to what authors seem to think they're writing about. (This led, incidentally, to a generation of graduate students who relentlessly "proved" that they were smarter than Rousseau, Wordsworth, James, Melville, etc.) In *The Freudian Body*, I was interested in the text simply going to pieces, and also in the way collapse itself is thematized in the idea of self-shattering (which I drew from Jean Laplanche). My interest in failure then continued in various ways—a culture without re-demptive power, certain failures in art and writing, homosexuality as a beneficent crisis of selfhood, and now what Ulysse Dutoit and I call, in our work on Caravaggio, a betrayal of the historical subject.

Important questions for me right now are: What is the relation between my interest in failure and my writing about homosexuality? And what is the psychic and/or political value of this insistence? Is it merely a recuperative move that ends up denying failure, or is it consistent with maintaining it? And in what way might these questions serve what I think is our most urgent project now: redefining modes of relationality and community, the very notion of sociality? All this also concerns the role of psychoanalysis in my work, first in revealing that failure, and then in revealing, after a certain point, a kind of failure within psychoanalysis itself—or its limited usefulness—for this sort of study.

Tim Dean: If your focus in *The Freudian Body* is on the points where the text collapses, fragmenting into a lack of coherence, what comes after this failure? Does it lead to a new place that is not simply a reconstitution of the previous one?

Kaja Silverman: That leads me to ask a question as well. Leo, you and I are people who write constantly against the self—against mastery and power. Both of us privilege the moment of undoing, and see it as some-thing which must either be endlessly repeated, or prolonged to infinity. It seems to me that your emphasis on failure needs to be thought about in this context. You valorize the moment of dissolution or "shattering" because you cannot imagine anything on the other side of that shattering except a reversion to the same. And it is that reversion—that unavoidable recuperation—which you seek to inhibit.

Bersani: I agree. I don't think of it as a going beyond, or that one can finally get rid of the self. That seemed to be the goal of the "schizophrenic" cul-tural politics of about twenty years ago, and now that strikes me as naïve and politically irresponsible.

Foster: But these terms, mastery and containment, seem too total. Often in your work you privilege failed subjectivity — just as Kaja has privileged masochistic masculinity — as a critical position. But that seems to project a subject that is successful, a social that is solid, against which these figures then appear as critical. Might your very insistence on shattered and/or supine figures make the symbolic order appear more intact than it is?

Bersani: It doesn't presuppose an intact order but rather one constantly straining toward mastery and containment — straining toward it in a suicidal way. It's very important to analyze that striving for containment in ethical and epistemological positions that presuppose a mastery over the object — to analyze them in terms of a movement toward mastery over the other that in fact masks and secretly promotes a suicidal self-dissolution. The crucial text here is *Civilization and Its Discontents*, which dissects the morality of civilization, its attempt to assert a self-contained mastery over disharmony, conflict, violence. That text suggests that there's no confident self-containment either on the subjective or the social level. The renunciation of aggressiveness multiplies the force of aggression; the socialized superego of civilization is itself constitutively self-destructive. So the question to ask is not whether such self-containment exists but what strategic purpose the insistence upon it serves. I think that purpose is to obscure or to repress the suicidal urge that underlies it.

For me, the culture of redemption is historically the obverse side of this suicidal movement. It is a shadow culture that does what the society has failed to do; it helps to repress the destructive impulses for which it is also meant to compensate. To what extent would the suicidal movement be exposed if there were no culture of redemption? It would be much more visible.

Foster: Hence your formula "the culture of redemption is the culture of death."

Bersani: Yes, because the culture denies the historical reality that it attempts to redeem, represses the suicidal impulse that is its very motivation. The culture of redemption is thus not mimetic, except in a very twisted way: it denies that to which it is related. Officially, it always presents itself as making the civilization intelligible — as a philosophically and aesthetically superior version of the reality that society lives historically. Of course, it reveals certain truths about this society, but not the truth of its suicidal movement or even the truth of its own obscuring function.

Dean: Leo, your distinction between a suicidal dissolution and a nonsuicidal self-dissolution is a very difficult one. It seems that it involves the effects of the superego not only on the ego but on social relations. In *The Freudian Body*, in your reading of *Civilization and Its Discontents*, you argue that the superego isn't simply an internalizing of paternal aggression so much as a folding back on oneself of one's own outwardly directed aggression — and that folding back is about a suicidal self-dissolution. What, then, is this other benign, nonsuicidal self-dissolution?

Bersani: To try and answer that I should refer to the part of *The Freudian Body* that interests me most — the discussion of masochism in relation to *Three Essays on the Theory of Sexuality*. And here I differ from Kaja because I still am interested in masochism — but in a masochism connected to, as you say, a nonsuicidal dissolution of the subject. Here we have to go back to the notion in Laplanche that sexuality is originally constituted as masochism. For me, Laplanche was suggesting, without saying this, that what is inherently destructive is also originally a mode of survival. This led to the speculation in the second chapter of *The Freudian Body* concerning the evolutionary purpose served by sexuality as *ébranlement*, as shattering. Perhaps the only way for the infant to survive the imbalance between external stimuli and the ego structures prepared to receive them is to find the pain of this imbalance pleasurable. This does not mean, incidentally, that *ébranlement* is an empirical characteristic of our sexual lives; it means that a masochistic self-shattering was constitutive of our identity as sexual beings, that it is present, always, not primarily in our orgasms but rather in the terrifying but also exhilarating instability of human subjectivity.

Two questions here: In what forms does this early threat to the constitution of our sexual selves persist in adult consciousness? And how does the originary experience of masochism enter into constructing intersubjectivity and sociality? These are crucial questions my subsequent work begins to address. That originary experience cannot be forgotten or done away with; we always revert to it in some way; there is always a memory of self-constitution that includes this masochistic coming-into-being of the sexual.

What interests me now is a productive masochism, which, thanks largely to the work on the visual arts that I have done with Ulysse Dutoit, I have begun to think in a nonbiological, perhaps even nonpsychological, way. It is a more spatial conception that brings masochism together with narcissism. In other words, I am now interested in masochism not as pleasure in pain so much as the pleasure of at once losing the self and discovering it elsewhere, inaccurately replicated.

Silverman: Why is it still masochistic?

Bersani: Because it still means a certain pleasurable renunciation of one's own ego boundaries, the pleasure of a kind of self-obliteration.

Silverman: But is that masochism or self-divestiture? Your new argument, in the Caravaggio work, about the extensibility of the subject and the communication of forms seems related to the old argument about self-shattering, but it's qualitatively different.

Bersani: It's important to me to talk about it precisely as masochism and narcissism and not as self-divestiture because self-divestiture approaches what I have tried to avoid, and that is any connection of these ideas to castration. This is a major point of difference between us: I am interested in a pleasure in losing or dissolving the self that is in no way equated with loss, but comes rather through rediscovering the self outside the self. It is a kind of spatial, anonymous narcissism.

Silverman: Your idea of a communication of forms seems to be really new and original. I think it's a mistake to fold it back into your earlier argument about self-shattering and masochism. That seems a reactive gesture, which prevents the communication of forms from achieving its own conceptual space. It suggests that you're still talking about body or psyche — about pleasure "trenching" on pain, or about what you thematize as psychic "detumescence" in "Is the Rectum a Grave?" [1987]. In fact, you're talking about form.

Bersani: What for you is a reactive gesture is for me a point of departure. Our move toward a correspondence of forms, in *Arts of Impoverishment* and now in the Caravaggio work, depends on a certain notion of masochism. If there weren't pleasure in giving up what our civilization insists that we retain — our ego boundaries — the communication of forms would never occur. So masochism is the precondition of this passage. However, when we talk about the correspondence of forms, it is true we are no longer talking about masochism per se, and in the Caravaggio work there is little use of the term.

Dean: Part of this debate is terminological: What are the intellectual and political implications of terms like masochism? But there is another term significant in your work by its absence. As you said a moment ago, you are keen to get outside a model based on castration. You are prepared to talk about loss but not with castration as its master term. Some might see your discussion of loss, then, as an idealization — even as a defense against castration. Can you elaborate on the role or nonrole of castration in your work?

Bersani: Okay, but to do so I need to retrace my itinerary — and Laplanche's.

Obviously they are different, but two notions in Laplanche are crucial for me: first, self-shattering (which is connected to the primacy of masochism in sexuality), and now the enigmatic signifier. But I want to take them in the direction of a productive masochism, and Laplanche does not. He talks about sexuality and the death drive, but never about how masochism might be exploited for a move into the correspondence of forms.

The notion of self-shattering is a somewhat solipsistic view of the sexual: the infant is born into sexuality by being overwhelmed by external stimuli, but it is a solitary situation. The notion of the enigmatic signifier places the birth of the sexual in a specific intersubjective context. And this has led me to a question that interests me very much: How do we rethink the constitution of the couple? And in what ways is this reconstitution the absolute precondition of any rethinking of sociality? That is the center of my work right now, not masochism.

So the notion of the enigmatic signifier places self-shattering in a new context — in the calling of the subject into a human community (as we termed it in *Arts of Impoverishment*). The question then becomes: What version of this calling do we have now, and what other versions can be produced? If we want to change the nature of our community, we have to rethink our originary call into it — how human organisms are made into human subjects. Beckett plays with this question in *Company* when he imagines somebody standing above a crib and calling. Where is the sound? the helpless infant asks. What is its nature? Is it attacking me? soliciting me? nurturing me? Of course, these questions are not linguistically formulated, and the disorientation is spatial, but it still involves a pleasure in the very pain of being disoriented.

The enigmatic signifier is a call like this: an adult addresses the infant with some message. For Laplanche the infant experiences this message as threatening; the adult is carrying so many sexual significations that he or she cannot help but overwhelm the infant. So how does the infant respond to these enigmatic signifiers? Laplanche says that it responds by taking the mass of what it can't understand and making it unconscious — that's his new version of primal repression. The repression puts the nonmetabolizable parts of the enigmatic message into the unconscious.

Dean: Are these things *made into* the unconscious, or do they already count as unconscious by virtue of their being enigmatic?

Bersani: What exactly is involved in primal repression is impossible to describe empirically. But Laplanche does talk about it as crucial to the very constitution of the unconscious.

The extraordinary thing, I think, is that this idea traces the end of psychoanalysis as a useful way of describing relationality. The Laplanchean unconscious, unlike the Lacanian one, is a mass of nonmetabolizable refuse, the waste of the enigmatic signifier; as such it is useless in describing relationality. For me the theory of the enigmatic signifier is one of the most moving events in the history of thought because it shows psychoanalytic thought refining itself out of existence. Laplanche would never admit this; he sees it as another step within psychoanalytic speculation. . . .

Dean: And I see it as another step in Laplanche's thought — toward Lacan!

Bersani: With the enigmatic signifier, the adult withholds what might complete the infant by giving it knowledge. The infant may then experience this unmasterable event as a kind of castration. More importantly, it seems to me, it begins the whole problematic of knowledge: What does the enigmatic signifier mean? This sets up the couple in a relation of paranoid fascination (and here there is a connection to Lacan): I need to know the message, but I am cut off from its sense.

There is no way to escape this confrontation, but there might be a way to rethink it — to rethink the constitution of the couple in order to move to a different relation to otherness, not one based in paranoid fascination but one that might use the masochistic element in the confrontation productively. As it is, the ego, in order to protect itself from the attack of the enigmatic signifier, becomes hyperbolically defended or armored. But might this very threat to the self open the subject, leading to a self-extensibility rather than a paranoid defensiveness? This is the move Ulysse and I trace in Caravaggio's painting: from the teasingly enigmatic eroticism of the portraits of boys to the nonsexual sensuality of physical contacts, extensions, and correspondences, from a problematic of knowledge (and interiority) to a kind of cartography of the subject, a tracing of spatial connectedness.

Silverman: As I indicated earlier, what interests me is the move you make beyond the categories we conventionally use to think the relational — categories like bodies and psyches. So I'm still very fascinated with that period of your and Ulysse Dutoit's writing that extends from *The Culture of Redemption*, through *Arts of Impoverishment*, to *Homos*. Think, for instance, of the following formulation in *Homos*: "His sexual preference," you write of a protagonist in Gide, "is without psychic content; there are no complexes, no repressed conflicts, no developmental explanations; only the chaste promiscuity of form repeatedly reaching out to find itself beyond itself." With a sentence like this, you help us rethink the relational in terms of design. You remind us that the ego is in fact a form, although we don't usually think about it that way. It is constituted through the imaginary incorporation of a series of external *Gestalten*, which Freud conceptualizes as abandoned love-objects, and Lacan as imagoes. There is a lot to be gained through thinking about the ego in formal terms. First, it's de-anthropomorphizing. It permits us to begin conceptualizing relationality outside the usual human categories, which have become very reduced in recent years through the insistence upon race, class, gender, etc. It helps us to understand that what we are at the level of the ego may be a much more complex issue than we are accustomed to imagining, having to do not only with mothers, fathers, lovers, etc., but also with line, shape, composition, color . . .

Bersani: That's exactly what we're interested in emphasizing. Furthermore, the very fact that the ego *is* a "form" in the sense you've just described should also have an effect on the way we think of our relations with "mothers, fathers, lovers." As I've suggested, the couple constituted by the enigmatic signifier raises the question of how the social is constituted — and other ways it might be imagined. It's very important to work on this imagining collaboratively, perhaps even to have workshops on ways to address the human that do not only repeat the originary situation of the enigmatic signifier — for mutual hostility, paranoid fascination, absolute separation between subject and object, impossible projects of mastery over otherness, all these are set up by the relationship put into play by the enigmatic signifier. For those of us interested in some other kind of sociality, what do we do? If we can't get rid of the relationship produced by the enigmatic signifier, perhaps it can be dis-essentialized, made less central than it is. What would this involve?

Dean: You've just mentioned the importance of collaborative projects, in which you have of course been involved in the books and essays coauthored with Ulysse Dutoit. What has your working together meant to you, and has the experience of working together been a model of what you just called "some other kind of sociality"?

Bersani: Very much so. It has been, and continues to be, an important and somewhat frightening experience. We have worked very closely together on the paintings, the sculpture, and the films we have chosen to discuss — but what has this "working together" meant exactly? When I get to the stage of actually putting together an essay or a chapter from our exchanges, I don't really discover that we've worked out differences to arrive at a common position, that some sort of intellectual consensus has been reached, or that the writing reflects or reveals the dialectical nature of our exchanges. Rather, I feel a kind of pull away from, even a collapse, of positions I might have taken, and identified as "mine," if I were working alone. Our collaboration has been a sort of beneficent assault on the integrity of our intellectual egos. I lose myself richly in these collaborations. Specifically, Ulysse doesn't need what most of us call "theory"—in particular psychoanalytic theory—in order to address and be addressed by works of art. For me, this has led to a certain intellectual instability in my work, which I don't regret at all, and which has even been visible in this conversation in the difficulty I had responding to Kaja about the persistence of masochism in the more recent work on the correspondence of forms. Perhaps the two don't "belong together" at all, but if they collide, that's okay.

One more word on the "calling forth" I mentioned a couple of minutes ago. How might a child be called forth into community in a less exclusively coupled way? Obviously, the principal responsibility rests with adults—how we constitute couples. This is future work connected to the upbringing of children, education, and art; those are three areas where the mode of calling might be modified in important ways.

The most difficult thing for the couple is to suggest to the child a call that is more disseminating than narrowing. As it is, the call seems to come only from one source. But this is just a transposition to the relation between adult and child of the way in which adults have been taught to think about the couple. Monogamy is very much involved here. In some ways the couple must be demonogamized in order for the enigmatic signifier to be dis-essentialized. Adam Phillips has just written a very interesting book on monogamy which led me to think—and I doubt that he would be happy with this effect of his work—that violence is inherent in monogamy.

Foster: How do you get from the extraordinary scene in Genet, recounted in *Homos*, where two men fuck on a Paris rooftop, totally indifferent to the world, all but oblivious to each other—how do you go from this wild scene, which is radically anticommunitarian, even antirelational, to your new version of the P.T.A.? I don't mean to be glib . . .

Bersani: It's not a question of being glib. Actually, your question interests me because it takes up, in modified form, a principal criticism of *Homos* made by certain gay and lesbian critics. I don't think you "get from" Genet to the P.T.A., or—to address gay concerns—to gay marriage or gay adoption (which of course will make the P.T.A. a universal concern). The issue is the difference between micropolitics and the kinds of questions I'm urging people to think about without abandoning struggles for particular reforms. To me, the interest of the writers that I look at in *Homos* — especially Gide and Genet — is not that they are relevant to specific policy issues that we may face today (for example, what the most effective AIDS activism might be) — they are not relevant to such issues — but rather, that they propose what are for the moment necessarily mythic reconfigurations of identity and of sociality. The problem with queer politics as we now define it is that, however broad its reach may be, it is still a micropolitics focused on numerous particular issues which there is no reason to believe will ever be exhausted if the fundamental types of community and relationality out of which such issues spring are not themselves questioned and attacked. And *that* activity has to be, at least for the moment, an activity of the intellectual imagination — one for which the micropoliticians often have no use or patience but which seems to me no less an activity and no more of a luxury than our immediate and our, of course, vital concrete struggles.

Silverman: But in your version of that reimagining, isn't a certain gay practice being valorized, in a displaced way? Aren't you making homosexuality redemptive? In *Homos*, cruising provides a way of conceptualizing a redemptive communitarianism, and in your present work nonmonogamy seems to function in a similar way.

Bersani: I would say productive, not redemptive; in my work, redemption concerns a compensatory relation to a suicidal society. Yes, the homosexual as a category does have a privileged position heuristically, but not as a social priority.

I am seeking a model of an address that leads not to paranoid fascination with the mysterious source of the address, but to a disseminating attention in which the child is not made to feel an imprisoning separation between himself and the other — a disseminating attention in which a narcissistic discovery of the self replicated outside the self would be possible. In what sense can a replicative model of relations help to modify the dangerous property relations fostered by the generative model of relations — the couple, the family, and the proprietary implications of those terms?

Dean: I wonder, in seeking a new model of sociality, whether retaining the term "couple" might lead to problems. The value of your account is that it's not really a couple at all, or if it is, it's one person coupled with something else that isn't another person. You pose a nonreciprocal relationship as the basis for relationality; there's a kind of depersonalization there. And the reason that homosexuality seems to work as a model is precisely because in certain kinds of gay sex (though not only there) there's a kind of de-personalization of sexuality, even a dehumanization — which is, of course, always an object of intense criticism. Isn't it that relation — not between persons but between a person and something that is nonhuman — that you want to build?

Bersani: Very much so. That gets to the connection between the interest Ulysse and I have had in the communication of forms aesthetically and the interest I have expressed more particularly in the homosexual as a model not only for the intersubjective but for the relation between the human and the nonhuman. But I want to focus on this question of privileging the homosexual.

As you know, my principal objection to queer theory is that it presents itself as a radical questioning of hegemonic heterosexism, whereas I think it has been a tame enterprise — tame because it largely consists in marshaling historical reasons for saying the homosexual did not exist before the middle of the nineteenth century (of course Foucault is very influential here, and some of this work is very interesting). From this claim has developed an apparently more radical position — that the heterosexual was also constituted recently, at the end of the nineteenth century or the beginning of the twentieth, as a category just as loaded with ideological and disciplinary implications, indeed with the homosexual needed as its support. Okay, that's what has been done, and I'm not against it.

Dean: But are you saying that's too tame?

Bersani: It's important, but when all that is said and done, the homosexual is left as the product of a disciplinary, malevolent society. And it is taken for granted then that we are politically very radical — which doesn't follow at all. You can be victimized and in no way be radical; it happens very often among homosexuals as with every other oppressed minority. So the question I wanted to raise in Homos is: Is there some kind of potential radicality, not in homosexuality historically, but in the homosexual as a category? It troubled me very much that, once the historical case was made about this evil society constituting us as homosexuals, it turned out that what we wanted was getting into the very system that has done us all this terrible harm. So my question became: Is there a model within the homosexual for thinking a different mode of sociality not based on the suicidal, paranoid relations that have governed dominant society?

Dean: This gives us the opportunity to make another important distinction, namely, that in academic discourse in the United States, Foucault's work has been used for historicist purposes. In queer theory there is an almost irresistible imperative to historicize sexuality. Your work is clearly influenced by Foucault in a different direction. How would you characterize what Foucault means to you?

Bersani: Foucault has been immensely important to me, but I obviously have mixed feelings about his work — or, more exactly, about his influence. There has been an absurd and reductive misreading of the first volume of the *History of Sexuality*, a reading that claims that "the homosexual" didn't exist before the middle of the nineteenth century. I don't think Foucault believed that for a single moment. I also think he would have been shocked by the frankly stupid confusion between the homosexual as a category of the psyche with elaborately defined characteristics (in large part, that *is* a modern invention) and the homosexual as an individual primarily oriented toward same-sex eroticism.

Foucault interests me mainly for what I take to be his fundamental project of rethinking relations. This is in particular what the first volume of the *History of Sexuality* is aiming toward. Of course, Foucault's polemic against the primacy of desire in our thought is a polemic against psychoanalysis, and his move from desire to pleasure remains schematic, unexplained. As I argue in chapter three of *Homos*, psychoanalysis, far from being the enemy of this project, actually complements it — but of course Foucault didn't see it that way. I'm very much interested in the role he gives to gay people in such a project, although, again, I'm bothered by the somewhat facile evocation in interviews of the happy gay couple and the idealizations of S/M as a privileged practice in de-genitalizing and expanding the field of the body's pleasures. Such idealizing goes against his truly powerful demonstrations of how all moves encounter points of resistance, and that the frictions (both physical and psychic) produced by these thrusts and counterthrusts of "power" must be taken into account in any enterprise of liberating relationality from the hegemonic model of domination and enslavement.

Dean: These issues evoke a word we have used only in passing: identity. *Homos* seems ambiguous in this respect: it argues both for and against a certain kind of identity.

Bersani: I think the homosexual might be crucial for constituting a relationality not based on identity. In dominant society today, we see a form of economics, of global capitalism, that is supernational, but this goes along with one of the greatest exacerbations of ethnic and nationalist violence ever seen throughout the world. Economic relations seem to have surpassed national limits at the same time that the most suicidal movement is carried out in the name of ethnic and national particularities. It is a blind or cover to think that we are beyond the ethnic and national — we are absolutely stuck in the particular in a horrendous way. This could endanger our system of global capitalism, given that the latter depends on conditions that are not riven by daily violence.

These are all matters of identity. And so it becomes extremely important — for all of us, though it may be more available to homo- sexuals — to imagine the possibility of nonidentitarian community. That is the work to be done (it is one reason why Giorgio Agamben interests me). And this is what the Genet scene on the rooftop and the correspondence of forms have in common: a peculiar notion of nonidentitarian sameness. Each man fucking the other replicates himself in the other, and they both replicate themselves outside, but there's no identity there. In the same way, the formal correspondences that Ulysse and I talk about in our three books are not identical — it's a kind of sameness that's not identity. Inac- curate replication, nonidentarian sameness: it corresponds to homosexual sex — not necessarily as practiced (very often the difference between the sexes is reconstituted and played out between two men or two women), but the homosexual as category, as sameness in which the relation to dif- ference would be a nonthreatening supplement to sameness. At his or her best, the homosexual is a failed subject, one that needs its identity to be cloned, or inaccurately replicated, outside of it. This is the strength, not the weakness, of homosexuality, for a nihilistic civilization has been built on the foundation of a (factitious) inviolable subject. This is so important because I think the only way we can love the other or the external world is to find ourselves somehow in it. Only then can there be a nonviolent relation to the external world that doesn't seek to exterminate difference. In this sense, "the homosexual" might be a model of this kind of com- munication of forms.

Dean: This sounds like a version of a question raised in *Homos*: how desire gets attached to persons.

Bersani: What we usually mean by desire between persons (something we understand psychologically, and therefore something quite different from the scenes in Genet and Gide I discuss in *Homos*) is by no means the model for the correspondences that interest us. In fact, the human itself has no ontological priority here. This "replacing" or "relocating" of the human perhaps started in the course of our work on Assyrian sculpture several years ago. During the writing of that book [*The Forms of Violence* (1985)], Ulysse made a remark to the effect that the repertory of forms in the universe is vast but limited; eventually all forms are repeated. In art, the space of that eventual encounter or "recognition" is condensed or shrunk. In studying the Assyrian bas-reliefs, we argued not that the narratives of violence somehow criticized themselves (there is not the slightest doubt for the Assyrians about the rightness and the glory of that violence), but rather that the sculptors also draw our attention to families of forms, thereby suggesting that murderous antagonism toward differ-ence (one race against another, the Assyrian hunters against animals) can always be turned away from, perhaps even set aside in, the pleasurable confirmation of a solidarity in the universe, a solidarity not of identities but of positionings and configurations in space, one that even ignores the apparently most intractable identity-difference: between the human and the nonhuman.

Dean: This issue fascinates me because I think our relation to the nonhuman is primary and predicates interpersonal relations rather than the reverse. It prompts me to ask about misreadings of *Arts of Impoverishment* that claim you're treating our relations with art works as an allegory for our relation to persons — with all the troubling ethical consequences that implies. But I think you're doing something much more interesting, by showing how our relations to art and our relations to other people are simply subsets of a much broader conception of relationality as such. In other words, inter-personal relationships don't determine relationality or sociality.

Bersani: Exactly. And Ulysse has helped me to see these correspondences not only in the visual arts but also in literature: our discussion of Beck-ett's *Worstward Ho* in *Arts of Impoverishment* is the analysis of a text so integrally constituted by inaccurate replications that we read backward as well as forward to confirm our memory of verbal configurations al-ready read. I think that I have always been interested in this without real-izing how directly useful it was and would continue to be (the section on Baudelaire in *The Culture of Redemption* "predicts" my own future work). Ulysse's formulations, made wholly outside a psychoanalytic frame-work, led me to a crucial modification of the "self-shattering" notion I had picked up from Laplanche. Identity-boundaries are violated not only as a masochistic phenomenon, but also as an effect of reaching toward one's own "form" elsewhere. This self-dissolution is also self-accretion; it is self-incremental. And so, thanks to the nonpsychoanalytic notion of the correspondence of forms, psychoanalysis is conceptually enriched by the category of a masochism identical to narcissism. . . . Identity is renounced in the pleasurable recognition of repetitions, that is, solidarity. The danger here—and this is addressed in the Rothko Chapel section of *Arts of Impoverishment*—is that correspondences might inspire the dream, or the wish, of a total unity of being, a sameness in which replication would be accurate and not inaccurate, and which would be equivalent to nothingness. Language, narrative, composition, articulation hold us back from this, so it can never be a question of simply being, for example, antinarrative, although narrative articulation is also the formal model for a universe of antagonistic differences.

Silverman: A "total unity" of being would also be completely immobilizing, not only metaphysically but also subjectively. And mobility is a central concern of the work you have done with Ulysse Dutoit. Because the two of you are concerned with the conditions under which we can *gravitate toward* rather than *contain* the forms which attract us, under which we can allow them their exteriority, your notion of the communication of forms can be seen as a way out of what Lacan calls "formal stagnation." Formal stagnation is what happens when we manage to achieve egoic consistency, when we succeed in sustaining for a long time an incorporative identification with a single form. You and Ulysse invite us to let go of the forms which we have imprisoned within our ego, in order to open ourselves up to the possibility of a whole new series of relationships, relationships which are in the first instance *aesthetic.*

Bersani: A final remark to suggest how different our emphasis on the aesthetic is from any so-called formalistic approach to art. Perhaps only an aesthetic grounded in the communication of forms can relieve the anxiety of castration. The enigmatic signifier is based on that which is missing, that which is being withheld from me, that from which I have been cut off. But in the nonsacrificial aesthetic we trace in the Caravaggio book, everything connects to and within the wholeness of Being (in an activity wholly different from the annihilating "unity of being" referred to in our discussion of Rothko). If we still have "secrets," they are now secrets not of interiority but rather of untraceable spatial disseminations; if there is still "concealment," it is the concealment of a visibility beyond the painting to which the painting directs us. Finally—and this is a major part of our demonstration—the artist himself paints his own connectedness to his work. The activity of Caravaggio's body in the work of his painting is figured in his painting by his occasional presence as a witness. The artist becomes a relational term within his own work; the latter makes visible the form of his implication in it. In this art, the communication of forms takes place, ultimately, as the artist's painted recognition of himself.

13

Beyond Redemption:
An Interview with Leo Bersani

with Nicholas Royle

NR: Is it possible? That's the first question I would like to ask. What is an interview? How might an interview be conceived in the light of your work?

LB: Well, I guess I have to admit it's a possibility to start with. The main problem with an interview is always that you feel it can take the direction of some kind of finalizing or conclusive statement about what you've done, becoming a summary of your work as if the end of a sentence had been reached. It changes the nature of the work you've done, to think of it as something that has that kind of conclusive, definitive quality. That, I think, is something that you sometimes feel in interviews and it's something I'd certainly like to avoid. On the other hand I think an interview can also almost entirely neglect what someone has done. But there must be some way in which you could give the sense of the interview as a moment in the activity of the person who's engaged in it and that of course would be the ideal one.

NR: I suppose I'm intrigued by the idea of the interview and the question of relationality as it figures in some of your more recent work, the idea of an interview as something which might not presuppose self-identical subjects, a different and new way of thinking about the space and form of the interview.

LB: Well, it's very difficult, because the very notion of the choice of someone for an interview implies that you have chosen your particular intellectual identity to speak with. It would be disingenuous to act as if there were no

Originally appeared in *Oxford Literary Review* 20. no. 1 (1998): 173–90.

identity involved here. But that's what I meant by the fact that if it could be thought of as part of the activity of a career or life of thinking about various questions, then it's not so much of an identity that can be summarized at the interview, but rather something like the Joycean idea of work in progress.

NR: It would also perhaps be the case that an interview has to fail, wouldn't you say? The notion of failure has a crucial place in your work. I wonder if you would like to say something about failure in this context?

LB: Well, that too is obviously a slippery concept. One could easily say to somebody who had written a dozen or so books of criticism and who talks about the necessity of failing: what can that possibly mean, if not something that's not very honest? But the notion of failure as I've been talking about it has to be very much situated in relation to another notion, one that was explored most thoroughly in *The Culture of Redemption* and *Arts of Impoverishment* (The latter written with Ulysse Dutoit). Any identification of failure with bad art is ridiculous and that's obviously not what I mean. Nor is it a question of failing to make sense. In the case of *Arts of Impoverishment* it seemed to us that the artists we talked about — Beckett, Rothko, and Resnais — were failing with respect to certain traditions and expectations connected to the medium in which they were working and that to a certain extent this inhibits a kind of appropriation of the work which we tend, as a result of a great deal of quite effective cultural training, to take for granted. That's what I mean by failure. And it obviously should be explained successfully in something like an interview. It would seem to me a cop-out to say: well, I can only fail to explain what I mean by failure in order to remain faithful to my idea of failure.

NR: Sure. I was thinking in particular of a kind of ethic of failure, as one perhaps finds in Beckett.

LB: Yes, the Beckett position is obviously the most radical: "I can't go on — I must go on." And you know I think Beckett is an extraordinary example because in some senses he was an astonishing universal man of letters. He did everything: criticism, novels, plays, radio, television, film. And yet I think one has to take very seriously the attempt to instil a kind of paralysis or immobility, an inhibiting movement, *almost* unreadability, almost (as in the Buster Keaton film) unlookability. It's an attempt to come as close as possible, in a certain sense, to a kind of non-existence, but that's a very difficult accomplishment. I think that when someone like Beckett talks about failure it really means: what are the modes of discourse which might be consistent with my sense that I don't want to write in accordance with the dominant cultural expectations of what writing should be? It is an extremely complex form of thinking that requires an extremely complex form of thinking about the nature of writing — which is hardly consistent with failure as simply giving up or not doing anything.

NR: Can I keep with the preliminaries for a little while if possible? I recall when I tried to introduce you to an audience in Finland some years ago (in 1991), I felt I didn't know how to describe you, because terms like "social critic," "cultural critic," or "literary intellectual" didn't and don't seem especially appropriate? Is there a noun for you?

LB: Well, I don't know. I mean I guess yes, I would like to fail in *that* respect — especially since I began working at a time when that kind of identification was assumed to be very easy in the academic world. It was taken for granted, when I first began to teach, that you identified yourself and could be introduced very easily — as the nineteenth-century French literary scholar, the Renaissance scholar, and so on. And as you know very well, the influence of French thinking, especially in the sixties and seventies, on titles and identifications and intellectual identities, at least in the United States, was extremely important because it began to make those sorts of identifications impossible: people began to be interested in kinds of work that were no longer easily classifiable in terms of traditional disciplines. It's interesting that you ask that, because there's going to be a colloquium in Paris in a couple of weeks on theory and subversion and I've been preparing a brief talk around this subject. I start by saying if there is one word I'd eliminate from my vocabulary it would be "theory" and I end by saying if there is another word I'd eliminate it would be "subversion." But none the less, the kind of disidentification process that I was talking about a couple of moments ago went under the very inadequate rubric of "theory." The reason I don't like calling it theory (although I realize it's much more cumbersome to talk about disidentification) is that it led to the quite stupid notion that there was no theory in literature unless you began to talk about it from a certain philosophical point of view. Whereas there is, I think, no important literary work that doesn't theorize about its own activity as it goes along. Unfortunately that seemed to get forgotten in many American universities, even by many of the best people actually, who insisted on having theory courses. I've always argued against that because it seems to me that the students then think of there being a distinct separation between something called literature and something called theory. I have always felt that one of the most interesting things that people like Derrida were trying to do was to practice a kind of writing where that distinction was no longer relevant. So what happened was interesting, and as usual the institution lags behind us. At Berkeley I was chair of a department of French literature, a department originally constituted on very traditional lines of centuries. So you'd hear people saying that we need a seventeenth-century person, but why did we need Foucault or Derrida or Lyotard or Laplanche, in other words all these people that we invited and who came but never "belonged" (in heavy quotation marks) to a literature department? Institutionally there was no reason for them to be there, except that there was enough flexibility in several of the best American universities to allow it to happen. So that you had a historian, a philosopher, a psychoanalyst spending a semester in a French literature department — which even at Berkeley several people in the department were quite unhappy with, but luckily at the time they didn't have the power, so it could happen. So if you were at all involved in any of that it becomes very difficult to know how best to describe what you are. I think you've probably felt the same thing with the kind of itinerary that you've followed. It's true that I began by being presentable in all senses of the word — respectable and also introduceable — as a specialist in modern French literature. But for me one of the marvelous things was a kind of interconnectedness. Alongside French literature, there were certain things that were happening in my life, such as a very personal connection with psychoanalysis, which I didn't have to think of as belonging outside of my professional specialty. There wasn't this kind of schizophrenic relation between my profession and whatever else I might be doing, that is, for example, my involvement with psychoanalysis or my being a gay man — as if all of this was sort of over there and then I had my unrelated career, of being in modern French literature. Rather there was some kind of infiltration and contamination, I suppose you might think of it as a foreign body in one's professional life — which became, in fact, not a foreign body in that life but which nourished it in various modes of interconnectedness. It was not at all that I suddenly began to talk only about psychoanalysis and homosexuality, and in fact I continue to be very interested in and continue to write on modern French literature — but in ways that, I think, do make it difficult to be introduced to someone as a specialist. That simply wouldn't cover the ways in which the boundaries have been blurred.

NR: Another preliminary sort of question I wanted to ask is about the concept of the œuvre. Do you think of producing or having produced an œuvre? Is that an appropriate term?

LB: No.

NR: Could you perhaps say a little bit about how one can or should talk about what it is that you have done or do? You don't like "œuvre" because it's too freighted with. . . .

LB: Well it's connected to — it has too many connotations of monumentalization and completion. The word just seems to me obsolete.

NR: That's interesting. There's an interview with Derrida (in *Acts of Literature*, ed. Derek Attridge) where he talks about his attachment to the concept of the œuvre. If one rejects this term, I wonder then how one should talk about a body of writing otherwise.

LB: Why is that? I mean, you don't require that kind of metalanguage in the context of other professional or artisanal activities.

NR: Such as . . . ?

LB: Such as being a plumber or a football player or a lawyer. I find it very irritating that people in the intellectual or academic world think of themselves as that different in what they're doing from what other people are doing. It's led to extraordinary pretentiousness on the part of unfortunately this same group that helped to break down some of those identity barriers in academic disciplines. You know, there was a time that I remember talking to one of my colleagues, soon after the AIDS epidemic broke out, who said only deconstructionists could really understand the immune system. Which struck me as, you know, an idiocy not to be believed, and that was someone acknowledged to be a quite brilliant so-called deconstructionist. But again, what you're asking is really about how what we do is to be identified. It is contrary to what interests me, not only because of the obvious scepticism about identifications in both of our interests in trying to work to dissolve that kind of security, but also because of the kind of aristocratic and hierarchical, differential assumptions that seem to me to underlie that. It implies a quite strikingly nondemocratic view of human work.

NR: Related to that, could I ask you another perhaps banal kind of practical, everyday question? How do you write?

LB: With a pen. No: what do you mean, how do I write?

NR: Well, if we're talking about an analogy with plumbers or football players, could you say a little about how you go about your business, the activity of writing? Is it easy? Is it painful?

LB: Well, first of all it's very fragile, so trying to think too much about it is something I'm not too anxious to do, because I think that you get a kind of reflex sense that you have to be faithful to the way in which you describe the way you work. I don't want that to happen. But generally I find — since you don't think only when you're sitting down and have your computer in front of you (or, in my case, my notebook) — that certain confrontations, meetings, movements, moments in everyday experience just seem to make things crystalize. Whether you're reading — and I mean reading without a project in mind — or talking to somebody, or just driving, I find that something begins, and you sort of think, well, it might be interesting to look at that, I think so-and-so has written something interesting about that or some friend has said something interesting about that — and then something begins to shape at that moment — and there's a long period of just jotting down thoughts, in a very scattered way, but then reading them over after two or three months you get to see the possibility of a book or an essay or something that would be a sustained argument.

NR: As you're writing your notes you are not sure what the essay or book might be?

LB: Well, as the notes collect you do begin to get closer to that, I think, although of course it's easier if it just happens around a single writer. For example, my book on Proust involved simply reading Proust material. Since it was my first book I can still remember the passage in *La Prison-nière* where I felt that something is going on here that I can't quite get by just reading it and I'd really like to work that out. I mean, writing is working out something — and in some funny, very naive way it just occurred to me that that's the way you write a book, that's the way you might *begin* to write a book, just because in reading you get stuck by something. It proliferates and goes out from that center. I find the work happens in two stages mostly. The first stage is really agony in a way. After getting those notes and feeling I really have something, I usually do an outline of each chapter, a sort of one-page summary of the argument. And then to begin to write is extremely painful.

NR: Do you write by hand?

LB: Yes, always by hand. And it's painful, partly because I tend, in addition to that shock of recognition that there's something I want to explore here, something that may seem to me, for whatever reason, incredible to think about — I tend to find that moment is accompanied or followed for me by a sense that I have my first sentence. And then I get this terrible feeling of fidelity to that sentence — that the book has to be written because I have that sentence. Now I know that that's not *exactly* the case, but I get very attached to these first sentences. I remember in PhD exams in English or Comp. Lit., one of the questions that was often asked was: what is the first sentence of *Pride and Prejudice*? This stuck in my mind not so much because of that first sentence (which is a marvelous sentence) but because I think I already had this kind of — I don't know — some kind of lightning thing about first sentences. I just get them. And it can be something that I've had some trouble with. I'm thinking of the essay that Ulysse and I did on Pasolini's *Salò* and Sade (called "Merde alors"). It began with: "The vagina is a logical defect in nature." Someone wanted to change it to: "According to Sade, the vagina is a logical defect in nature." And I refused, saying it will be quite clear that we're not saying this as *our* statement, but it's got to stay, as the first shock.

NR: "There is a big secret about sex: most people don't like it."

LB: Yes, yes.

NR: Is this [the opening sentence of "Is the Rectum a Grave?"] a good example of what you're talking about — as if in a sense everything issues from that first sentence?

LB: Yes, in that essay what I say about various kinds of terror of gay sex and the attitude toward pornography — and, near the end of the essay, the celebration of an ascetic *jouissance* — is all connected, I suppose, to that aversion. I feel the first sentence is extremely important in almost getting a high, or at least I hope that it gives a kind of high — it gives me a high and I hope it gives the reader a high. But at the same time I don't really want the essay to be entirely faithful to its first sentence, at least not in a very literal way. Although in some respects the talk I did yesterday does work in that way: "Psychoanalytically speaking, monogamy is cognitively inconceivable and morally indefensible." I think the talk does more or less follow that, as divided into two parts: the first sentence is almost an outline of what's going to come. But then what's marvelous about writing, I think, is that — when you're accomplishing something, when it's going along smoothly (I think maybe tennis players feel this during a very good long rally) — a great deal of energy is being used but at the same time it's as if it's really one of these rare moments in existence where there is this extraordinary ease of a kind of steady, expansive *going out*. It's just happening. It's coming. And the sexual connotation of "coming" here is only partly relevant — because it's not so much an explosive pouring out, it's really just a kind of — it's funny, it's the maximum of activity with the maximum of peace, and it's the maximum of inward concentration with also the maximum of giving, of moving out, expansiveness.

NR: So it's something that is in accord with what you say, in various contexts, about radical passivity?

LB: In a way, yes, a passivity that's not deadening, where actually the distinction between activity and passivity doesn't seem relevant any more. I think that's very important. One of the stultifying things about the way people talk about sex is the distinction between activity and passivity. In one of the psychoanalytic sections in the book on Assyrian sculpture that Ulysse and I wrote [*The Forms of Violence*] — and I can't remember now the context or why we talked about it — but we were trying to say how wrong it is to talk about male sexuality (and I don't mean just gay male sexuality but I mean genital male sexuality in either a gay or a straight context) as "active," as if it could be only active. In a sense the male orgasm is impossible without passivity. It's a very nice and extremely pleasurable example of a moment when there is a kind of — at its highest intensity — a breakdown of that distinction. But I think it exists in other things as well. I think that the writing process can be an example of that.

NR: There's a letter in which E. M. Forster describes the experience of writing *A Passage to India* as "voluntary surrender to infection." It's volitional, in some sense, but the power isn't yours, or is only yours by not being yours.

LB: Yes, it's almost like a kind of open secret that you keep about writing. You wouldn't write if you weren't interested in what we vaguely call ideas, but at the same time I don't think people would be interested in your ideas if there weren't something else going on in your writing — which is a little more difficult to get at — even though people are very hesitant to talk about it, partly because they don't know how to talk about it and partly because they may be slightly afraid of it and somewhat afraid of themselves in it as well. It's very rare to feel that you have what *seems* like a total adequation to language. We're usually not aware of the gap between the body that we're happy to live in and this language which is not a creation of that body but on which we depend and which we use instrumentally so easily. Of course people have talked about that famous "otherness of language" — but I think it becomes very physical and felt when you write, because it's after all something that you're trying to express but at the same time there's something foreign in the operation and that's very particular to writing and I think that's different from the other kinds of professions that one might engage in. I mean the language is to writing what the football is to football but for the football player the football itself is not something that's troubling, that is, this difference between the object and the person using it is not troubling. Whereas, in writing, you want to be identical to that foreign object from which you're different. And I guess what happens in certain moments is that language comes to *realize* a certain rhythm in yourself—and it really is a rhythm where I can't distinguish between mental and physical. For example at the beginning of Chapter 3 ('The Gay Daddy') in *Homos*, I've made almost palpable in the writing a rhythm of movement towards Foucault (towards the things he was talking about—gay love and gay sex) and movement away (from his desexualizing of the gay threat). It's a fluctuation, a kind of respiration almost, that's fast, slow, changes its pace and its spacing, and it actually embraced, actually coerced language into embracing its undulations. And it comes out in that particular passage as a humor or irony or distancing, to use a series of recognizable critical terms which, at the same time, don't exactly describe the specific coincidence between the rhythms of body and that which is foreign to the body. Maybe that's the peace and expansiveness I was talking about before. The inherent foreignness of language momentarily becomes simply like the clothing of your most intimate rhythms and that's an extraordinary correspondence. It might even be the sort of biological foundation of my interest in what Ulysse and I have been calling the correspondence of forms. It's a correspondence where you realize that there is a mode in which *your* moving through space coincides with the circulation of something entirely indifferent to you, which is language, and that there was a junction, something happened, there was an intersection which is extremely peaceful because you're out of yourself at the same time.

NR: A coitus?

LB: Perhaps.

NR: I wonder if we could link this to what Malcolm Bowie was talking about yesterday. The kind of attention he was giving to your writing seemed to me to represent something new in terms of the ways in which I've seen your work being written about. In his distinctive deployment of quite classical terms like "style" and "irony," and in his discussion of what he names that "perverse epigrammatic intensity" which he takes to be characteristic of "the later Bersani," his paper did seem to be engaging in fascinating ways with these difficulties of how one might talk about writing, your writing in particular.

LB: Yes, I think what he was talking about was in different terms the thing that I've just been trying to describe. I think that in distinguishing between some of the first things that I've written and some of the more recent things it was as if he was saying that that kind of coincidence of rhythms—impersonal and linguistic rhythms *and* my most intimate rhythms — was happening more, recently, than it had before, so I was very interested in that. It's difficult to talk about but I like very much his almost irritation at those phrases that might qualify that, as if I were a little afraid of that happening all the time. In fact I find more and more that I cut out phrases like "it might be said that" or "so to speak" or "precisely," all these words that don't mean anything, but that are ways in which language treacherously provides us with phrases with which we remind ourselves and others that *we* are really not talking, we're really only *using* the language. So that interested me very much, as a kind of warning. It's funny — when you watch people at a lecture listening to you: I've always felt, for example, that on the few occasions I've spoken when Malcolm's been there, that's he's *hearing* the kind of thing that I was talking about. I feel that there are certain people who are not just hearing the so-called ideas but they're also actually participating themselves, when you do it successfully, in that rhythmic concordance between a system of intellectual and physical respiration and the system of language.

NR: This may be simply to do with my own sense of rapport with your work, but I am often struck by a sense of comic energy, a feeling that there is something immensely funny happening somewhere.

LB: When I was working on the beginning of the Foucault chapter in *Homos* with the man who translated it into French we were both not exactly hilarious but we found it very funny. But it's not always or ever simply funny. Thinking about the kind of coincidence that I was talking about, that one reaches very rarely, that anybody reaches very rarely, I think (except the greatest writers, say, Shakespeare or Dante, who seem to write almost all the time that way) — but where I feel I come closest to it, for example in *Homos*, is in two very different modes: at the beginning of that Foucault chapter and at the very end of it, where there's that little lyrical thing — which really has nothing to do with any of the ideas in the book — about two men fucking: this isn't humorous in the way that the beginning of the chapter perhaps is but still, I just felt totally at ease in writing that in some way, and I don't think it was for psychological reasons. I just think the language hits something there. There's also a passage that I'm very attached to in the essay on *Salò* and Sade, a passage on the aesthetic about which I remember just feeling sort of frightened in writing it, because I really felt that there was a kind of intimacy in me about what this art was like, that I had never even understood until the moment I was writing this passage, and it was very, very strange, and that wasn't funny either.

One of my most intimate rhythms has been important to me in teaching, at least when I have been most successful, and it's very annoying to some students, as if I'm being frivolous or not taking myself seriously. It doesn't bother me to be dismissive of my own ideas when I teach. I mean, I want to be as rigorous as possible, thinking about these ideas, but at the same time I would hate very much to be identified as, in all seriousness, a "such-and-such." You know in the United States there are department meetings at the university where people say "we need a Marxist critic" and "we need a psychoanalytic critic," and the number of times people have said to me "you've been a psychoanalytic critic, haven't you?" I *hate* that. (Reviewers, incidentally, have consistently said that *Caravaggio's Secrets* is a psychoanalytic study, which it is *not*.) I've had troubling classes when students have tried to read things psychoanalytically and I've sort of trashed psychoanalysis. In various ways now I'm moving away from psychoanalysis, but even when I was most involved in it, it seemed to be very uninteresting to sort of be really faithful to it in a way, and there is something comical about that, I mean comical about being willing to leave lots of points at rest as you go along. I think the beginning of "The Gay Daddy" chapter is that. Here's this statement from Foucault about why these two guys are happy. In a sense what's interesting about it is that it's against everything I've ever thought — but that's why I like it. I mean I like it and I don't like it. There's always something funny in sort of *walking along* with someone — and it's slightly affectionate and slightly mocking at the same time. That strikes me as a very healthy combination, in order to avoid what I think is a very bad form of passion, when passion — either in sexual relations or even intellectual relations — comes to be obsession, and a lot of political passions are obsessions, just as a lot of romantic passions are obsessions. It may seem as if you lose yourself in that kind of passion but in fact it's extremely self-affirming in a bad sense, an appropriative and tyrannical form of passion. Whereas this other thing, of being sort of laughing a little at that with which you're walking along, whether it's Foucault or your own ideas, seems to me to be very good. And that may be the source of what you're thinking of.

NR: In what you've just said I can't help hearing a sort of etymological playing out of "parody," of song, of something beside itself, walking beside oneself perhaps. Just recently when I was rereading "Is the Rectum a Grave?," I was very struck by how much it seems to be an essay about parody. Perhaps I could recall a couple of brief quotations from the essay? The first is: "Parody is an erotic turn-off, and all gay men know this." The second is the sentence that runs: "The ultimate logic of MacKinnon's and Dworkin's critique of pornography — and, however parodistic this may sound, I really don't mean it as a parody of their views — would be *the criminalization of sex itself until it has been reinvented.*" You would like to take a distance from the notion of parody, even while engaging or at least invoking it?

LB: Yes, I feel somewhat inconclusive about that. I'm a little suspicious of the term "parody." I know that when people use that word they often are willing to say that there's a certain affection included in the parodistic movement or there can be, but a parody is a kind of mocking if somewhat affectionate imitation of something, right?

NR: There is something affirmative about it, you mean?

LB: Well, there can be. One of the things I argue against in *Homos* is the extraordinary importance that at some point Judith Butler had given to the notion of the subversive effect on dominant cultural models of parodies of those models. Here parody would not be affectionate, because it really is trying to undermine and subvert those forms. Butler, if I'm reading her correctly, was thinking of parody as having a possible, real, politically subversive function, because it exposes things in the model that are then weaker as a result of the parodistic confrontation. But the model can also be unaffected, or even strengthened, by the "affirmative" side of parody, by a complicity between it and its object. In "Is the Rectum a Grave?" I was talking about two different kinds of parody. First, there is the gay leather thing which has been defended as a parody of a certain type of machismo masculinity. (As David Miller has brilliantly said, the body you wouldn't dare fuck with — the serious straight machismo — becomes, in the gay version, the body you may indeed be allowed to fuck.) My argument was that there is also a great deal of complicity in the parody, and that it really is paying tribute to what is being parodied. The second kind is the parody of women in gay campy conversation, which certainly includes complicity (as in the machismo leather scene with machismo maleness), but is also heavy mockery, and really quite nasty toward women. I mean I think it's part of the misogyny in gay life and that kind of deliberate effeminate campiness is connected to the — what I've always found disgusting — near idolatry of those actresses who represented a bitchy and destructive femininity, like Bette Davis in some of her movies, or, even worse, the worship of Judy Garland — you know, the woman as a total sort of extraordinary, talented being and at the same time a total drugged wreck. What better way to murder a woman than to take Judy Garland as a heroine? So anyway, just as a conclusion: I'm not sure I would want to use the word "parody" for the kind of comic "walking alongside" that we've been talking about.

NR: Yes, sure. Can we go back for a moment (if we ever left it) to psychoanalysis? You see yourself as moving away from psychoanalysis, and that seems to have to do with what you talk about as different ways of being in the world.

LB: Ulysse and I have been discussing presences of the subject in the world that are not effects of interpretation, projection or identification. The art we've studied suggests, in different ways, that we are *already in the world* (even before we appeared in it . . .), there are always relations, and not simply because we interpret and project and introject the world, and it's that distinction between ways of being in the world that I'm now interested in talking about.

NR: So it's the idea of what you were talking about (in "Against Monogamy"), the idea of a self that is not identificatory?

LB: Yes, a self that is not simply a self of interpretation. But of course I'm not really "leaving" psychoanalysis, as you can see from my talk yesterday, especially in my comments on *Civilization and Its Discontents*. It's one of the books I just came back to: I reread it and discovered that there was a whole other thing going on — other than what I had previously seen. I had never paid that much attention to it but in *Civilization and Its Discontents* Freud is saying something like: "You know I'm not really saying much that is new, but then, finally, *here* is a psychoanalytic idea." I didn't talk about that in *The Freudian Body*, except in passing, and now (with "Against Monogamy") it's the center of what I am saying about *Civilization and Its Discontents*. *Civilization and Its Discontents* is funny in the way that there is all this somewhat banal respectability in much of the early chapters of the main text and then two or three of these footnotes have these wild things about sniffing and how we had to give up doing the only thing we really wanted to do, which was go round on all fours sniffing women. The "rational" part of the text is more faithful to an ideal or model in traditional philosophy, a certain model of seriousness, one that goes under the rubric of truth and knowledge; seriousness vehicles the notion that philosophy gives us truth and/or knowledge. Freud in his most interesting moments undercuts any security about what knowledge or truth might mean. This is also the case with the Caravaggio book, where we say that Caravaggio is an early figure in the history of the suspicion, fatal to philosophy, that truth cannot be the object of knowledge, that there is no such thing as truth. I think truth is the basis of the kind of seriousness that I'm interested in helping to do away with.

NR: Can I ask you about teaching, about how you teach and how you feel about teaching? Perhaps this could be linked up to something you referred to in the discussion yesterday, about the idea of teaching in such as a way as "not to say anything *absolutely*."

LB: Yes, I'm more and more interested in that (it is, I think, a phrase of Robert Walser) because people of course ask more and more: What are the practical modes of this? What can one do, what's open to us in changing modes of relationality? These are the questions the Caravaggio book and *Homos* and even *The Culture of Redemption* seem to invite. I mean, if we don't have a redemptive culture what do we or might we have?

NR: Beyond redemption, you mean?

LB: Yes. It's very difficult. I understand why people ask that question, but at the same time you can't do everything at once. I mean, you do have to go through a kind of speculative, rather non-immediately-politically-viable stage of reflection and a lot of it may turn out to be finally just disposable, but that's all right: it's like writing first drafts, you throw away some of it. Of course very specific things need to be done politically, and we should engage in those struggles. In gay life we are far from having all the rights we should have. For instance, I think gay marriage as an ideal for the gay community is completely uninteresting, but I certainly would fight for the right for gay men and women to have it. So there are all these things that are fairly obvious and necessary struggles, but beyond or in addition to that, I'd say, I'm energized by attempting to imagine new modes of relating and relationality. And some of these new modes are ways that exist anyway, but which we seem trained, culturally, not to notice, for example in a kind of connection to the other and to the outside that I was describing in relation to the process of writing, or in the ways in which I can "walk alongside" Foucault *now*, or in the "formal correspondences" Ulysse and I trace in the visual art we've written about. And as teachers we have a rare opportunity to experiment with some of the shifts in modes of connecting that I'm interested in. That is what teaching is: it's a sustained time and space where you do nothing but see how a group of people are going to connect. It's really extraordinary in that way. In teaching, a certain type of group-work can be done, which might slowly disseminate into a fairly significant part of society. It would be a matter of how modes of connectedness subtly change within a society. Literature also does this. Literature does finally have an effect on the way in which people instinctively and intuitively relate and connect. And I think teaching can also do that. It can train us, among other things, in a kind of impersonal intimacy, an intellectual and nonpermanent friendship. Pedagogy and friendship are modes of extensibility less glamorous than public sex (a current queer favorite) but perhaps more worthy of exploration. Foucault's interest in friendship in his final work, Derrida's work on the politics of friendship — I mean, why talk about that now if not because there's a sense of these new relations? To redefine friendship would be a political move. A political move, for example, in opposition to a certain notion of the most important relation as being the (usually married) couple. That's my interest in the "Monogamy" essay, for example.

NR: It makes me think of a phrase that you and Ulysse Dutoit use in the Caravaggio book. You talk about his paintings as constituting a sort of ontological laboratory. I'm now thinking that perhaps that is what your work suggests an interview should also be. Linked to that, finally, I'm also wondering if, all along — in relation to everything you have been saying about rhythm and respiration and connectedness — we haven't also been talking about music. Could you say anything about this? What is your relation to music?

LB: It's a very poor relation. I have this sort of fantasy plan that — except I keep thinking of other things to do. I mean I struggled when I was a kid with studying piano for ten or twelve years. I resisted it a great deal as a lot of kids do, but now I'm more and more interested in music. I'm very ignorant about it, but I've always thought I wanted to develop it. It interests me more than anything else now, but in the depths of ignorance. It may not be what I will do, either in terms of the composers that I'm going to mention or in terms of even whether I'm going to do it, but I feel that much of what I've been trying to do I would understand better if I could understand what's going on in certain pieces of Schubert and late Beethoven. And that's all I can say about that.

NR: Thank you very much.

Index

abstinence, premarital, 122, 123–24

"Advice to Doctors on Psychoanalytic Treatment" (Freud), 156

aesthetic subject, 83–167; in Almodóvar's *All About My Mother*, 80; as mode of relational being, 142; psychoanalysis and, 139–53; self-loss in, 69–70

Affect Theory, 67–68

Agamben, Giorgio, 183

aggression: comes to include everything, 99; in demand for sexual relation, 51; Freud on narcissistic enjoyment in, 64, 65, 127; Freud on sex and, 64, 126–32, 134, 136; in internalizing authority, 98; *jouissance* as inseparable from, 150; *jouissance* of, 136; oceanic feeling associated with, 126, 127, 132; psychoanalysis on human destructiveness, 63–64, 65, 79; renunciation of aggressiveness multiplies its force, 173. *See also* violence

AIDS: displacement in discourse about, 27; media coverage of, 5–9; monogamy as consequence of, 25, 85; as pretense for oppression of gays, 6–8; promiscuity associated with, 3, 5, 16, 17, 27; public and political responses to, 4–9; Reagan administration response to, 4–5, 6–7; research, 4, 27

A la recherche du temps perdu (Proust), 58

All About Eve (film), 71, 78, 79, 80

All About My Mother (Almodóvar), 71–82

Allouch, Jean, 66, 109

Almodóvar, Pedro, 70–82; *All About My Mother*, 71–82; *The Flower of My Secret*, 74; *Labyrinth of Passion*, 81; *The Law of Desire*, 75–76; *Matador*, 75; *Pepi, Luci, Bom, and Other Girls on the Heap*, 73, 81; repetition in work of, 75, 76, 80; *Women on the Verge of a Nervous Breakdown*, 82; on women talking, 73–74, 82

Altman, Dennis, 12

anal sex: attitudes toward passive role in sex, 18–19; Freud on, 123; homophobia and *jouissance* of, 133; potential for multiple orgasms of, 18; self-annihilation associated with, 29–30

And the Band Played On (Shilts), 7n

Arcadia (Florida), 5, 16–17, 18

Aristophanes, 55, 56–57, 117–18

art: the aesthetic and, 70, 185; as affirmation of solidarity in the universe, 100; of Almodóvar, 70–82; as anticommunitarian, 34; defining gay art, 31; diagrams universal relationality, 142; failure in, 188; as form-giving and form-revealing, 104; Godard in reformulation of the aesthetic, 167; homoeroticism found in, 34, 42; human subject's capacity for exceeding its own subjectivity in, 139; impotent aesthetics, 171; is there a gay art?, 31–35; as model for new relational modes, x; negativity in, 34; and politics, 35; Proustian, 160–61; psychoanalysis on work of, 140; as site of being as emergence into connectedness, 104, 118. *See also* aesthetic subject

Arts of Impoverishment (Bersani and Dutoit): on Beckett's *Westward Ho*, 184; on calling of subject into human community, 176; on correspondence of forms, 175; on ego-dissolving self-extensions into the world, 34; on failure in art, 188; on impotent aesthetics, 171; on nonerotic sensual exchanges, 131n; on relations between human and nonhuman, 87, 184; on Rothko Chapel, 185

ascesis, 30, 48, 58–59, 61, 69, 193

Assumption of the Virgin (El Greco), 165–67

Assyrian sculpture, 142, 183–84, 194

Balzac to Beckett/Center and Circumference in French Fiction (Bersani), 171

Barthes, Roland, 32

Bataille, Georges, 24, 25, 25n25, 109
bathhouses: closing of, 5; hierarchy and com-
    petition at, 12, 29; ideal cruising in, 60
Baudelaire, Charles, 171, 184
Baudelaire and Freud (Bersani), ix, 28, 171
Beckett, Samuel, 34, 103–4, 176, 184, 188–89
being on top: Foucault on, 59; MacKinnon
    and Dworkin on significance of, 21; as
    never question of just physical position,
    23; power represented by, 19; struggle for
    power as consequence of, 25
Beyond the Pleasure Principle (Freud), 100,
    127, 131, 159
bisexuality, 89–92, 126
blacks: collaborating with their oppres-
    sors, 15; gay men compared with, 9–10;
    violence of inequality, 20
Blood Wedding (Lorca), 78
Boffey, Philip M., 5n2
Bollas, Christopher, 94, 97, 162
Boswell, John, 18
Bowen, Otis R., 6, 7
Bowie, Malcolm, 195
butch-fem lesbian couples, 12
Butler, Judith, 32, 38, 40, 90, 196

Califia, Pat, 22
camp, 14, 198
Caravaggio, 35, 135, 142, 175, 177, 185–86,
    199–200
Caravaggio's Secrets (Bersani and Dutoit), 35,
    131n, 135, 172, 177, 196, 199–200, 201
Cartesian dualism, 154, 155–56, 157, 160, 162
castration, 54, 175–76, 185
catharsis argument, 21
Chartreuse de Parme, La (Stendhal), 50
child abuse, 22, 27, 29, 99, 132
childhood sexuality, 22, 29
Christian right, 37, 123
Civilization and Its Discontents (Freud): on
    aggression and the sexual, 64, 126–32, 134,
    136; on antagonism between civiliza-
    tion and sexuality, 50, 93; arrives at idea
    worthy of psychoanalysis, 98, 199; on
    bisexuality, 90, 126; on civilization and
    individual unhappiness, 120; "everything
    past is preserved," 99, 131, 149; footnotes
    of, 125, 126; on guilt, 68; on internal-
    ization of authority, 96; on loving thy
    neighbor as thyself, 63; on narcissistic
    enjoyment in destruction, 65, 79; as
    not speaking psychoanalytically, 97, 121,

127, 199; on oceanic feeling, 99, 124;
    oceanic textuality of, 128; paradoxes in,
    98, 128–29; on self-containment, 173; on
    sexual repression, 125–32
"'Civilized' Sexual Morality and Modern
    Nervous Illness" (Freud), 121–25, 130
community: art as anticommunitarian, 34;
    in bathhouses, 29; calling forth into,
    176, 179; cruising for conceptualizing
    redemptive communitarianism, 180; fam-
    ily conflicts repeated in, 96; Genet's view
    of, 33, 179; identity as communitarian,
    37, 86–87; in pastoral view of sex, 22, 34;
    redefining, 38, 43
Company (Beckett), 103–4, 176
confidentiality, 6
conscience, 52, 88, 97–98, 128–29
control, loss of, 24
conversation, sociable, 46–47
Cooper, Dennis, 34
coquetry, 47, 60
countertransference, 156
couple, reconstituting the, 178–80
cruising, 57–62; as an ascesis, 69; for concep-
    tualizing redemptive communitarianism,
    180; ideal, 60; phallocentrism of, 28; as
    promiscuous, 57; seen as relationally in-
    novative, 59; as sexual sociality, 57, 61; as
    training ground in intimacy, 60–62, 69
Culture of Redemption (Bersani), 171, 173,
    177, 184, 188, 200
cut of being, 147, 150

Davis, Bette, 72, 198
Dean, Tim, 110–11
death: death drive, 65, 67, 68, 79, 100, 131,
    137, 159, 176; sex associated with, 61–62
Deleuze, Gilles, 111n14, 161
depth psychology, 139, 156
Derrida, Jacques, 189–90, 191, 201
desire: as construction, 76; defensive func-
    tion of, 79; essentialism in schemes
    of, 39; Foucault on power and, 157;
    Foucault's distinction between pleasure
    and, 135, 182; founding, 151; how it gets
    attached to persons, 183–84; Lacan on
    object and cause of, 159; Lacan's excesses
    of, 100–101; Lacan's theory of, 110–11; as
    lack, 110–19, 135, 138; power to see it ev-
    erywhere, 144; psychoanalysis on origins
    of gay male, 53–55, 88, 89; psychoanaly-
    sis' tendentious accounts of, 105